The Complete Kitchen Guide

The COMPLETE KITCHEN GUIDE

The Cook's Indispensable Book

Lillian Langseth-Christensen / Carol Sturm Smith

Illustrated by Lillian Langseth-Christensen

GROSSET & DUNLAP PUBLISHERS, NEW YORK

ISBN: 0-448-01402-5

1971 Printing

To Our Husbands—Dick and Stan

Contents

This book is for people who cook—for everybody who has ever been exasperated by a recipe reading "bake until browned," "boil until tender," "cook until done" without even hinting at the length of time it will take. This book answers the questions. It is the most complete single volume of non-recipe cooking information available.

THE COMPLETE KITCHEN GUIDE is the direct result of our years of working together. It is impossible to estimate the amount of time we have spent searching for such information to complete a recipe accurately and fully to our satisfaction. This book is the outgrowth of that searching.

We have compiled this book because it contains information that should be readily and quickly available.

Many people and organizations have been extremely helpful, and we would particularly like to thank: Mr. John von Glahn of the Fisheries Commission; Herbert Bain of the American Meat Institute; Mr. Selig of the United Fresh Fruit and Vegetable Association and Mr. Bernard Lewis of their Public Relations firm; The Agriculture Research Service of the United States Department of Agriculture; General Foods Kitchens; Fleischman's Yeast; National Canner's Association; National Wheat Growers Association; Hershey Chocolate Corporation; American Institute of Baking; American Meat Institute; National Live Stock and Meat Board; National Dairy Council; United States Department of the Interior, Fish and Wildlife Service; Wheat Flour Institute; Standard Brands Incorporated; and Birdcliff Game Birds.

Lillian Langseth-Christensen
Carol Sturm Smith

Introduction

The differences in style, material and cost of cooking utensils can be staggering. But good pots, pans and knives and a reasonable number of kitchen aids are indispensable for good cooking. A suggested list of basic equipment heads the descriptions.

There are very few rules that apply to the buying of utensils. There are very few absolutes. Buying the equipment with which you will cook requires numerous choices, based on convenience, sturdiness, necessity and often on storage space.

1 ᘒ
Equipment

Pots and Pans   Pots and pans can be very expensive and it is worth spending time making comparisons. It is better to have a few good utensils than a complete set of pots and pans that conduct heat poorly.

Always purchase pots and pans with matching covers—with the exception of omelet or pancake pans. It is convenient to have all-metal utensils which can be used both on the stove and in the oven.

Cast Iron   Although heavy, cast-iron utensils are excellent because the heat is conducted evenly. Cast-iron should be "seasoned" before use; scour thoroughly, dry, rub generously with oil and heat in a hot oven for about half an hour. Cast-iron omelet or pancake pans are generally wiped clean with paper towels. If iron utensils rust, scour and reseason before using. Oil lightly after washing to help prevent rusting, and dry quickly over high heat. Do not use for cooking acid foods, such as dishes with wine, because the cast iron will discolor it.

Enameled Cast Iron   Perhaps the best all-around pots and pans are enameled cast iron. These utensils are very heavy; they conduct heat evenly and are easy to keep clean. (Soaking in hot soapy water for a few minutes and a sponge usually does the job. If the enamel discolors, try using a mild copper cleanser—avoid using steel wool on the enamel if possible.) Available in many different sizes, shapes and beautiful colors, these can be brought to the table for serving. Enameled cast-iron pots and pans are expensive, but worth it.

Copper   Heavy copper is an excellent heat conductor, and copper utensils are favored by many gourmet cooks. But there are some drawbacks to take into consideration before investing in these very expensive utensils. Copper must be lined for safe cooking; this is most often done with tin. With use the tin will wear off, and the copper must be retinned. Copper is a beautiful addition to a kitchen, but time-consuming to keep clean, for it tarnishes easily. Copper utensils that are shellacked should be emersed in boiling water and the shellac scrubbed off before using for the first time.

Stainless Steel   Alone, stainless steel is a poor heat conductor, but stainless steel utensils are quite good when the bottoms are of cast aluminum, and they are easy to keep clean. Copper-bottomed stainless steel is less satisfactory unless the copper is fairly heavy.

Aluminum   Heavy aluminum is a good heat conductor, but thin aluminum is not. All aluminum will discolor some foods, particularly dishes containing egg yolks or acids, and aluminum utensils eventually become unattractive in appearance.

"No-Stick" Utensils   "No-stick" pots and pans are available in a wide range of weights and prices. Some are excellent, particularly the heavy-duty ones, and some are inadequate. It is no longer necessary to use special cooking equipment with some of these products because they do not scratch as was the case with the early "no-stick" equipment. Before using, season the pots and pans according to manufacturers' directions. The special attraction of these utensils is the ease in cleaning them.

Knives   Carbon steel may rust and need more scouring (with steel wool), but these knives hold an edge better than stainless steel. Knives should be kept sharp at all times—have a knife sharpener handy and use it as often as needed. Have a professional sharpen them several times a year. Knives should be washed and dried immediately after use and stored away from other utensils which might dull the edges.

Wood in the Kitchen   An assortment of wooden spoons and spatulas is a must. Wood will not discolor food and can be handled safely while stirring hot foods because heat is not transferred. Keep separate wooden utensils for foods containing garlic.

Wooden planks and carving platters must be seasoned before use: rub wood well with oil and heat in a 200–225° F. oven for about 1 hour.

Wooden salad bowls are either wiped clean with paper towels or rinsed quickly in water and mild soap and then immediately dried thoroughly.

Glass   Glass utensils are handy for seeing the cooking process, such as in a coffee pot or double boiler, but most glass utensils should not be used over direct heat.

Pottery   Pottery utensils are used primarily for baking purposes and rarely on the top of the stove (always use an asbestos mat to keep pottery from direct top-of-the-stove heat). Care should be taken to prevent cooking foods from spilling on unglazed pottery to prevent cracking.

Suggested Kitchen Equipment (Asterisk indicates essentials)

Cooking and Baking

* Baking Dish with Cover (1½ quart)
  Bread Loaf Pan (9x5x3″)
* Broiling Pan
  Coffee Maker
  2 Cookie Sheets
  3 Cooling Racks for cakes, and breads
* Covered Frying Pan (10″)
* Covered Saucepans (1 quart, 2 quart, 3 quart)
  Custard Cups

* Double Boiler
  Frying Pan (6″)
  Icing Spatula
  Kettle with Cover (4–6 quart)
  Muffin Pan
  Pepper Grinder
  Pie Plates, 8″ and 9″ diameter
  Roasting Pan with Rack (13x9½x2″)
  Salt Shaker
  2 Cake Pans (8½″)

THE COMPLETE

KITCHEN GUIDE

Teakettle
Teapot
2 Wire Whisks

Preparation Utensils

* Bottle and Jar Opener
* Can Opener
  Colander
* Cutlery Set (butcher knife, bread knife, French chef's knife, 2 paring knives)
* Cutting Board
  Funnel
  Graters
* Kitchen Shears
* Lemon and Orange Squeezer
  Long-Handled Fork
* Pancake Turner
  Pastry Blender
  Pastry Cloth
  Rolling Pin and Cover
* Slotted Spoon
* Strainer
  Tongs
  Vegetable Brush
  Vegetable Peeler

Measuring and Mixing

* Liquid Measuring Cup

* Mixing Bowls (convenient sizes)
  Rotary Egg Beater
* Rubber Scrapers
* 1 Set Dry Measuring Cups
* 1 Set Measuring Spoons
  1 Spatula (7″ blade)
* Wooden Spoons

Miscellaneous

Baster
Candy Thermometer
Dutch Oven
Flame-Tamer
Garlic Press
Gelatin Molds
Griddle
Kitchen Timer
Knife Sharpener
Ladle
Meat Thermometer
Melon Ball Cutter
Oven Thermometer
Pastry Brush
Potato Masher
Soufflé Dish
Vegetable Slicer

Apple Corer   A small tubular appliance for removing the entire core and seeds of apples.

Apple Corers

Asbestos Mat   An asbestos mat is used to protect cookware from direct heat.

Baster   A small appliance with bulb for basting.

Bean Pot   A covered pot of crude heavy crockery, made especially for the slow cooking of beans.

Biscuit Cutter   Small utensil for cutting dough into rounds.

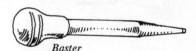
Baster

Blender   An electric appliance used for blending, mincing, grating, chopping and liquefying.

Bottle Opener   A small utensil for removing caps from bottles.

Bottle Stoppers   Used for recapping opened bottles.

Bread Box   A metal ventilated container with lid or opening for storing bread.

Bean Pot

Bread Pan   An oblong utensil for baking bread.

Brown Paper   A heavy paper used in the kitchen for lining pans.

Brushes   Used for cleaning kitchen equipment.

Bottle Openers

Brushes

Butter Boards

Butter Curler

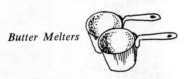
Butter Melters

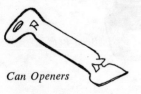
Can Openers

Butter Boards   Ridged wooden boards for rolling butter balls.

Butter Curler   A device for making curls of butter.

Butter Melter   A small heavy metal utensil for melting butter.

Cake Pan   A utensil of varied shapes used for baking cake. May contain a center tube.

Cake Rack   A small metal framework utensil for cooling cakes and pastries.

Cake Tin   See cake pan.

Canner   A large cooking utensil with a cover, handles and a jar rack used for canning foods.

Cannisters   Containers used for storing staples, in a set of four progressive sizes with tight fitting lids to preserve freshness. Available in a variety of materials, shapes and colors.

Can Opener   An appliance used to open cans—may be manual or electric.

Carving Board   A large wooden board for carving meats, usually grooved to catch meat juices.

Cake Pans

Cake Rack

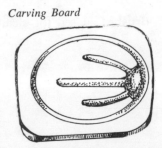
Carving Board

Casserole, Round, Covered A covered utensil of oven-proof pottery, metal or glass with one or two handles, in which food may be baked and served. Most casseroles can be used on top of the stove. Available in many designs and the following sizes: 1 quart, 1½ quart, 2 quart, 2½ quart, and 3 quart.

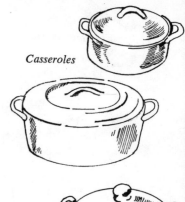

Casseroles

Chafing Dish A double dish for cooking or keeping foods warm at table. May be electric or alcohol burning.

Charlotte Molds Molds in graduated sizes with sloping sides used for baking charlottes, often tin-lined.

Cheesecloth A thin, unsized, loose-woven cotton cloth used for straining and other kitchen purposes.

Chicken Fryer A deep skillet with a cover, used for frying chicken or as a casserole.

Chopper A mechanical device or blade with a handle used for chopping foods.

Chopping Board A thick wooden board used as a surface for chopping.

Chopping Bowl A wooden bowl used with a rounded chopper.

Chopping Board

Choppers

Charlotte Mold

Chafing Dish

Clam Opener

Clam Opener   A metal device used for opening clams.

Cocktail Shaker   A container for mixing the ingredients of a cocktail.

Cocotte   A French casserole with a tight-fitting lid.

Coffee Grinder   A large device used for grinding coffee beans. May be manual or electric.

Coffee Pot   A covered pot in which coffee is prepared or served.

Colander   A vessel with handles and with the bottom or lower part perforated for draining liquid from foods.

Cookie Cutters   Small utensils for cutting dough into various shapes.

Cookie Press   A hollow cylindrical container which is filled with batter or soft dough which is then pressed through various disks or tubes onto a cookie sheet.

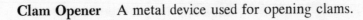
Cocktail Shakers

Coffee Pots

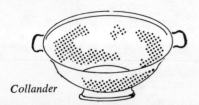
Collander

Nested Cookie Cutter

Cookie Cutters

Cookie Presser

Cookie Sheet A rectangular metal sheet designed for baking cookies and cake sheets, although also used for other baking purposes.

Cork Screw A device used for removing the cork from a bottle.

Custard Cups Small deep ovenware bowls.

Cutlery Implements for use in cutting, serving and eating food.

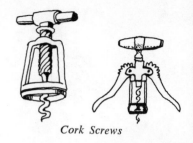

Cork Screws

Deep-Fat Fryer An uncovered cooking utensil with a perforated, meshed or sieve-like insert basket with one handle.

Dish Pan Large deep pan used for washing dishes.

Dish Towel A cloth used for drying dishes.

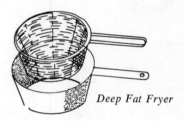

Deep Fat Fryer

Double Boiler Two nested, handled saucepans, equipped with a single cover. The purpose is to cook food over boiling or simmering water or to keep food warm.

Double Fry Pan Two hinged shallow pans—rectangular or semicircular. One acts as a cover for the other. Each side has a handle.

Doughnut Cutter Small utensil for cutting doughnuts.

Dutch Oven A deep, iron cooking pot equipped with a cover. Used for cooking pot roasts and stews. Comes in various sizes.

Double Boiler

Egg Beater

Egg Beater   A handled utensil for beating eggs.

Egg Poacher   A covered pan with a special egg holder, or a separate device for poaching.

Egg Slicer   A small appliance which slices hardcooked eggs by means of tightly stretched wires. The appliance can be obtained with an arrangement to slice eggs across or lengthwise.

Enamelware   A utensil coated with enamel to protect from rust and the action of acids.

Feather Brush   A few white feathers tied together for brushing or glazing foods.

Fish Boiler   A long narrow kettle suitable for boiling whole fish such as salmon.

Flan Ring   A circular strip of metal for baking tarts and pies on a cookie sheet.

Flour Sifter   A device used for sifting flour.

Fluted Knife   A knife with a zig-zag edge for decorative cutting.

Fluter   A tool used for edging piecrusts.

Food Mill   An appliance used for sieving and puréeing foods.

Egg Slicer

Feather Brush

Salmon Boiler

Flan Ring

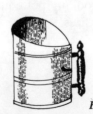
Flour Sifter

Food Mill

Foil A very thin sheet of metal, such as aluminum, used for wrapping foods, etc. Comes in rolled form.

Fondue Service Consists of a fondue pot over an alcohol flame and fondue forks, used for cooking and serving cheese or meat fondues.

Forks Pronged or tined devices.

Freezer Paper A heavy white paper used in wrapping foods in preparation for the freezer.

Fruit Juicer A device used to extract the juice from fruits.

Frying Pan A shallow pan for use over direct heat, with or without a cover. Frying pans are available in many sizes and of many metals. The following sizes are available: 5″, 5¾″, 6½″, 7″, 8″, 9½″, 11″ and 13″.

Funnel A conical-shaped vessel with a tube at the point used to transfer liquids or powders into narrow-necked containers or bottles.

Garlic Press A device used for extracting the pulp and juice from garlic cloves.

Glasses Vessels made of glass or other materials used for beverage containers.

Grapefruit Spoon A pointed spoon used for separating and eating grapefruit sections.

Forks

Frying Pan

Funnel

Grapefruit Spoon

Garlic Press

(11)

Grater A kitchen tool used for grating cheese, nutmeg, lemon peel, etc.

Gratineer Dish or tin in which gratineed food is baked.

Griddle A flat, uncovered, handled, heavy utensil, with or without a pouring lip. Most often used for pancakes.

Grill A metal rack with evenly spaced bars; comes with or without legs or as two grills hinged together with a long handle.

Ham Boiler A large pot used exclusively for boiling hams.

Hibachi A small self-contained grilling unit with a compartment capable of holding hot coals and a removable grill on top. Of Oriental origin, often used for barbecuing shish kebab.

Icebox Containers Tight-lidded containers of various sizes and shapes for storing foods in the refrigerator.

Graters

Ice Cracker A handled device for cracking ice.

Ice-Cream Freezer Electric or hand-turned container for making homemade ice cream.

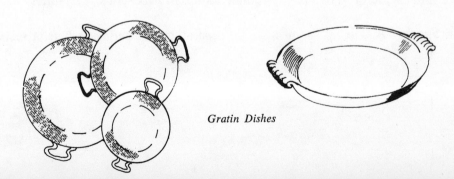

Gratin Dishes

Ice-Cream Molds   Variously shaped vessels for freezing ice cream, aspics, mousses and puddings.

Ice-Cube Crusher   A device, either manual or electric, for crushing ice cubes.

Ice-Cube Trays   Compartmented trays to be filled with water and frozen to make ice cubes.

Ice Pick   Sharp pointed awl-like implement used for cracking large blocks of ice.

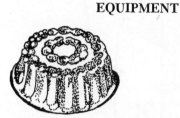

Ice Cream Mold

Jar Opener   A grasping device for removing jar lids.

Jigger   A measuring glass for alcohol—available in 1-, 1½- and 2-ounce sizes.

Kettle   A cooking utensil with or without cover, equipped with two side handles, available in 1- to 6-quart sizes.

Kitchen String   Heavy white string for tying meat and trussing fowl.

Knife Sharpener   Device used for sharpening steel knives.

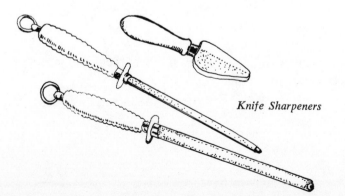

Knife Sharpeners

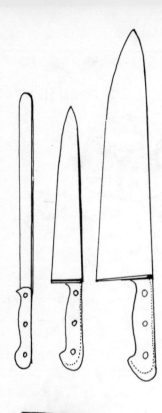

Knives Sharp-edged tools for cutting, carving, slicing, chopping, etc.

Ladle A long-handled utensil with a rounded cup base used for serving liquid foods such as soups and stews.

Larding Needle A special needle used for pulling strips of larding pork through meats.

Loaf Pan A rectangular utensil of standard loaf size, designed for baking bread and cake loaves.

Mallet A wooden hammer used to chop ice, or to flatten meat or poultry.

Marmite A French cooking pot.

Measuring Cups Used for measuring liquid, solid or dry ingredients.

Measuring Spoons Graduated spoons for measuring liquid, solid or dry ingredients.

Meat Grinder A device used to grind meat. Available in hand or electric forms, also as attachment to electric mixers.

Meat Slicer Small electric appliance for slicing meats.

Melon Baller A long-handled utensil with a rounded base for scooping and shaping melon, potatoes or other fruits and vegetables into balls.

(14)　　　*Knives*

Cleaver

Boning Knife

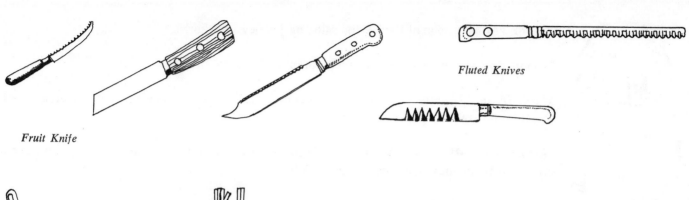

Fruit Knife

Fluted Knives

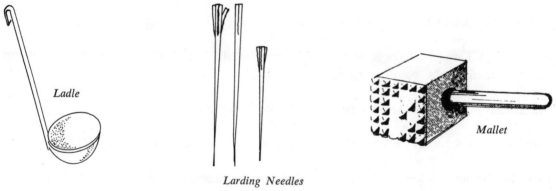

Ladle

Larding Needles

Mallet

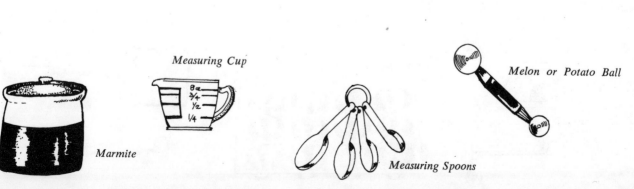

Marmite

Measuring Cup

Measuring Spoons

Melon or Potato Ball

(15)

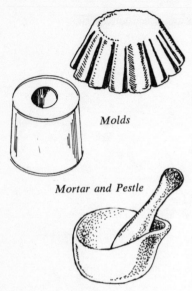

Molds

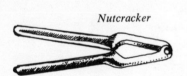

Mortar and Pestle

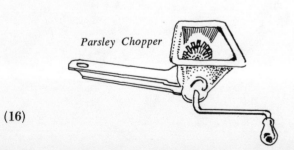

Nutcracker

Parsley Chopper

Mincer (Mouli)   Small device for mincing parsley and herbs.

Mixing Bowls   Bowls for use in preparation and mixing of foods.

Mold   A metal, pottery or earthenware container, for shaping hot or cold desserts, cakes or puddings, sweets, jellies or aspics.

Mortar and Pestle   Used for grinding herbs, spices and nuts to a fine even pulp, also used occasionally for making sauces such as aïoli.

Muffin or Cupcake Pan   A sheet-like pan containing 12 deep cups.

Needle and Thread   A large needle and coarse white thread are used in the kitchen for sewing stuffed meats, poultry and fish.

Nutcracker   An instrument for cracking the shell of a nut.

Omelet Pan   A round heavy cast-iron or copper pan used exclusively for omelets.

Pancake Turner   A long-handled utensil for turning pancakes and other foods.

Muffin Tin

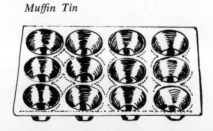

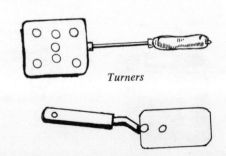

Turners

Paper Napkins, Towels Disposable napkins made of paper. Paper towels have a variety of uses.

Parchment Used for cooking meats, fish or vegetables in folded paper and for other kitchen purposes.

Pastry Bag A funnel-like paper or cloth bag fitted with a metal tube. Any soft mixture such as butter cream is forced through the tube for decorating or garnishing.

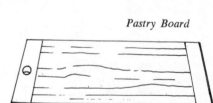

Pastry Bag and Tops

Pastry Board A large thin wooden board used for rolling out dough.

Pastry Blender A handled wire utensil for cutting fat into dry ingredients.

Pastry Brush A small brush used for brushing the surface of unbaked cookies or pastries with egg white or glaze.

Pastry Cloth A cloth on which to roll out pastry dough.

Pastry Board

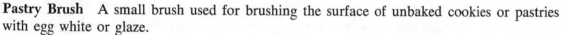

Pastry Wheel A fluted wheel on a handle used to cut pastry.

Pepper Mill A device used for grinding peppercorns in various stages of roughness.

Pastry Blender

Pastry Wheel

Pastry Cloth

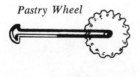

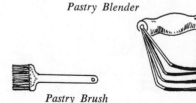

Salt Shaker and Pepper Mill

Pastry Brush

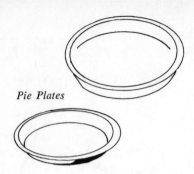

Pie Plates

Pie Pans or Plates   Round, sheet utensils with sloped sides, in standard sizes.

Pie Rings   (see Flan Ring)

Plastic Wrap   Thin sheets of plastic in roll form for covering and wrapping foods to preserve freshness and prevent spoiling.

Potato Peeler   A utensil used to strip the skins of potatoes.

Potato Peeler

Pot Holders   A cloth device used for protecting hands from hot cookware. Available in many sizes, colors and forms.

Pressure Cooker   An appliance for cooking foods under steam and with pressure.

Punch Bowl   A large bowl from which to serve punch or other mixed beverages.

Reamer   A device used to extract juice from fruits.

Ricer   A utensil designed for pressing potatoes and similar cooked vegetables through a perforated container, the resulting product emerging as strings about the diameter of a grain of rice.

Pot Holders

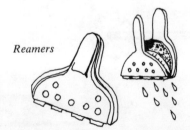

Reamers

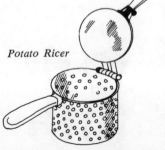

Potato Ricer

Roaster   A heavy pan, with or without a rack or cover, used for roasting meats and poultry.

Rolling Pin   A cylindrical piece of wood or other material for rolling out dough.

Rolling Pin Cover   A stockinette cover for rolling pin to facilitate rolling dough.

Rotisserie   A kitchen appliance with motorized spit for broiling meats.

Salad Basket   A small wire basket in which to shake freshly washed greens dry.

Salad Bowl   A large bowl, usually wood, in which to prepare and serve salad greens.

Salad Server   A separate spoon and fork or hinged spoon and fork for serving salad.

Salt and Pepper Shakers   Containers with perforated tops from which to shake salt or pepper. Usually the holes in the pepper shaker are fewer and smaller.

Sauce Boat   A utensil for serving sauces or gravy.

Saucepan   A medium-deep cooking utensil with one handle and a slightly rounded bottom, used with or without a cover. Available in several sizes.

Scales   A device used for weighing ingredients.

Roaster

Salad Basket

Salad Set

Saucepan

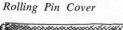

Rolling Pin Cover

Saucepan with Lids

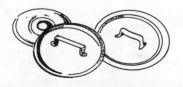

Rolling Pins

(19)

Kitchen Scissors

Scissors   An instrument for cutting, consisting of two cutting blades with crossed handles, and held together in the center by a pin.

Scoop

1. A large ladle used for dipping or skimming liquids.
2. A round bulb on a handle with a special device used for scooping out even portions of ice cream, rice, mashed potatoes or other foods.

Scoop

Scrapers   Rubber spatulas for scraping out bowls and for folding in beaten egg whites and cream.

Shears   A double-bladed cutting implement.

Shrimp Deveiner   Small gadget for peeling and deveining shrimp in a single and easy motion.

Sieve   An apparatus with meshes through which the finer particles of a pulverized or granulated substance are passed, to separate them from the coarser particles.

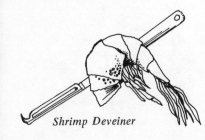

Skewer   A pointed wood or metal tool used for shish kebab or for closing openings of stuffed meat.

Skillet   A handled cooking utensil of various sizes used with or without lid. May be obtained in the following sizes: 5″, 5¾″, 6½″, 7″, 8″, 9½″, 11″ and 13″.

Shrimp Deveiner

Sieve

Scrapers

Shears

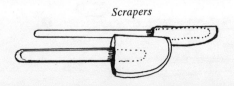

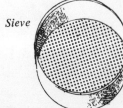

Skimmer   A device used to take off top surface of grease, cream, etc.

Slicer   A kitchen device for slicing evenly.

Slotted Spoon   A long-handled spoon with openings used for removing solid foods from liquid.

Snail Pan   A pan, containing six or twelve depressions, used for cooking and serving snails.

Soufflé Dish   A straight-sided oven-ware baking dish used for soufflés.

Spatula   A handled utensil both flat and thin for spreading.

Spoons   Kitchen utensils used for stirring, serving and eating.

Spring Form   A deep cake pan with a special side clasp which allows the rim to be removed from a cake.

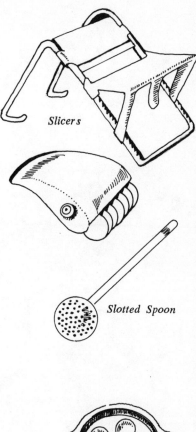

Slicers

Slotted Spoon

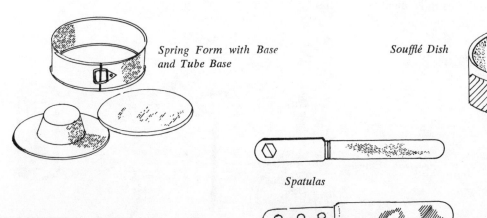

Spring Form with Base and Tube Base

Soufflé Dish

Spatulas

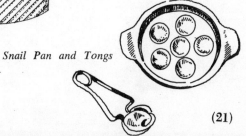

Snail Pan and Tongs

(21)

Fruit Juicer

Squeezer   A utensil for extracting juices from citrus fruits.

Steam Cooker   A large covered kettle equipped with a rack with hook-like handles.

Stew Pot   A large pot with tightly-fitting lid used for stewing foods.

Strainer   A device used to hold back solid pieces while liquids pass through.

Teapot   A vessel with a spout, in which tea is steeped and from which it is served.

Tea Strainer   Used to separate tea leaves from brewed tea.

Thermometer   An instrument used for determining accurate temperature—especially meat thermometers and candy thermometers. Oven thermometers are also available.

Timers   Devices for accurately timing cooking foods, may be electric or manual.

Toaster   A small, usually electric, appliance for toasting bread.

Steamer

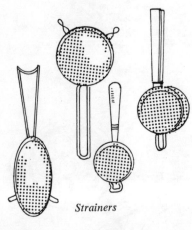

Strainers

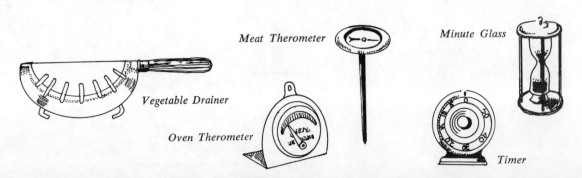

Meat Therometer

Minute Glass

Vegetable Drainer

Oven Therometer

Timer

(22)

Tongs   A scissor-type device for lifting and turning meats and vegetables without piercing; also used for serving.

Tray   An open receptacle with a flat bottom and a low rim for holding or carrying articles.

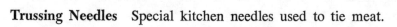

Tongs

Trivet   An ornamental metal plate on very short legs for use under a hot dish at a table, or on stove as an asbestos mat or for steaming puddings in pots.

Trussing Needles   Special kitchen needles used to tie meat.

Vegetable Brush   A small stiff-bristled brush for scrubbing vegetables.

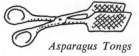

Vegetable Scoop   A handled utensil with a rounded base for scooping. (see Scoop)

Asparagus Tongs

Waffle Iron   A utensil for cooking waffles, having two metal parts hinged together and shutting upon each other with projecting studs on the insides; may be electric or manual.

Waxed Paper   Paper with a coating of white wax and other ingredients.

Wine Basket   A basket which permits the wine bottle to rest horizontally during serving.

Trivet

Wine Basket

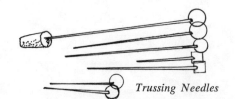

Trussing Needles

(23)

THE COMPLETE

KITCHEN GUIDE

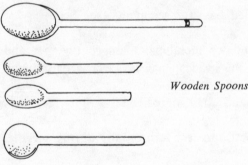

Wire Whisk

Wine Rack   A wooden or wire device for storing unopened wine bottles on their side.

Wire Basket
1. A utensil that suspends foods for frying in deep fat.
2. A small wire utensil for shaping and frying foods in deep fat

Wire Whisk   A whipping or beating device.

Wooden Picks   For securing foods that might open in cooking. Also used for serving appetizers.

Wooden Spoons   Long-handled spoons made of wood.

Wooden Spoons

Acidulate   To make sour or acid in a moderate degree, usually with lemon or lime juice or vinegar.

Bake   To cook in dry heat, in an enclosed oven.

Barbecue   To cook slowly over hot coals or embers, or under a broiler unit, basting often with a marinade or highly-seasoned liquid. The sauce is also called barbecue, as is the food cooked in this manner.

Bard   To cover uncooked lean meat or fish with slices of larding pork to prevent surface drying during cooking and to give flavor.

Baste   To moisten cooking foods—usually baking or roasting meats or poultry—with melted fat, juices, sauces, marinades, wines, pan drippings or other liquids. Basting helps to keep the surface of cooking foods moist, noticeably helps in browning and crisping skin.

Batter   A semi-liquid mixture, usually of eggs, milk and flour, thin enough to pour well or capable of being dropped evenly from a spoon.
   Beating is done with a wooden spoon, a wire whisk, an egg beater, an electric mixer or for pancakes and waffles.

Beat   A process of adding air to a mixture to make it smooth and/or incorporate additional ingredients.
   Beating is done with a wooden spoon, a wire whisk, an egg beater, an electric mixer or a fork.

Bind   To unite ingredients with a sauce such as mayonnaise.

2 ❧
Dictionary of Cooking Methods

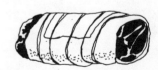

Barding

Blanch
1. To pre-cook foods for a short period of time by plunging them into boiling liquid.
2. To aid in skin removal of fruits and some vegetables.
3. To scald shelled nuts until the thin outer skins are sufficiently loosened to remove easily.

Blend   To mix ingredients together thoroughly. Also to use an electric blender.

Boil
1. To bring liquid to a temperature of 212° F. at sea level (see p. 268 for Altitude Adjustments). When boiling, bubbles rise and break on the surface.
2. To cook foods in boiling liquid.
3. Boiling over high heat is often called a fast or "rolling" boil.

Bone
1. To remove, by extracting from the inside, the carcass and bones of a bird.
2. To remove bones from meat or fish.

Braise   To brown foods slowly in a small amount of fat. Then add a small amount of liquid and cook in a tightly-covered utensil.

Bread   A coating of bread crumbs, cracker crumbs or meal. The crumbs are made to adhere by first dipping food in liquid or beaten egg.

Broil   To cook by dry heat, generally underneath a broiler unit (see also Grill).

Butter   To rub the cooking utensil to be used with butter (or fat) to prevent foods from sticking.

Candy
1. To cook in a heavy syrup—as with fruits, peels and ginger—until transparent.
2. To cook in syrup, brown sugar, sugar or honey such as candied yams.

Caramelize   To melt sugar and boil it until a characteristic brown color and flavor develop. Used to flavor soups and sauces, in icings and candy.

Carve   To cut meats into serving portions (see Carving, p. 125).

Chop   To separate into pieces using a sharp knife or chopper.

Clarify
1. To clarify butter: heat until melted, then carefully pour liquid into another utensil, leaving the creamy residue behind.
2. To clarify stock: add eggwhites, broken egg shells, or raw ground meat to clear, fat-free stock and simmer uncovered for about 20 minutes.

Coat   To cover food completely with a glaze, aspic, mayonnaise, sauce or icing.

Chopping

Coat a Spoon   A term used to describe thickness of sauces or custards which adheres to back of inverted spoon.

Coddle   To cook eggs gently in water just below boiling.

Cream   To work butter or shortening with a wooden spoon until soft and consistent, especially for batters. To work together fat and sugar until creamy and light.

Creamed   Foods cooked in or served with a plain or flavored white sauce or cream sauce.

Crisp
1. To make crisp by immersing in cold water or refrigerating; said particularly of salad greens.
2. To crisp foods by heating in oven.

Cubing

Cube   To cut foods into ½- to 1-inch squares. Larger cubes are often called chunks.

Cut   To sever food with a knife or scissors.

Cut In   To work with a pastry blender or two knives until solid fat and dry ingredients are evenly and finely divided, especially in making doughs.

Cutting In

Decant   To carefully pour liquid into a second container to separate the residue.

Deglaze   To loosen the drippings caked on a utensil after cooking by adding water, broth, wine or other liquids to make a sauce.

Degrease   To remove fat from surface of liquids.

Dice   To cut into small even cubes less than ½-inch square.

Dicing

Disjoint   To separate joints of poultry or break into pieces.

Dot   To cover the surface of food with small amounts of butter before baking or broiling. Usually said of gratineed dishes.

Dough Mixture of ingredients, always containing flour, fat, egg or liquid. Thick enough to knead or roll but too thick to pour or stir. Doughs are usually finished when they leave the sides of the mixing bowl clean.

Dredge To coat evenly with seasoned flour, fine crumbs or meal, etc. Particularly with chicken and meat for stews.

Dredging can be done by placing dry ingredients in a paper bag, adding foods to be dredged and shaking the bag vigorously.

Fruits and nuts are dredged in unseasoned flour to keep them suspended in cake batter while baking.

Dress
1. To cover with a dressing, as salads and vegetables.
2. To stuff a bird or meats.
3. To garnish.

Drip A method of preparing coffee.

Drippings Fat and meat juices accumulated in a cooking pan.

Dust To sprinkle lightly with flour, sugar or any light ingredient.

En Papillote To place meat in parchment paper or envelope with other ingredients and bake in oven.

Filter
1. A method of making coffee.
2. To strain through a fine cloth or paper.

Papillote

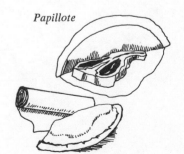

Flake
1. To shred in thin pieces.
2. To pull apart food that separates into natural divisions.

Flambé To ignite a warm alcoholic beverage added to any suitable dish.

Flip To turn a pancake or fritter.

Float
1. A flavoring liqueur floated on top of an alcoholic beverage.
2. Cream or light substance floated on soups or stews.

Flute To edge a pie crust by pinching or impressing with a fluter or the fingers.

Fold
1. To incorporate fragile substances as beaten egg whites or whipped cream into a heavier substance. The process is a very light folding over, done with a spatula, rubber scraper or wooden spoon.
2. The first and second turns made when sliding an omelet out of the pan.

Folding

Fricassee
1. To cook in liquid, usually applied to poultry or veal cut into pieces. Food served in a cream sauce based on the cooking liquid.

Frost To ice or glaze a cake, fruit or other foods.

Fry

1. To cook in a pan or on a griddle in a small amount of fat, also called pan-frying or sautéing.
2. To cook in deep fat, or to immerse completely in fat, known as deep-fat frying (see Chart, p. 269).

Garnish   To decorate foods before serving, as with parsley, radishes, olives, nuts, etc.

Glacé   To coat with a thin layer of boiled sugar syrup.

Glaze   To coat with sugar syrup, jelly or meat juices.

Gratinee   To cover cooked food with a sauce, sprinkled with crumbs or cheese and dotted with butter and browned under a broiler or in the oven.

Grating

Grate   To process foods on a hand grater or other mechanical device to obtain fine-to-coarse particles.

Grill   To cook by direct heat, particularly over a fire or hot coals.

Grind   To crush into minute pieces, particularly with peppercorns and other similar hard spices.

Hydrogenate   A process in which hydrogen is combined with an unsaturated compound, such as oil, to form solid or semi-solid fat.

Ice   To decorate a cake or pastry with icing.

Julienne   To cut into even matchlike sticks, particularly potatoes and carrots.

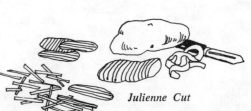
Julienne Cut

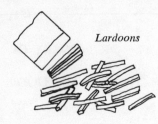

Lardoons

Knead   To work dough by pressing, stretching and folding with the hands.

Lard   To insert strips of larding pork, lardoons, into meat with a larding needle.

Leavening   A raising agent such as yeast, baking powder, etc.

Marinate   To let food soak in a liquid-acid mixture usually wine and oil.

Macerate   To let fruits stand in flavored liquid, usually wine or liqueur.

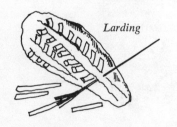

Larding

Mask   To cover surface of food completely with mayonnaise mixed with aspic or other thick sauce or to cover with jelly.

Measure   All measures should be level and exact. To measure accurately use standard measuring cups and spoons.

To measure dry ingredients, use a set of metal or plastic cups (available in ⅛-, ¼-, ⅓-, ½-, 1- and 2-cup sizes). Fill cup, place on level surface and smooth off excess with flat blade of knife or spatula.

Sifted flour and powdered sugar should be spooned lightly into the cup measure; brown sugar should always be packed tightly. When measuring other ingredients, as ground nuts, rap the top of cup to settle ingredient evenly before leveling.

To measure liquid ingredients, set a glass measuring cup on a flat, level surface and fill liquid to indicated measure level.

To measure solid ingredients, use either type of measuring cup unless measuring by displacement method. (To obtain 1 cup butter by displacement: fill a 2 cup glass measuring cup with 1 cup cold water and add enough cold butter to bring the contents to the 2 cup mark.)

Measuring Cups

To use measuring spoons, fill spoon with liquid or solid ingredient. Hold spoon level and smooth off any excess solid ingredient with flat edge of a knife (see Weigh p. 38).

Melt   To heat solid food until it is liquefied.

Mince   To chop food into very minute pieces.

Mix   To combine and shake or stir ingredients so that they are evenly distributed.

Mold   To prepare food in a specified shape by setting or gelling in a mold.

Pan-broil   To cook uncovered over direct heat, in a very hot frying pan. Any accumulating fat is poured off.

Pan-fry   To cook in hot fat over direct heat.

Parboil   To partially cook by boiling for a short time; cooking is completed by another method.

Parch   To dry and brown by direct heat; applied to nuts.

Pare   To cut off any outside covering, as skin or rind.

Pasteurize   To preserve liquids, e.g., milk and fruit juice, by heating to 140° F. to 180° F. to destroy certain microorganisms and arrest fermentation.

Peel   To remove the outside covering with a knife, peeler, etc.

Fish Mold

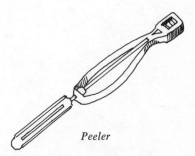

Peeler

Pickle   To preserve, steep or season in a solution of salt, vinegar, spices, etc., for instance, cucumber or herring.

Plank
1. Placing broiled or grilled meat or fish on a wooden plank, surrounding it with piped potatoes and cooked vegetables and returning to oven to brown lightly.
2. Baking or broiling meat or fish with vegetables on a wooden plank.

Poach   To cook food gently in a barely simmering liquid.

Pot Roasting   To cook large cuts of meat in little liquid in a tightly covered kettle.

Pound   To strike with a heavy blunt instrument to tenderize and/or flatten.

Powder   To shake dry ingredients through a fine sieve over food surface.

Preheat   To allow the oven, broiler or other cooking appliance to heat to the required temperature before placing in food.

Pressure-cooking   To cook foods in steam under pressure in a special utensil.

Punch Down   To strike risen dough with the fist to allow gas to escape and fresh oxygen to reach the yeast.

Purée   To mash or crush solid foods into a soft mass, e.g., a purée of green peas.

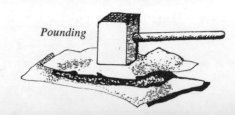

Pounding

Ream   To squeeze out juice, usually over the recipe.

Reduce   To reduce the quantity of a liquid by boiling down.

Render   To melt fat from fatty meat and tissue.

Rest   To allow dough to lie before using.

Rewarm   (see Warm)

Rice   To put potatoes through a ricer before mashing.

Rise   To let yeast dough rise in a warm place until double in bulk or as recipe specifies.

Roast   To cook in an enclosed oven by dry heat. Can also be done in hot ashes or sand, etc.

Reaming a Lemon

Roll Out   To flatten dough with a rolling pin to desired thickness for pie crust and before cutting into cookies, noodles.

Sauté   To brown or cook in hot fat or oil. To fry.

Scald
1. To dip into boiling water.
2. To heat milk to just below boiling.
3. To immerse almonds in boiling water in order to skin.
4. To dip fruits and vegetables in boiling water to facilitate drawing off the skin or shell.

Scale To remove the scales from fish with a knife or scaler.

Scallop To bake in a sauce. Usually with bread or cracker crumbs.

Score
1. To cut narrow gashes in fat, to prevent meats from curling.
2. To cut narrow crisscross lines in fat side of ham or roast.
3. To cut even shallow lines in cucumbers with a fork or scoring knife for decoration.

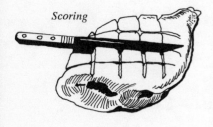

Scoring

Sear To brown meat by a short exposure to intense heat. When meats are seared before roasting, roasting time has to be reduced.

Season To render more palatable by adding a spice or relish. Usually taken to mean adding salt and pepper.

Separate
1. To place egg whites and yolks in different utensils.
2. An undesirable sauce condition in which the ingredients separate.

Shred To tear or cut into long, narrow pieces with a knife or hand or mechanical shredder.

Shuck To remove shells of oysters or clams or corn husks.

Sieve To separate out lumps in dry ingredients.

Sift To put dry ingredients through a fine sieve.

Simmer To cook just below the boiling point, in a liquid, usually at a temperature of 190° F.

Skewer
1. To thread foods on a skewer for cooking.
2. To secure openings over stuffing.

Skim To remove a top surface of fat, cream or scum.

Sliver To cut into even, long, thin strips.

Steam To cook foods by direct or indirect application of steam.

Steep To soak in a liquid, to extract flavor, color, etc.

Sterilize To steam, cook or boil foods in order to destroy living microorganisms.

Stew To cook by simmering in liquid to cover. Foods, particularly cubed meats, cooked with vegetables in this manner.

Stir To blend ingredients uniformly by mixing together with a circular motion.

Strain To remove solid foods from liquid by pouring through a sieve, strainer or colander.

Stuff To fill cavity of bird or pocket in meat with forcemeat, stuffing or dressing.

Test with a Straw To insert a straw or wooden pick in the center of a cake to test for doneness. The cake is done when the straw comes out clean.

Toast To warm, crisp and brown with dry heat.

Truss To prepare whole poultry for cooking by securing wings and legs with string or skewers.

Uncork (see p. 254)

Unmold To loosen the contents of a mold. Three methods of unmolding:
1. Immerse mold in hot water, then carefully invert onto a serving platter and remove mold.
2. Invert mold onto a serving platter; then wrap mold with kitchen towel, wrung out in very hot water. Remove the mold.
3. Run blade of thin knife around edge of mold and invert as above.

Warm Warm platters and plates by placing them:
1. In a low oven, not over 200° F.
2. In dishwasher or electric plate warmer.
3. On electric buffet tray.
(Rewarm)
1. Rewarm leftover foods, soups and sauces in the top of a double boiler, over boiling or simmering water.
2. Rewarm baked dishes and casseroles in a low oven.
3. Rewarm clear soups in a saucepan over low heat.

Weigh To ascertain the weight of, on a kitchen scale. If food has to be weighed in a container, weigh the container separately before or after weighing food. Add or subtract quantity until correct weight is reached. Weigh meats in order to determine roasting time.

Weigh Down   Place a weight on, to flatten or extract moisture.

Whip   To beat rapidly to induce expansion and fluffiness by beating in air, particularly heavy cream and eggs.

Wrap   To cover fresh or cooked foods to prolong their freshness, to retain crispness of vegetables and greens and to prevent absorption of flavors and odors.

When using plastic bags: press out all air, after filling and before sealing or tying.

Washed salad greens and parsley may be stored in plastic bags without deterioration for several days.

It is always preferable to use fresh herbs. If you are not fortunate enough to have an herb garden of your own, herbs are often available at fruit and vegetable stands in season. Some herbs grow well in a sunny kitchen. A good way to familiarize yourself with various herbs is to blend 1 to 1½ tablespoons of the chopped fresh herb into ¼ cup softened butter. Spread on plain crackers and taste.

Dried and crushed or ground herbs are readily available. Substitute less than a teaspoon of ground or about 1 teaspoon crushed herbs for 1 tablespoon of fresh herbs. Crushed herbs can be soaked in a small amount of liquid (oil, brandy, wine, stock, water, etc.) before using, which will intensify and enhance the flavor. Add the soaking liquid to the recipe with the herb if desired.

Purchasing Dried Herbs

1. Buy small amounts of the best dried herbs available—this is no place to economize.
2. Store herbs in tightly-covered containers away from strong light.
3. Crush dried herbs between your fingers before using to release all of the flavor.
4. Herbs lose strength with age, so do not hesitate to discard herbs that have lost their aroma and taste—even if the bottle is nowhere near empty.

Tarragon Vinegar   When fresh tarragon is plentiful, fill about 2 cups of the leaves and a few stalks into a gallon container. Fill container to the brim with a good cider vinegar and let stand several months. Decant as much as desired and refill container with additional cider vinegar. If preferred, use much less vinegar and let tarragon infuse for 2 weeks or so; then strain.

3

Herbs

Herbs

Name	Origin	Type of Plant	General Uses	Use in or with	Market Forms
Angelica	Syria	Perennial herbaceous plant. Use root, stems and leaves	Baking, confectionary, flavoring, tea, garnishing	Fruit cakes, breads	Candied, jarred
Balm (Balsam) Also: Sweet Balsam Lemon Balsam	Greece and Southern Europe	Perennial	Flavoring, liqueurs, garnishing	Soups, stews, salads	Fresh
Basil	Tropical Asia	Annual bush	Vinegar flavoring, garnish, Italian recipes	Stews, tomatoes, cheese, fish, soup, stuffing	Fresh, dried
Bay (Laurel)	Rome, Southern Europe	Perennial evergreen shrub or tree	Flavoring leaf usually removed before serving; herb bouquet, perfumes	Stews, marinades	Whole leaf, fresh or dried
Bergamot	Turkey	Variety of mint, also small fruit	Mint flavors, perfume		Fresh
Borage	Aleppo	Hardy annual plant	Candied flowers, Pimms cup, flowers	Pickles, salads, claret cup	Garden
Bouquet Garni (Herb Bouquet)	France	Composed bouquet of bay leaf, parsley and thyme	Flavoring soups and stew	Soups and stews, remove before serving	Homemade or small herb bags and jars or cans
Burnet (Pimpinella)	Northern Countries	Annual	Vinegar, tankards	Salads, beverages	Fresh
Catmint (Catnip)	England	Perennial	Bee forage flavoring	Sauces	Wild, fresh dried
Chervil	South Europe	Annual parsley-like aromatic herb	Vinegar flavor	Salads, soups, dried peas	Fresh, dried

Angelica

Lemon Balm

Basil

Bay

Bergamot

Borage

Bouquet Garni

Burnet

Catmint

Chervil

Name	Origin	Type of Plant	General Uses	Use in or with	Market Forms
Chives	Asia and Europe	Perennial self-seeding	Sauces, garnish, chive butter, substitute for onion	Vichyssoise, salads, chive cheese, potatoes, eggs	Frozen, dried, fresh-potted plants
Dill	Mediterranean	Annual	Sauces, garnish	Pickles, fish, vinegar, mayonnaise, lamb, cauliflower	Fresh, dried
Fennel	Mediterranean	Perennial	Raw as celery with antipasto, flavoring, garnish	Sauces, mayonnaise, fish, blanched leaves	Fresh as celery
Garlic	Far East	Bulbous herb	Garlic butter, garlic salt, garlic vinegar, aromatic	Lamb, soups, salads	Fresh, dehydrated flakes
Horseradish	European	Herb plant with pungent root	Flavoring and garnish	Sauces	Roots stored in sand, bottled grated, dehydrated
Lovage	Mediterranean	Perennial	Candied	Confectionery	Fresh, dried
Marigold	South Europe	Self-seeding	Leaves in salad, flowers for coloring, petals good flavor in stew or soup	Buns	Fresh
Marjoram	North Africa	Perennial	Vinegar flavor, garnish, flavoring, especially in soups, salads, stuffing	Used in beer and ale prior to discovery of hops	Fresh, dried
Mint	Mediterranean	Perennial	Flavor vinegar or apple jelly, garnish	Juleps, ice tea, lemonade, lamb, fruits, sauce, onions, candy, chewing gum, and toothpaste	Fresh and dried, bottled mint sauce, crystalized leaves

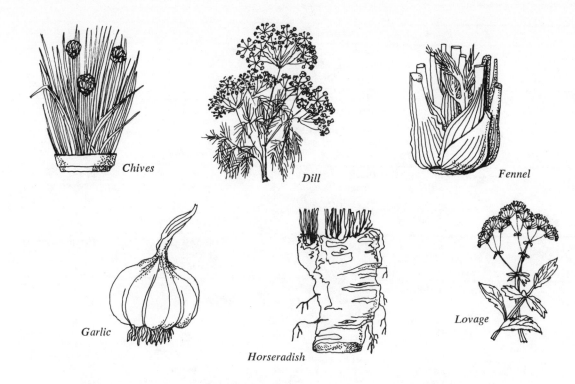

Chives

Dill

Fennel

Garlic

Horseradish

Lovage

Marigold

Majoram

Mint

Name	Origin	Type of Plant	General Uses	Use in or with	Market Forms
Nasturtium	American	Annual	Seeds and flower buds for flavoring, flowers for garnish	Salads	Fresh
Oregano	North Africa	Perennial	Flavoring mushrooms and pizzas	Italian recipes	Fresh, dried
Parsley	Sardinia	Biennial	Herb bouquet, parsley butter, garnish	Sauces, vegetables, fish, stews, eggs, potatoes	Fresh, dried, dehydrated
Rosemary	South Europe	Perennial shrub	Immortalized as romantic symbol by Shakespeare, Ben Johnson, Sir Thomas More, etc.	Lamb, shell fish, pork	Fresh, dried
Rue	South Europe	Perennial shrub	Seasoning	Young leaves in claret cup, fish sauces	Fresh, dried
Saffron	Biblical	Type of crocus bulb	Flavor, color, Henry VIII so fond of it in his food he forbade its use by court ladies to dye their hair	Breads, rice, fish, soups	Dried shreds, powdered by the milli-gram
Sage	North Mediterranean	Semi-perennial bush	Seasoning, especially pork sausage, baked fish, cheese. Hot sage milk drunk by Hollanders after skating.	Pastas, chicken, lamb, veal, onions, stuffings, sage tea	Fresh, dried
Savory	Mediterranean	Summer annual Winter perennial	Seasoning poultry, sausage and boiled fish	Peas, beans, dried leaves, syrups and conserves	Fresh, dried, powdered

Nasturtiums

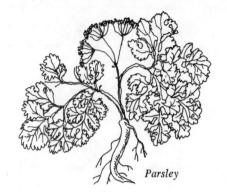

Oregano

Parsley

Rosemary

Rue

Saffron

Sage

Savory

Name	Origin	Type of Plant	General Uses	Use in or with	Market Forms
Sorrel	Europe	Perennial	Soup, sauce	Leek, potatoes, spinach, fish	Fresh
Tansy	Europe	Perennial	Garnish, flavoring	Puddings, omelets	Fresh
Tarragon	Southern Russia, Siberia	Perennial, if protected	Vinegar, herb bouquet, flavoring	Meat, chicken, eggs, fish sauces, bearnaise sauce; leaves—fresh or dried in salads	Fresh, dried, preserved in vinegar
Thyme	Near East	Perennial	Herb bouquet, sausage herb. Flavor: poultry stuffing, meat loaf, burgundy sauce	Tomatoes, stews, meat	Fresh, dried
Woodruff	European	Perennial	Flavoring wine bowls	May wine, peach and strawberry bowls	Dried

Sorrel

Tansy

Tarragon

Thyme

Woodruff

Spices, condiments and flavorings, such as vanilla, are used to enhance the flavor of food and also, in the case of salt, as a preserver.

Ground spices, like dried herbs, tend to loose flavor, so it is advisable to purchase small quantities of high-quality spices. Store them in tightly covered containers and replace those that have lost their strength.

4 ∂

Spices, Condiments and Flavorings

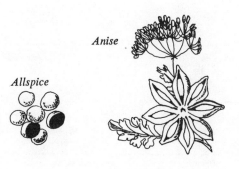

Allspice

Anise

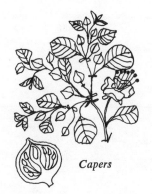

Capers

Spices, Condiments and Flavorings

Name	Origin	Type of Plant	General Uses	Use in or with	Market Forms
Allspice	South America, Central America, Mexico	Myrtle tree	Seasoning	Spiced baking, puddings, sauces, meats and pastas	Ground
Anise, Aniseed	Egypt, Greece, Asia Minor	Annual	Flavoring, garnish	Soups, salads, pot-herb, liqueurs, cookies, breads, absinthe, anisette	Seeds, ground
Capers (buds)	Mediterranean	Bud of a low prickly shrub	Garnish, flavoring	Sauces, fish, vegetables, appetizers, Vitello Tonato	Pickled bud

Name	Origin	Type of Plant	General Uses	Use in or with	Market Forms
Caraway Seeds	Arabia	Biennial	Flavoring	Breads, kraut, beefs, confectionary, liqueurs	Dried seeds
Cardamon	East Indian	Perennial plant	Flavoring	Beverages, food	Dried seeds
Celery Seed	Europe	Seed of a stalk and shoot vegetable	Flavoring	Dressings, casseroles	Dried seeds
Chili Powder	Mexico and South America	Pepper & herbs	Spicing	Mexican recipe sauces	Powder
Cinnamon	Malaya	Bark of a cinnamomum tree	Flavoring	Sugar, puddings, confectionary, cinnamon toast, beverages	Bark, ground
Chutney (see Sauces)					
Cloves	East Indian	Tree	Flavoring	Ham, onions, soup, beets	Whole, ground
Coriander Seeds	Near East	Annual	Flavoring	Breads, soup, alcoholic beverages	Seeds
Cumin	Near East, Far East, Egypt	Dwarf plant	Flavoring as caraway	Indian dishes, sauerkraut, German breads, Scandinavian breads	Dried seeds
Curry Powder	India	Contains: ginger, cumin, turmeric, coriander, cayenne, fennel, lime juice, etc.	Seasoning and spicing	Curries, soups, sauces and Indian recipes	Bottled, canned
Dill Seed	Southern Russia, Mediterranean	Annual	Flavoring	Cucumbers, pickles, dressings, vinegar	Dried seed, ground

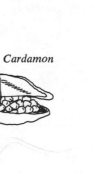

Cardamon

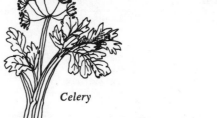

Celery

Caraway

Chili

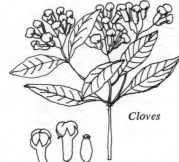

Cloves

Cumin Seeds

Curry Powder

Coriander

Dill Seeds

Name	Origin	Type of Plant	General Uses	Use in or with	Market Forms
Extracts: Vanilla, Lemon, Orange, Coffee, Mint, Almond, Walnut, Maple, Rum, Fruit, Berry	Various	Vanilla bean, fruit trees, berry bushes, lemon and oranges, maple trees, coffee bean, walnut and almond trees, mint leaves, rum from sugar	Flavoring	Confectionary, desserts, baking	Bottled
Fennel Seed	Mediterranean	Perennial	Flavoring	Liqueurs	Seeds
Ginger	India, Borneo	Perennial	Flavoring	Ginger ale, ginger beer, curries, breads, confectionary	Carton, root, green-fresh, ground, conserved, candied, crystalized
Juniper Berries		Berry of evergreen shrub or tree	Flavoring	Game, ragouts, gin and liqueurs	Whole, ground
Mace	Tropical America	Dried outer covering of nutmeg kernel	Flavoring	As nutmeg, but stronger, tomato juice	Ground
Monosodium Glutamate	Orient	Chemical extracted from plants	Enhancer	Heightens natural food flavors	Powder in shaker
Mustard Seeds, Ground (Dry Mustard or Mustard Flour)	East India	Seed of mustard plant ground	Flavoring	Sauces, dressings, appetizers and salads as is; or moisten with liquid and use as prepared mustard	Bottled, canned
Mustard Seeds, Whole	East India	2 infinitesimal seeds in each mustard pod	Flavoring	Salad dressings, in making sausage and pickling spices	Canned, bottled
Mustard, Prepared	East India	Ground seeds, commercially moistened and prepared	Flavoring	Sauces and dressings, with meat, smoked meats, eggs and fish	Jarred

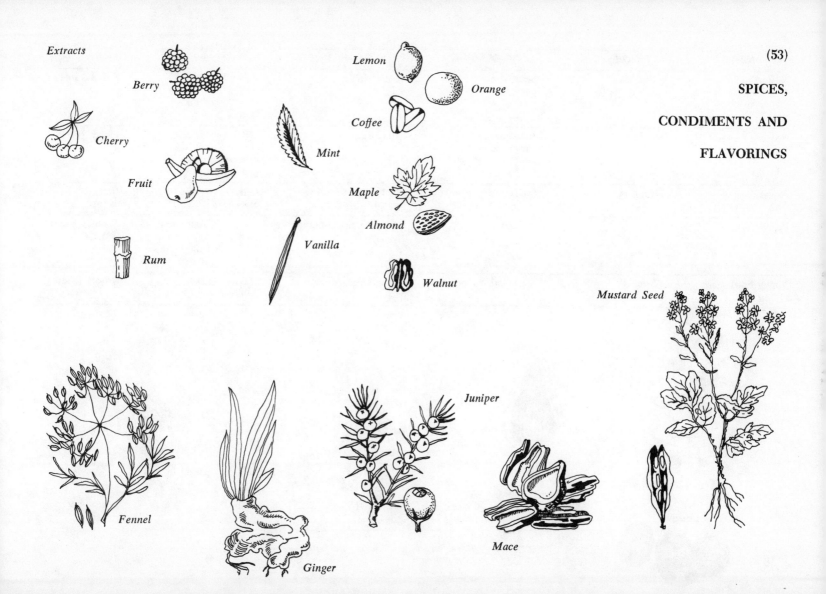

Extracts

Berry

Cherry

Fruit

Rum

Mint

Vanilla

Lemon

Orange

Coffee

Maple

Almond

Walnut

Mustard Seed

Fennel

Ginger

Juniper

Mace

Name	Origin	Type of Plant	General Uses	Use in or with	Market Forms
Nasturtium	America	Seed of an annual plant	Flavoring	Seeds in salad, pickles and beverages, also flower buds in salads	Dried seeds
Nutmeg	India	Root plant of ginger family	Flavoring	Egg nogs, cocoa, chocolate, meat, dried bean and pea soups	Hand grated, ground
Paprika	Hungary	Sweet red pepper	Coloring, flavoring, garnish	Gulyas, paprika chicken	Bottled, canned
Peppercorns	India	Annual	Flavoring, seasoning	Whole in soups and stews, ground seasoning for almost all food except desserts	Whole, ground
Poppy Seed	Asia	Seed pods of poppies	Flavoring, garnish	Baking, breads and rolls	Whole seeds

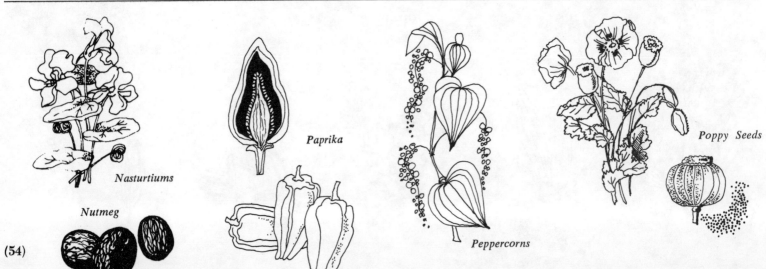

Nasturtiums

Nutmeg

Paprika

Peppercorns

Poppy Seeds

(54)

Name	Origin	Type of Plant	General Uses	Use in or with	Market Forms
Saffron	Biblical	Type of crocus bulb	Flavor, color	Breads, rice, fish, soups	Dried shreds, powdered by the milligram
Salt	Salt deposits and sea water	Deposits or evaporated sea water	Seasoning and preserving	Almost all seasoning of foods except desserts	Sea salt, rough salt, table salt, rock salt
Sesame Seeds	India	Annual plant	Flavoring, garnish	Breads, chicken recipes, cookies	Dried seeds, toasted dried seeds
Soy Sauce	Asia	Bean	Spicing, flavoring	Oriental recipes, spareribs	Bottled
Turmeric	India	Root plant of ginger family	Color, flavoring, substitute for saffron color	Curried recipes, dressing, relishes	Ground
Vanilla Bean & Seeds	Tropical America	Tree	Flavoring	Place vanilla bean in powdered sugar container or grate for desserts	Extract made from seeds, dried bean

Saffron

Sesame Seeds

Turmeric

Vanilla

(55)

Tender, high in nutritional value but low in calories and cholestoral-associated fat, fish and shellfish have long been ingredients of great gourmet dishes. Fish is often simply cooked, and enhanced with a fine sauce.

The two most important factors in successful fish cookery are to obtain the freshest fish available and to cook it for the shortest possible time.

Here are some pointers for determining the freshness of fish:

1. Look for fish that has been packed in ice.
2. The eyes should be clear and bulging—not sunken and dull.
3. The scales should lie flat and be bright and shiny.
4. The gills should be pinkish red to red.
5. There should be a "fresh fish" smell, not an unpleasant one.
6. The flesh should be firm and it should spring back when it is indented or pressed with the fingers.
7. The fish should be free of any "slime."

5.
Fish
and
Shellfish

Amount to Buy

1 pound whole or round fish serves 1 person.

1 pound drawn fish serves 1 person.

½ pound dressed or pan-dressed fish serves 1 person.

⅓–½ pound fish steaks serve 1 person.

⅓–½ pound fish fillets serve 1 person.

Cooking Methods   It should be remembered that fish does not require tenderizing; the cooking process is only to develop its flavor. It requires less cooking time than meat and should be cooked just before it is eaten.

Baking   In order to bake fish successfully, be sure of its exact weight so that it can

Whole or Round Fish

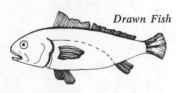

Drawn Fish

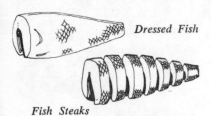

Dressed Fish

Fish Steaks

Fish Fillets

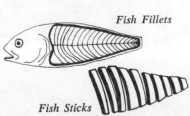

Fish Sticks

be cooked the proper length of time. Whole fish should be baked with the head on if possible. It seals in the juices and prevents a dried or toughened cut end.

Rinse fish quickly in cold salted water, dry it with a damp cloth or drain it on paper towels. Place in an open baking pan on buttered foil or brown paper. Bake in a 400° F. oven according to time chart. Stuff or baste fish according to individual recipes. If fish is stuffed, secure opening with skewers or sew with kitchen thread.

Steaming The secret of perfectly steamed fish is to use very little water. Cover the pot tightly and steam fish exactly the right length of time.

Use a deep pan or fish kettle with a tightly-fitted cover. Fill pan with 1½ to 2 inches of water and bring to a boil. Know the exact weight of the fish as it is ready for steaming. Wrap fish in cheesecloth or muslin so it can be removed from the rack without breaking when it is done. When water is boiling place fish on rack, lower into pan and cover pan tightly. Reduce heat to simmer after water returns to a boil.

Cooking Time For steaming fish, a chart of times and temperatures is not necessary. Simply remember this: Fish less than 2-inches thick require 1 minute of steaming for each ounce of weight. That is why knowing the exact weight of the fish is so important.

Fish over two inches thick requires different times, depending on the variety. Steam approximately 8 to 12 minutes per pound, or follow recipe directions.

Do not add salt or vinegar to steamed fish until after cooking is completed. Other seasonings, such as garlic, wine, parsley, celery or onion, should be added to the pan at the beginning of the cooking period so that the flavors will have a chance to blend.

Pan Frying To pan fry, heat butter, margarine or oil in a skillet, dip fish in flour and then in a mixture of 1 beaten egg and ⅓-cup milk. Then roll fish in cornmeal or fine bread crumbs. Fry on both sides until light brown.

For a simple fried or sautéed fish, use butter in the pan and leave out the cornmeal or bread-crumb coating. Sauté fish on both sides until light brown. Remove to heated serving dish. Sprinkle with chopped parsley. Salt and pepper to taste. Melt a little extra butter in the pan and pour over the fish.

Broiling   Broiled fish fillets take between 5 and 10 minutes to cook depending on the variety of fish. Never turn fillets while broiling them. Baste according to chart. Using aluminum-foil boats will save cleaning up later and also will add flavor by retaining fish juices around the fillet during cooking period.

Filleting Fish

Fresh Fillets   Wipe fillet dry with damp cloth. Lightly dust it with flour, cornmeal or cracker crumbs. It is important to preheat broiling compartment and pan under full heat (550° F.) for 10 minutes or follow directions of range manufacturer for preheating. Place fillet on preheated broiling pan 2 inches from source of heat. Baste fillet evenly with butter, margarine, shortening or oil. Broil fillet the length of time indicated on chart. Do not overcook.

Frozen Fillets   Cook them frozen but allow a little more cooking time. Place frozen fillets 3 inches from the source of heat. Be sure to baste evenly over the entire surface of the fish.

Steaks   Steaks may be cut to any desired thickness. Average thickness will vary from ½ to 1 inch. Wipe steak dry with damp cloth. Lightly dust it with flour. Preheat broiling pan and compartment at full heat (550° F.) for 10 minutes or follow instructions of range manufacturer for preheating. Place steak on preheated broiler pan.

Brush top of steak evenly with butter, margarine, shortening or oil. Make sure steak is 2 inches from source of heat (see chart for Broiling Fish Steaks). Place still frozen steaks 3 inches from heat and cook slightly longer.

Fish steaks are best broiled a shorter period of time on the first side. Thus, the second side or side which will be served up will be a rich golden brown. Fish steaks take between 6 and 10 minutes of broiling, depending on the variety of fish and thickness of the steaks. Use aluminum-foil boats to save flavor and cleaning up later.

Darne

Split Fish   Any fish weighing less than 4 pounds may be split for broiling. Split fish cooked with bone left in is juicier and has more flavor. You may have the fish split where you buy it or do it yourself at home. Slit the underside of the fish all the way down to the tail. Then, keeping the knife pressed against the backbone, slice the fish in two along its entire length.

Dust split fish with flour. Preheat broiling pan and compartment at full heat (550° F) for 10 minutes or follow directions given by range maker. Place split fish on preheated broiler rack as specified on chart for Broiling Split Fish. Baste surface evenly with butter, margarine, shortening or oil. Use aluminum foil for more flavor and less work later.

Whole Dressed Fish   Whole dressed fish, like steaks, must be broiled on both sides. Only fluke and flounders are not turned while broiling. Preheat broiling compartment and pan at full heat (550° F.) for 10 minutes or follow range maker's directions. Wipe fish with damp cloth. Lightly dust the fish with flour. Brush or spread top side of the whole fish evenly with butter, margarine, shortening or oil. Place fish, basted side up, on preheated broiling pan (see chart for Broiling Whole Dressed Fish). Broil first side according to chart. Season and turn. Baste second side evenly. Use aluminum-foil boat to keep juices around fish while broiling.

Barbecuing Fish   Fish cooked on an outdoor grill or barbecued. Allow one 1-inch thick fish steak per person. Marinate fish steaks 30 minutes before grilling. Broil on grill about 3 minutes on each side, 5 inches from coals. Brush each side with butter or marinade before grilling.

Fish steaks may be wrapped in foil with accompanying ingredients or barbecue sauce and grilled 3 inches from coals for about 10 to 12 minutes.

Whole small fish may be cooked by either method on an outdoor grill or pan fried over an outdoor fire.

Timetable for Broiling Fish Steaks

Type of Steak	Thickness	Time on 1st Side in Minutes	Time on 2nd Side in Minutes	Extra Bastings
Cod	½ inch	3	5	1
	1 inch	5	5	1
Salmon	½ inch	3	3	
	1 inch	3	5	
Swordfish	½ inch	3	3	
	1 inch	3	5	
Fresh Tuna	½ inch	3	3	
	1 inch	4	5	
Halibut	½ inch	3	3	1
	1 inch	4	5	1
Striped Bass	½ inch	3	3	1
	1 inch	4	4	1

Timetable for Broiling Split Fish

Name of Fish	Distance from Source of Heat in Inches	Thickness of Fish	Broiling Time in Minutes
Bluefish	3	¾ inch	8
Bonito Mackerel	3	½ to 1½ inches	10
Croaker	2	¾ inch	8
*Carp	6	½ to 1½ inches	12-14
Cisco (Lake Herring)	3	¼ to 1 inch	9-11
Hake	3	1 inch	6-8
Mackeral	2	¾ to 1 inch	8-10
Mullet	3	¼ to 1 inch	10-12
Porgy	3	½ to 1 inch	6-8

Name of Fish	Distance from Source of Heat in Inches	Thickness of Fish	Broiling Time in Minutes
*Pike	3	¼ to 1¼ inches	8-10
Sea Bass	3	½ to 1 inch	6-8
Weakfish	2	½ to ¾ inch	6-8
Whitefish	3	½ to 1½ inches	10-12
Whiting	3	¼ to ½ inch	6-8

*(Carp and Pike should be basted twice during the broiling period instead of the single basting recommended for the other varieties.)

Timetable for Broiling Fish Fillets

Name of Fish	Thickness of Fillets Vary from	Baste During Broiling	Broiling Time in Minutes
Bluefish	¼ to ¾ inch	Once	6
Carp	¼ to 1¼ inch	Once	8-10
Cisco (Lake Herring)	¼ to ½ inch	Once	5-7
Cod	½ to 1 inch	Twice	8-10
Flounder	¼ to ½ inch	Once	5-7
Fluke	¼ to 2/3 inch	Twice	5-8
Haddock	1/3 to 2/3 inch	Twice	5-8
Hake	¼ to ½ inch	Twice	6-8
Mackerel	¼ to 1¼ inch	Once	6-8
Mullet	¼ to ¾ inch	Twice	6-8
Pike	¼ to 2/3 inch	Once	6-8
Pollock	½ to 1 inch	Twice	6-8
Porgy	¼ to ⅝ inch	Twice	6
Sea Bass	¼ to ½ inch	Twice	5
Sole-Lemon	¼ to ¾ inch	Twice	5-8
Sole-Gray	¼ inch usual thickness	Once	5
Weakfish	¼ to ¾ inch	Twice	6
Whitefish	¼ to ¾ inch	Once	6-8
Whiting	¼ to ¾ inch	Twice	5

Timetable for Broiling Whole Dressed Fish

Name of Fish	Distance from Source of Heat in Inches	Time on 1st Side in Minutes	Time on 2nd Side in Minutes
Bluefish	3	4	5
Butterfish	3	4	5
Carp (up to 3 pounds)	6	12	14
Cisco (Lake Herring)	6	4	5
Croaker	6	5	8
Flounder	3	10	White Side up— don't turn
Fluke	3	8	White Side up— don't turn
Mackerel	6	3	5
Mullet	6	5	9
Pike	6	5	8
Porgy	3	3	6
Sea Bass	6	5	6
Swellfish Tails	3	5	6
Weakfish	6	3	5
Whitefish	6	5	8
Whiting	6	4	5

Timetable for Baking Fish

Name of Fish	Thickness in Inches	Baking Time Head On	Baking Time Head Off
Small Fish		Minutes Per Ounce	Minutes Per Ounces
Bluefish	1½	1½	2
Butterfish	½ inch	3	
Croaker	1½	1½	2
Flounder	1 inch	2	
Herring	1 inch	1½	2
Mackerel	2½	2	1
Pike	2¼	1¼	1

Name of Fish	Thickness in Inches	Baking Time Head On	Baking Time Head Off
Porgy	2	1	1¼
Sea Bass	1½	1-2/3	2
Mullet	2	1½	2
Weakfish	1½	1-2/3	2
Whiting	2	1¼	1½
Large Fish Pieces		*Minutes Per Pound*	*Minutes Per Pound*
Carp	2½	12	16
Cod	2¾	9	12
Florida Mackerel	2½	17	19
Haddock	3¼	10	14
Halibut	2¾		11
Salmon	2¼		11
Spotted Sea Trout	3½	14	15
Striped Bass	2½	12	16
Whitefish	1½	15	16

Fresh Water Fish Chart

Name of Fish	Market Form	Approximate Weight in Pounds	Cooking Method See Cooking Directions and Charts
Bass	Whole, drawn (lean)	¾-1	Bake, broil, steam, boil
Buffalofish (Big mouth, Red mouth, Small mouth, Gourhead) Winter Carp	Whole, drawn, dressed or steaks (lean)	2-25	Bake, broil, pan-fry, deep fat fry
Burbot (Fresh water Cod or Cusk)	Whole (lean)	2½-3	Bake, broil, steam
Carp	Whole, dressed (lean)	2-8	Bake, steam, pan-fry, deep fat fry

Bass

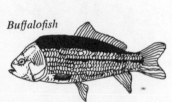

Buffalofish

Burbot

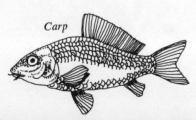

Carp

Catfish

Name of Fish	Market Form	Approximate Weight in Pounds	Cooking Method See Cooking Directions and Charts
Catfish (Bullhead)	Round, dressed, (lean)	1-40	Bake, broil, pan-fry, chowder
Gar (Garfish, Garpike)	Round, dressed, fillets (lean)	2-5	Bake, pan-fry, broil
Lake Herring (Cisco)	Whole, drawn (fat), fillets	1/3-1	Pan-fry, broil, deep fat fry
Lake Trout	Dressed, drawn (fat), fillets	1½-10	Bake, broil, fry
Mullet, white sucker or red fin	Whole, drawn, filleted (medium fat)	2-6	Bake, pan-fry, broil
Perch (see Yellow Perch)			
Pickerel, Jack, grass pike and Northern pike	Whole, dressed, fillets (lean)	2-10	Bake, broil, fry, chowder
Pike, yellow pike, pike perches, walleye	Whole, dressed, fillets (lean)	1½-5	Bake, broil, fry
Sauger pike, Sandpike	Whole, dressed, fillets (lean)	1-1½	Broil, bake, fry
Sheepshead, fresh water Drum	Whole, fillets (lean)	1½-8	Bake, broil, boil, steam
Smelts	Whole, dressed, fresh, frozen (lean)	⅛ (2 ounces)	Fried, breaded and fried, deep fat fry, broil, bake

Garfish

Herring

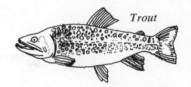
Trout

Mullet

Perch

Smelts

Sheepshead

Pickerel

Pike

(65)

Name of Fish	Market Form	Approximate Weight in Pounds	Cooking Method See Cooking Directions and Charts
Trout (brook, speckled, mountain, rainbow) (Classified as game fish)	Whole, dressed, drawn, fresh, frozen, hatchery raised or self caught (fat)	1-2	Boiled, steamed, breaded and fried, fried
Whitefish	Whole, dressed, fillets, fresh frozen (fat)	1-6	Bake, broil, deep fat fry, pan-fry
Yellow perch, Lake perch	Whole, fillets, fresh, frozen (lean)	½-1	Bake, broil, deep fat fry, pan-fry
Yellow pike (see Pike)			

Whitefish

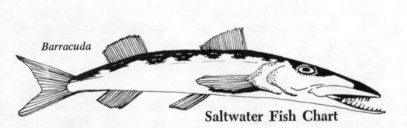

Barracuda

Yellow Perch

Saltwater Fish Chart

Name of Fish	Market Form	Approximate Weight in Pounds	Cooking Method See Cooking Directions and Charts
Barracuda	Whole, dressed, steaks, (lean)	3-6	Bake, broil, boil or steam
Bass: Sea, Striped	Steaks, fillets, whole or drawn (lean)	½-4 50-125	Bake, pan-fry, deep fat fry, broil
Black drum or Sea drum, Red or Redfish	Whole, steaks, fillets (lean)	1-40 2-25	Bake, boil, steam, chowder

Sea Bass

(66)

Black Drum

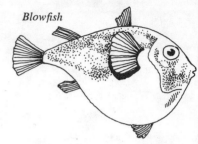
Blowfish

Name of Fish	Market Form	Approximate Weight in Pounds	Cooking Method See Cooking Directions and Charts
Blowfish	Dressed (lean)	¼-1/3 4-6 ounces	Fried
Bluefish	Whole (lean)	½-8½	Bake, broil, deep fat fry or pan-fry
Blue runner	Whole, steaks, fillets (lean)	1-7	Bake, broil, deep fat fry or pan-fry
Bonito	Drawn, steaks, canned, (fat)	4-10	Broil, boil, bake, steam
Butterfish	Whole (fat)	¼-1¼ (8 ounces)	Pan-fry, broil, bake
Cod	Whole, fillets, steaks, salted, smoked	10-100	Broil, bake, boil, steam, chowder
Crevalle, Blue runners	Whole or drawn (lean)	½-7	Broil, bake, deep fat fry, pan-fry
Croaker or hardhead, Tomcod	Whole, drawn, fillets (lean)	1-2 1¼	Bake, chowder, pan-fry, broil, boil or steam
Cusk	Drawn, steaks and fillets (lean)	1½-10	Bake, broil, boil, fry, steam
Drum, black or red (see Black drum)			
Eel, common	Whole, live, dressed (fat)	1-5	Broil, fry

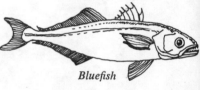
Bluefish

Bonito

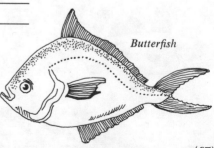
Butterfish

Eel

Croaker

Cusk

Cod

(67)

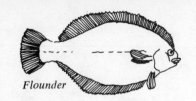

Flounder

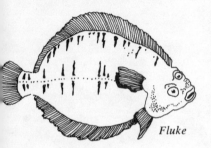

Fluke

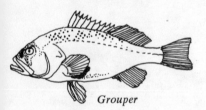

Grouper

Haddock

Name of Fish	Market Form	Approximate Weight in Pounds	Cooking Method See Cooking Directions and Charts
Flounder: dab, lemon or grey sole, dover or English, blackback	Whole, fillets, fresh, frozen, steak (lean)	1-5, 1-7, ¾-4, 1-2½, ¾-2	Bake, fried, breaded and fried, deep fat fried, casseroled, poached, steam, chowder
Fluke, Summer flounder	Whole, fillets (lean)	1-5	Bake, broil, broil, steam, fry, chowder
Grouper, (sea bass)	Steaks, fillets, whole, drawn, dressed (lean)	5-12	Bake, broil, boil, steam, chowder
Haddock	Whole, fillets, frozen, drawn, smoked, salted (lean)	1½-7	Bake, broil, boil, steam, chowder
Hake, red, white or common	Whole, drawn, dressed, fillets, (lean)	2-5	Bake, steam, boil, chowder
Halibut	Steak, smoked, drawn, dressed, fresh, frozen (lean)	5-75 some larger	Broil, bake, steam, boil, chowder
Herring (see Sea Herring)			
Kingfish, King whiting	Whole, drawn (lean)	¾-3	Bake, broil, fry
Lingcod, Blue cod	Dressed, drawn, steaks, fillets (lean)	3-20	Broil, boil, steam

Hake

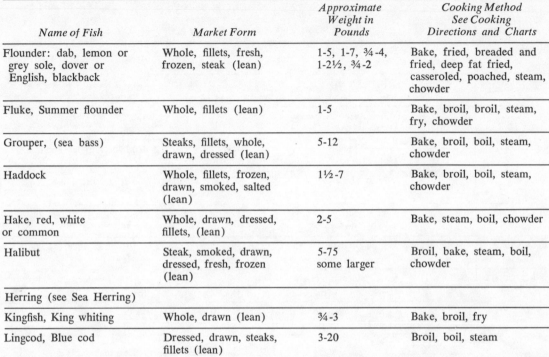

Kingfish

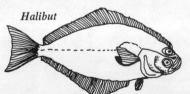

Halibut

Herring

Lingcod

(68)

Name of Fish	Market Form	Approximate Weight in Pounds	Cooking Method See Cooking Directions and Charts
Mackerel, King mackerel, Spanish mackerel	Whole, drawn, steaks, fresh, frozen, smoked, salted, canned (fat)	½-2½ 5-20 & larger 1-4	Bake, broil, fry
Mullet	Whole, fillets (lean)	½-3	Bake, broil, boil, steam, chowder
Perch or ocean perch, red perch, rosefish	Whole, fillets (lean)	½-2	Broil, fry
Pollock, Boston bluefish	Whole, drawn, dressed, steaks, fillets, smoked (lean)	1½-12	Bake, broil, boil, steam, chowder
Pompano	Whole, fresh, frozen (fat)	½-3½	Bake, broil, boil, steam
Porgy or Scup	Dressed, whole, drawn (lean)	½-1½	Broil, bake, fry
Red fish, red drum, channel, spotted ban	Whole, drawn, dressed, fillets (lean)	2-25	Bake, boil, steam, chowder
Red snapper, gray snapper, mutton fish, yellowtail	Whole, drawn, dressed and fillets (lean)	2-20	Bake, broil, boil, steam
Rockfish, striped Bass	Drawn, dressed and fillets (lean)	2-25	Broil, bake, fry
Sablefish or black cod	Dressed, steaks, smoked (fat)	3-15	Broil, bake, boil, steam

Mackerel

Mullet

Pollock

Pompano

Ocean Perch

Red Snapper

Red Drum

Rockfish

Sablefish

Porgy Scup

(69)

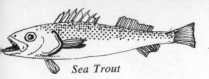

Sea Trout

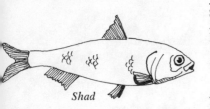

Shad

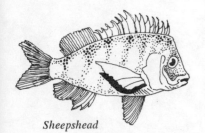

Sheepshead

Name of Fish	Market Form	Approximate Weight in Pounds	Cooking Method See Cooking Directions and Charts

Salmon:
Atlantic or Kennebec
Pacific Salmons:
  bluefish, sockeye or red,
  chinook or king, chum,
  dog or fall humpback or
  pink silver or coho
	Dressed, whole drawn, sections or halves per pound, slices or steaks, smoked, canned, frozen steaks	5-10
		
		5-12
		5-30 & larger
		5-10
		3-10 & larger
		6-30
			Poach, boil, Broil, bake, fry, smoke

Sardines	Whole, smoked, canned (fat)	⅛	Fry
Scrod or Cusk	Steaks, fillets (lean)	1½-10	Broiled, fried, baked
Sea Bass (see Bass)			
Sea herring, alewife, gray herring	Whole, smoked, salted (fat)	2-4 ounces	Broil, boil, steam, deep fat fry, pan-fry

Sea trout: gray,
  spotted,
  white
	Whole, drawn
	Whole, drawn, dressed
	Whole (lean)
		1-6,
		1-4,
		½-1½
			Bake, broil, fry

Shad (with or without roe)	Whole, drawn, fillet, canned (fat)	1½-5	Bake, broil
Sheepshead	Whole, fillets (lean)	¾-10	Bake, broil, fry
Skate	Dressed (lean)	1-20	Bake, boil, broil, fry

Skate

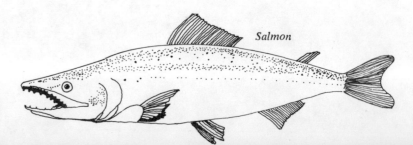

Sardine

Salmon

(70)

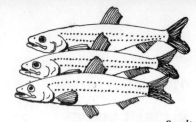

Smelts

Name of Fish	Market Form	Approximate Weight in Pounds	Cooking Method See Cooking Directions and Charts
Smelt	Whole (fat)	2 ounces	Fry
Sole, lemon sole, Dover sole	Whole, fillets, fresh, frozen (lean)	¾-4 1-2½	Fry, sauté, bread and fry, gratineé, poach
Striped bass (see Bass)			
Sturgeon	Smoked (fat)	Sliced	Considered a great delicacy
Swordfish or broadbill	Steaks, fresh, frozen, canned (lean)	50-800	Bake, broil, pan-fry
Tile fish	Whole, drawn, steaks (lean)	4-18	Bake, boil, broil, steam
Tuna: Little tuna or bonito, Albacore or longfin, bluefin	Drawn, whole, steaks, fresh, frozen (fat), canned Whole, drawn, steaks (fat)	4-10, 15-25, 75-1,000 & larger	Broil, boil, pan-fry, steam, bake
Whiting, silver hake	Drawn, whole, fillets (lean) smoked, salted	4-18	Bake, broil, fry
Wolffish	Drawn, dressed, steaks, fillets (lean)	8	Bake, broil, boil, fry, chowder

Sole

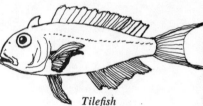

Tilefish

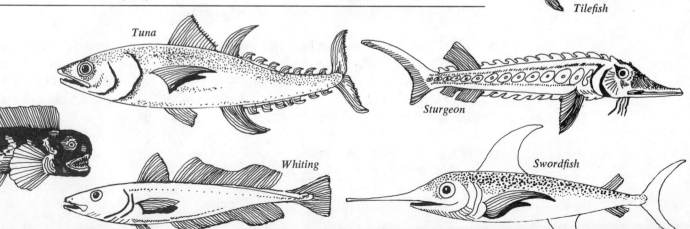

Tuna

Sturgeon

Whiting

Swordfish

Wolffish

All leftover fresh, frozen or canned fish and many smoked and salted fishes lend themselves to casseroles and chowders; some also lend themselves to salads and soups, according to individual recipies.

Happy Marriages   boiled potatoes, parsley, butter, white wine, flavored herb sauces, cucumbers, salads, eggs, cheese, gratineed dishes, vegetables, and crumbs all go well with fish.

Lean fish, being low in calories and high in protein and minerals are an excellent diet food. All shellfish are classified as lean.

Salt Fish (Salt mackerel and salt herring)   Prepare salt fish for cooking by removing dark parts and thin black membrane. Soak fish, meat-side-down in cold water overnight, or longer if a less salty fish is preferred. Drain well, place skin-side-down in a pan, cover with fresh water and bring to a boil, pour off the water and repeat twice. The third time the water comes to a boil, reduce heat and simmer 30 minutes. For broiled fish, pat dry after draining the second time and broil as recipe suggests, omitting salt.

Salt Cod   Follow salt fish directions, soaking fish 24 hours and changing the water several times. Bring to a boil in water to cover—drain and repeat 3 times. Remove bones, flake the fish and use for codfish balls or as recipe requires.

Smoked Fish   Smoked haddock, preserved by smoking and salting, is called Finnan Haddie. Smoked herring are called Kippers. To freshen Finnan Haddie, place in water or milk or a combination of water and milk to cover—bring to a boil and let stand over low heat for 25 minutes, do not simmer. Kippered herring should be covered with cold water. Bring water to a boil, take out kippers and use as recipe requires.

Shellfish—Servings Per Person
    1½ pound lobster per person—served in shell.

⅓ pound lobster meat per person.
1 lobster tail per person.
1 pound crab in shell per person.
⅓ pound crab meat per person.
6–12 oysters on half shell per person.
6–12 clams on half shell per person.
12–16 mussels per person.
8 average shrimp per person.
⅓ pound scallops per person.
12–36 steamed clams per person.

Buying Shellfish   Oysters, mussels and clams are bought alive in the shell. Shells should be tightly closed to indicate mollusks are alive. Oysters and clams are also sold as fresh or frozen shucked meats. Lobsters should be alive unless purchased as boiled lobster. Shrimp is sold fresh or frozen, head off. Some is marketed as cooked, peeled and deveined shrimp. Crabs are sold alive in the shell as hard shell (year round) and soft shell (warm months only). Crabmeat and lobstermeat are sold fresh-cooked in pry-open tins. Rock lobster tails are the frozen tail sections of ocean crayfish. Be sure they are frozen solid when you buy them. Scallops are economical buys, having no waste. There are two types, bay and sea scallops. Bay scallops are small, less plentiful and more expensive than the larger sea scallop. Mussels are sold in the shell alive, by the pound.

Cooking Clams   Hard clams come in three sizes—large, medium and small. Largest is the popular chowder clam.

Next in size is the Cherrystone clam which is famous as the "clam on the half-shell." The Littleneck, smallest of the three, is used widely for clam cocktails and clam fritters.

"Steamers" are by far the most popular soft clam. There are three favorite ways of preparing them. As a steamed clam in the shell with a butter-base sauce; removed from the shell and fried; or for clam soup or broth, for which they are well adapted both in tenderness and flavor.

Large soft clams, featured as "soft clams in shell," are much less widely known due to their comparative scarcity.

Although Cherrystone (hard) clams are frequently steamed, they are not referred to as "steamers." Small Cherrystone clams and soft clams may be steamed with equal success.

Allow 1 quart of clams per person. Scrub clam shells with a stiff brush under running water. Steam in a Clam Steamer or large kettle with a tightly-fitted lid. Allow ¼ cup water for 2-quarts clams. Steam about 14 minutes, or until shells are opening, but not entirely open. Strain and serve clam juice separately. Mussels are steamed in the same way, or follow individual recipies.

Cooking Lobster   The simplest way to prepare lobster in the kitchen is to thrust the lobster head first into boiling water (3 quarts of water and 3 tablespoons of salt for a one-pounder). Cover and boil 10 minutes for one pound, and 3 minutes for each additional pound. Don't overcook. As soon as it's cool enough to handle after boiling, split it down the front from head to tail. Force the two halves apart with the fingers. Take out the intestinal vein which runs the length of the tail and the stomach. In dressing the stomach cavity, the green liver or tomalley may be removed or not depending on individual taste. Some remove it for mixing with bread crumbs, salt and pepper as an added delicacy. If it's a female lobster, a red roe or coral may be found in the stomach cavity. This is edible and is enjoyed by most lobster lovers. A small dish of melted butter to which a few drops of lemon juice have been added should be served with the lobster. Serve split, with claws cracked with a hammer or provide nutcrackers for cracking the claws and small oyster forks to get meat out of the legs.

Cooking Rock Lobster Tails   Rock lobster tails are imported frozen from Australia, New Zealand and South Africa. They range in size from four ounces to one pound and over. The over-one-pound size are split in half lengthwise and marketed as "splits." An 8-ounce tail makes a normal serving (for defrosting, see Freezing Section p. 272).

For boiling tails allow 5 minutes for 4-ounce tails, 6 minutes for 5-ounce tails, etc. In broiling, place tails, shell side up, 4 to 5 inches below flame. Broil all sizes for 5 minutes, shell side up. Then turn tails and broil, flesh or underside up, 6 minutes for 4-, 5- and 6-ounce tails; 7 minutes for 7- and 8-ounce tails. For tails to 1 pound allow 8 to 9 minutes broiling with the flesh side up. For added juiciness and tenderness place a little water in the bottom of the broiling pan.

For Grilled Lobsters or Lobster Tails   Allow 1 live lobster weighing 1½ pounds per person, or 1 fresh frozen lobster tail weighing 12 ounces.

Kill live lobsters by inserting long pointed knife in cross at center back where head meets shell. Quickly lower knife to cut through length of back. Spread out the two halves, remove intestine, crack claw shells and grill for 20 minutes, 5 inches from coals. Brush with butter sauce according to recipe directions.

Rock Lobster Tails   Defrost and cut through underside of shell. Split open and flatten. Grill shell side down for about 16 minutes, 4 inches from coals, turning once. Brush with butter or sauce according to recipe directions.

Cooking Shrimp   One pound of fresh shrimp will serve three persons. Keep shrimp tightly wrapped in refrigerator or on ice until ready to cook. If shrimp is not to be eaten immediately keep them in the stock in which they were cooked and store them, covered tightly, in the refrigerator to have them plump and juicy. In cooking, shrimp should always be simmered in a covered sauce pan not longer than 5 minutes. *Do not boil shrimp.*

To simmer one pound of shrimp, use 1 cup of water, 1 teaspoon of salt, 4 peppercorns, one-half lemon, sliced, and one-half stalk of celery. Simmer the stock 5 minutes before adding shrimp. Cooking time should be reckoned from time stock returns to simmer after shrimp have been added. To cut down cooking odor given off by shrimp with excessive iodine content, shell before cooking; lemon in the water also reduces cooking odor. A simple tool which shells and deveins shrimp at the same time is a great help. There are several types available.

Cooking Oysters   Many oyster enthusiasts like their oysters served raw on the half-shell. For the great number who like them cooked, there are oyster dishes which are easy

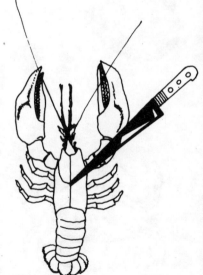

Killing a Live Lobster

to prepare. Two simple, widely known cooked oyster dishes are the oyster stew and oyster fry.

Oyster stews are always best cooked over water. This means the stew pan should be placed in a larger pan which contains the water.

Fried oysters need just one minute of frying on each side. In any cooked oyster dish, always add oysters as the last ingredient. Baked oysters require only a few minutes.

Cooking Scallops   The shucked scallop is the muscle that controls the shell. Scallops are so tender, particularly the small bay scallops, they can be eaten raw. Be careful not to overcook them. A few minutes poaching in liquid will suffice, or a light sautéing in butter.

Cooking Mussels   (see Cooking Clams p. 73)

Shellfish Chart   All shellfish are classified as "lean".

Clam

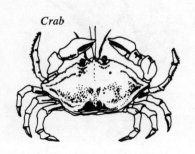

Crab

Name	Market Form	Weight	Cooking Method
Abalone	Headless, raw, steaks Canned	2-5 ounces 1 pound	Broil or fry

Clams:
  hard-shell
 	
  soft-shell
	Live, fresh, frozen in
	shell, shucked in shell,
	shucked, canned, smoked
		100-250 per gallon
		80 per bushel
		45 per bushel
		200-700 per gallon
			Steam, halfshell, fry,
			bread and fry, bake, broil

Crab: hard-shell	Live in shell, cooked, canned, frozen	¼-1 pound	Baked, steamed, boiled, fried
soft-shell	Live in shell, cooked, canned frozen	1/7-1/3 pound	
dungeness	Live in shell, cooked, canned	1¼-2½ pounds	
king (Alaska king)	Live in shell, cooked, canned, frozen	6-20 pounds	
rock, stone	Live in shell, cooked, canned, frozen	1/3 pounds	

Name	Market Form	Weight	Cooking Method
Lobster:	Live in shell, frozen in tins, canned	¾-4 pounds	Baked, boiled, broiled, steamed
spiny or (rock lobster)	Live in shell headless raw	1-4 pounds ½-2 pounds	
rock lobster tails		1-4 pounds	
	chicken	¾-1 pounds	
	quarters	1¼-1½ pounds	
	large	1½-2½ pounds	
	jumbo	3-4 pounds	
Mussels, sea	Live in shell, canned, smoked	55 per bushel	Steam
Oysters:	Fresh or frozen	80 per bushel	Steamed, eaten raw, baked, boiled
Eastern	Live in shell, shucked	150-200 per gallon	
Pacific	Live in shell, shucked	80 per sack	
Olympia	Live in shell, shucked, canned, canned smoked	48-240 per gallon 120 per sack 2,200-2,400 per gallon	
Scallops:	Fresh or frozen shucked		Fried, breaded and fried, broiled, scalloped baked
bay		100-150 per gallon	
sea		250-350 per gallon	

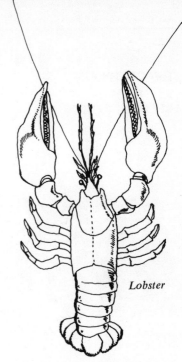

Lobster

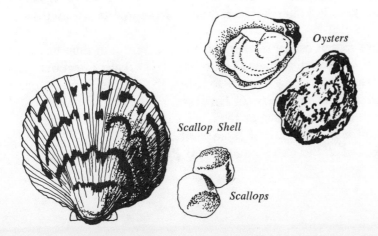

Oysters

Scallop Shell

Scallops

Mussel

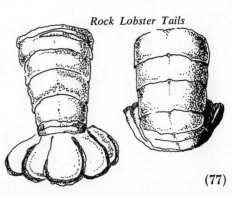

Rock Lobster Tails

(77)

Shrimp

Name	Market Form	Weight	Cooking Method
Shrimp: "Green" are uncooked,	Frozen in shell, frozen peeled and cleaned, canned		Boil, broil, bake, fry
white, prawn,	Headless raw in shell	12-17 per pound	
pink grooved,	Headless raw in shell	12-70 per pound	
brown grooved,	Headless raw in shell	12-70 per pound	
ocean and pink shrimp	Headless raw in shell	100-275 per pound	
Shrimp Sizes:			
	extra colossal	less than 10 per pound	
	colossal	10-15 per pound	
	jumbo	21-25 per pound	
	large	31-35 per pound	
	medium	43-50 per pound	
	small	51-60 per pound	

Storing Fish and Shellfish   Fresh fish should be eaten as soon after purchasing as possible. Store in coldest part of refrigerator until time to cook.

Store cooked fish in coldest part of refrigerator for as short a time as possible.

Store fresh and frozen shellfish the same way as fresh or frozen fish. Live shellfish should be kept in the refrigerator at medium temperature. Do not try to keep live shellfish, particularly lobsters, alive by placing them in water because they will rapidly drown and die.

Freezing Fish and Shellfish   Store frozen fish in freezer and keep frozen until time to use: Never refreeze after thawing. Cook unthawed or thawed according to package directions.

Thaw at refrigerator temperature only long enough to allow for ease in preparation. If preferred, frozen fish, tightly enclosed in a waterproof bag, may be thawed by immersing in cold running water. This is the quickest method of thawing. Do not allow the water to touch the fish itself. It is not desirable to thaw fish at room temperature.

Frozen shell fish can be defrosted in the same manner (see Freezing Section, p. 272).

Methods for Preparing Crabs and Crab Meat

Soft-Shelled Crabs   Crabs with new soft shells that have recently shed their old ones are called soft-shelled crabs. The shells are cooked and eaten with the crabs.

Select active live crabs and have them killed and prepared for cooking at the fish market. Use as soon after preparation as possible and store in refrigerator until used. If they have to be prepared at home, lay one crab at a time, shell side up on a wooden board and insert a sharp knife directly between the eyes and about ½ inch behind them, or turn crab on its back and cut off the entire head ½ inch behind the eyes. Turn crab over, shell-side-up, turn back the two pointed ends on either side and scrape out the sponge or feathers. Cut off the apron, or tail, which is folded under the crab. Rinse in cold water, pat dry with kitchen towels, dredge with flour and proceed as recipes suggest.

Hard-Shelled Crabs   Select active crabs, rinse and cook live, as lobsters. Drop each crab, head first, into a large kettle of boiling water with 2 tablespoons sea or rock salt added per quart of water, or 1 teaspoon table salt per quart. Cover and boil 20 to 25 minutes according to size.

Drain, as soon as crabs are cool enough to handle, crack claws with a nut cracker and crack the shells. Break off the apron, or tail, which is folded under the body by pulling it back against the body.

If crab shells are to be used with a baked stuffing, do not crack them. Lift off shells and dry them before stuffing. Remove gills, sponge or feather and intestine and pick out body meat with an oyster fork and wooden pick.

Crab Meat   Buy crab meat fresh, frozen or canned. All varieties have to be picked over to remove bits of shell and tendons. Thawed frozen crab meat, and canned crab meat should be well drained before using unless recipe specifies otherwise.

Oyster Crabs   Sometimes found in oysters, oyster crabs are small and can be eaten shell and all. They are considered a great delicacy and are often combined with oyster, crab meat or other seafood dishes.

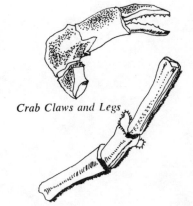

Crab Claws and Legs

Frogs' Legs   Only the hind legs of frogs are edible. Fresh frozen frogs' legs can be purchased at many frozen food counters. They have to be thawed, rinsed and dried before being prepared according to recipe directions.

To prepare fresh frogs' legs: Rinse in cold water. Draw off skins, which come off easily in one piece, and place frogs' legs in a bowl. Pour boiling water over them and soak for 5 minutes. Drain and dry well and use as recipe requires.

Fresh frogs' legs can be ordered from fish markets and come ready for use.

Snails   Snails are available live, canned or frozen. The live ones take several hours to clean. Canned snails are usually pushed into shells (which can be purchased), covered with a herbed garlic butter and baked until the butter browns and sizzles. Recipes for the herbed garlic butter usually appear on the can. Some packages include the canned snails, the clean shells and an envelope of dehydrated herbs to be stirred into the butter. Frozen snails-in-shells, covered with the prepared butter, can be purchased at specialty markets. They only require heating until the butter browns.

Fresh snails must be soaked in salted water, 3 tablespoons salt to 1 quart water, for 1 hour. Wash thoroughly in running water, scrub shells with a stiff brush and boil in lightly-salted water for 30 minutes. Remove snails from shell as soon as they are cool enough to handle, slice off hard outside "door." Place a little garlic butter in each shell and return snails to shells. Cover with more garlic butter and bake in medium oven until butter browns and sizzles, or follow recipe directions. Serve 6 to 12 snails to a person. If fresh snails are obtainable, the best are those that feed on grape leaves in a vineyard.

Eat with snail forks and use snails clips to hold them—or draw out of shells with nut picks and soak up the snail butter with sliced French or Italian bread.

Terrapin   The finest of the turtles and tortoises is the Diamond-Back terrapin from the Chesapeake Bay. Terrapin comes canned or fresh. If fresh it should be alive when purchased. One medium terrapin serves 2. The easiest way to kill a terrapin is like lobster. Plunge it, head first, into boiling water and boil for 10 minutes. As soon as it is cool enough to handle, remove head, claws and rough skin of legs and neck with a coarse towel. Return it to boiling water, add soup greens and boil 45 minutes. Cool terrapin in cooking water, drain and place back-down on a wooden board. Cut body from shell with a sharp knife and remove sac, gall, sandbags and intestine. Cut meat in pieces, including heart and liver, and prepare as recipe requires.

Since meat and meat products account for a percentage of the food budget, it is important to purchase from a reliable butcher or in a good supermarket. If you are dissatisfied with your meat purchases, shop around until you are satisfied. It is worth being choosy.

Learning about the various cuts of meat and the best cooking methods for each is a difficult and confusing task. In the long run, however, it is an extremely economical thing to do. This chapter lists the meat cuts according to their best cooking methods, with timetables for various weights, thicknesses and desired degree of doneness, as well as meat thermometer readings where applicable.

It is possible to use this chapter in lieu of recipes for many meat dishes—and also as a cooking-suggestion guide for previously unfamiliar cuts.

6 ❧
Meat
and
Game

Beef Beef is graded by the United States Department of Agriculture in the following order: prime, choice, good and standard. (You will rarely find the lower grades—i.e., commercial, utility, cutter and canner—in your supermarket.)

The tenderest cuts of beef are the ribs and loin. These should be cooked by dry heat, i.e., broiled, pan-broiled, charcoal-grilled, oven-roasted or on a rotisserie.

Beef For Roasting Beef for roasting should be well-aged. (Well-aged beef is dark in color; ask your butcher.)

Select Standing rib roast that is well-marbled, with a layer of fat on the outside.

Well-marbled, boneless rib-eye roast.

Well-marbled tenderloin with a thin fat covering.

Meaty and tender sirloin tip roast.

Any of the following ground meat for meat loaf: chuck, neck, brisket, plate, shank, flank or heel of round.

Roasting Directions Season roast with salt and pepper. Place fat side up on rack (not needed for standing rib) in open roasting pan. A meat thermometer inserted into the center of the thickest muscle, not touching bone or fat, indicates doneness. Do not sear. Do

Tip

Boneless Rib-Eye

not add water. Do not cover or wrap in foil. Roast in a slow oven (325° F.) to desired doneness.

To roast tenderloin: follow same procedure except place meat in a very hot oven (450° F.) for 45 to 60 minutes or to an internal temperature of 140° F. Tenderloin is best when served medium-rare or rare.

Timetable for Roasting Beef

Market Form	Weight in Pounds	Approximate Roasting Time at 325° F. in Hours[1]	Approximate Minutes Per Pound	Meat Thermometer Temperature in ° F.	
Rib roast, standing (bone in)[2]	4	1¾	18-20	140	rare
		2	30-33	160	medium
		2	33	170	well-done
	6	2	20-22	140	rare
		2½	25-27	160	medium
		3	30-32	170	well-done
	8	2½	20-26	140	rare
		3	23-25	160	medium
		4½	33-37	170	well-done
Rib roast, boned and rolled[3]	4	2	30	140	rare
		2½	37	160	medium
		3	45	170	well-done
	6	3	30-35	140	rare
		3½	35	160	medium
		4	40	170	well-done

Rib Roast

Rolled Roast

1. Reduce time approximately ⅓ for rotisserie cooking.
2. Ribs which measure approximately 6 inches from back bone to tip of ribs. If ribs are cut longer, allow less time.
3. Roasting times based on 4 pound roast with 4½- to 5-inch diameter; 6 pound roast, 5½ to 6 inch diameter. Roasts of smaller diameter require less cooking time.

Beef rump and sirloin tip roasts of top quality may be oven-roasted by following the directions for the rolled rib roast; braise as pot roast if lesser quality.

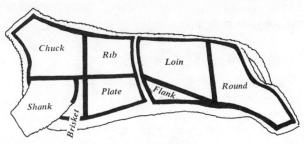

Beef For Broiling

Select   T-bone steak that is well marbled with some tenderloin.

Porterhouse steak is fine-grained and should be well-marbled, with large tenderloin.

Sirloin steak is coarser grained and has a wedge, round, pin or double bones, and some tenderloin.

Well-marbled loin strip steak (boneless).

Filet mignon is boneless slices of tenderloin and should be well-marbled.

Rib steak is well-marbled and should contain a meaty "eye."

Rib-eye steak (also called delmonico steak) is boneless.

Minute steaks are mechanically tenderized slices of lean beef.

Ground beef patties or hamburgers made from chuck, neck, brisket, plate, shank, flank or heel of round.

Flank steak (a less tender cut) is boneless, and is sometimes broiled and cut in thin diagonal slices (London broil).

Broiling Direction   Set temperature control at broil or 500° F. as recommended by equipment manufacturer. Place steaks on grill or on rack in broiling pan. Allow 2 to 5 inches between surface of steak and heat. The thickness of the steak and the degree of doneness desired determine the distance steaks should be placed from the heat and the length of cooking time. Use manufacturer's instructions. Broil steaks until well-browned on one side, season with salt and pepper, turn and continue broiling until steak is cooked to the

Tournedos

Rib Steak

Boned Roast

Sirloin

Porterhouse

T-Bone

Loin Strip

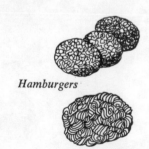

Hamburgers

desired degree of doneness. Check doneness by cutting slit near the bone to check the color. Red is rare; pink is medium; brown is well done. Season second side.

Timetable for Broiling Beef at 500° F.

Market Form	Thickness in Inches	Weight in Pounds	Total Approximate Cooking Time in Minutes		
			Rare	Medium	Well-Done
Sirloin steak	1	1½-3	10	14	18
	1½	2½-4	16	20	26
	2	3-6	22	26	32
Porterhouse steak	1	1¾-2	10	14	18
	1½	2-3¼	16	18	26
	2	2½-3¾	22	22	30
T-bone steak	1	1-1¾	10	14	18
	1½	1½-2¼	16	20	26
	2	2-3	22	26	32
Rib steak	1	¾-1	10	14	18
	1½	1-1¼	16	20	26
	2	1¼-1¾	22	26	32
Rib-eye steak (Delmonico steak)	1	½-1	10	14	18
	1½	1-1½	16	20	26
	2	1½-2	22	26	32
Loin strip steak	1	1-1½	10	14	18
	1½	1½-2	16	20	26
	2	2-2½	22	26	32
Filet mignon	1	2/3-1	6	9	12
	1½	1-1½	8	12	14
	2	1½-2	12	18	24
Hamburger	1	1/3	8	12	14
London broil	1-1½	2-3	10	—	—

*Boneless Outside
Chuck Roast*

Boneless Chuck

Top Round

Tenderloin

Plate Beef

Rolled Plate Roast

Cross-Cut Shanks

Standing Rump Roast

Rolled Rump

Rib Roast

Liver

*Chuck or Blade
Bone Roast*

*Chuck or
Arm Bone Roast*

English or Boston Roast

Pan Broiling Directions Heat a heavy skillet. Brown meat on both sides, adding a small amount of fat if necessary to avoid sticking. Reduce heat and continue cooking until meat is of the desired doneness. Pour off fat as it accumulates. Season before serving.

Timetable for Pan-Broiling in a Heavy Skillet

Market Form	Thickness in Inches	Weight in Pounds	Total Approximate Cooking Time in Minutes		
			Rare	Medium	Well-Done
Sirloin steak	½	1-2	6	10	
	1	1½-3		16	
	1½	2½-4		22	24
Porterhouse steak	½	1-1½	6	10	
	1	1½-2		14	
	1½	2-3		20	22
T-bone steak	½	1	4	8	
	1	1½		14	
	1½	1½-2		20	24

Timetable for Broiling Steaks and Ground Beef at 350° F.

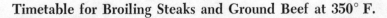

Cut	Thickness in Inches	Approximate Total Cooking Time in Minutes		
		Rare	Medium	Well-Done
Filet mignon	1	6	10	—
Hamburger	1	12	16	20
Club	1	12	16	20
Delmonico	1	12	16	20
Rib	1	12	16	20
T-bone	1	12	16	20
Porterhouse	1	16	20	24
Sirloin	1	16	20	24

Steak

Cut	Thickness in Inches	Approximate Total Cooking Time in Minutes		
		Rare	Medium	Well-Done
Top round	1	16	20	24
Chuck	1	18	22	28
Filet mignon	1½	10	14	—
Hamburger	1½	15	20	25
Club	1½	20	24	28
Delmonico	1½	20	24	28
Rib	1½	20	24	28
T-bone	1½	20	24	28
Porterhouse	1½	24	28	32
Sirloin	1½	26	30	34
Top round	1½	24	28	32
Chuck	1½	28	34	40
Filet mignon	2	16	20	—
Hamburger	2	18	22	28
Club	2	28	32	38
Delmonico	2	28	32	38
Rib	2	28	32	38
T-bone	2	28	32	38
Porterhouse	2	32	36	40
Sirloin	2	34	38	42
Top round	2	33	36	42
Chuck	2	36	40	45

Market Form	Thickness in Inches	Weight in Pounds	Total Approximate Cooking Time in Minutes		
			Rare	Medium	Well-Done
Rib steak	1	1	4	10	
	1½	1½-2		18	22
Rib-eye steak	1	¾	7	12	
(Delmonico)	1½	1		20	24

Minute Steaks

Market Form	Thickness in Inches	Weight in Pounds	Total Approximate Cooking Time in Minutes		
			Rare	Medium	Well-Done
Loin strip steak	½	1	4	8	
	1	1½		12	
	1½	1¾-2		20	24
Minute steak (European)	½	½	½		
	1	1	¾	1	
Filet mignon	1	½-¾	6	9	12
	1½	1-1½	10	14	18
Ground beef (hamburger)	1½	1/3	8	10	12

Pan-Frying Directions   Pan-frying rather than pan-broiling is necessary when meat has very little fat or when meat is breaded or floured. Procedure is the same as for pan-broiling except that fat is added first.

Timetable for Pan-Frying in Small Amount of Fat in a Heavy Skillet

Market Form	Thickness in Inches	Total Approximate Cooking Time in Minutes		
		Rare	Medium	Well-Done
Any steak cut	1	10	14	20
	1½	14	20	26
	2	20	26	30
Ground beef (hamburger)	2	10	12	14

Ground Beef

Beef for Braising, Boiling or Stewing in Liquid   Less tender cuts of beef—chuck, shank, brisket, plate, flank round and ox joints—should be cooked by moist heat.

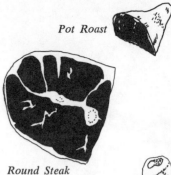

Pot Roast

Directions for Braising   Brown meat slowly on all sides in 2 tablespoons hot fat in a Dutch oven or other heavy utensil. Season with salt and pepper. (Because salt draws out meat juices, it is better to season the meat after browning; or if the meat is coated with flour, seasonings may be added to the flour.) Add a small amount of liquid (about ½ cup). Cover and cook over low heat or in moderate oven (350° F.) until tender. Add more liquid as needed. Allow 2 to 2½ hours for steak and 3 to 4 hours for pot roasts, depending upon thickness. Vegetables may be added during the last 45 minutes of cooking.

Round Steak

Timetable for Braising Beef

Market Form	Thickness or Weight	Amount of Liquid	Braise on Stove or 350° F. Oven Time in Hours
Pot roast, rump chuck, heel of round	3-5 pounds	½ cup	3½-4
Round or chuck steak	1-1½ inches	½ cup	2-2½
Flank steak	1½-2 pounds	½ cup	2
Short ribs	6 Serving Pieces	1 cup	2-2½
Stewing beef	1½ inch pieces	1 cup	2½-3
Ox joints	2 inch sections	2 cups	3-3½

Flank

Short Ribs

Beef for Broiling or Stewing in Liquid

Directions for Boiling Beef   Place meat in kettle, cover with water, cover kettle and cook over low heat until tender; add vegetables as recipes direct.

Stewing Beef

Oxtail Joints

(91)

Timetable for Boiling Beef in Liquid

Market Form	Weight in Pounds	Approximate Total Cooking Time in Hours
Corned beef	8	4-5
Brisket	8	4-5
Plate	8	4-5
Shanks	4	3-4
Stewing beef	1½ inch pieces	2½-3
Tongue	3-4	3-3½

Corned Beef

Brisket

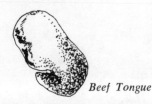

Chipped Beef

Beef Tongue

Tripe   the very muscular lining of the stomach of cattle. There are several sections of lining, resulting in various forms of tripe, three of which are honeycombed. Fresh tripe is complicated to prepare—it must be washed well in several changes of water, soaked, and blanched before cooking, although some tripe is available pre-cooked.

Storing Beef   Store meat as soon as you return from the market. Loosen wrapper on fresh meat before storing in fresh food or meat compartment of refrigerator. If meat is not store-wrapped, wrap loosely. Do not store beef longer than 2 or 3 days in refrigerator. The smaller the cut the sooner it should be used. Leftover beef should be cooled uncovered, then immediately covered or wrapped and placed in refrigerator.

To Freeze at 0° F. or Lower   Wrap securely in freezer paper. Recommended maximum storage time for properly wrapped beef is 6–8 months; ground beef, 3–4 months; and beef tongue, 3–4 months.

Cooking Frozen Meats   Cooking methods are the same for frozen meats as for fresh meats only the total cooking time varies.

Roasting hard-frozen beef requires approximately ⅓ to ½ again as much time per pound as fresh meat. Place meat on rack in 325° oven, do not cover, baste or add liquids. Use meat thermometer after meat is about half done.

Broiling hard-frozen steaks requires from ¼ to ¾ more broiling time than fresh steaks. Place broiler rack in such a way that surface of steak is 4 to 5 inches from heat source.

Pan-Broiling hard frozen steaks requires ¼ to ½ again as much as for fresh meat.

Braising hard-frozen beef requires approximately the same cooking times as fresh meats. Thaw meat slightly only if it is to be dredged with flour.

Boiling hard-frozen beef requires no longer cooking time than fresh meat, except for very large cuts, when a little more time may be needed.

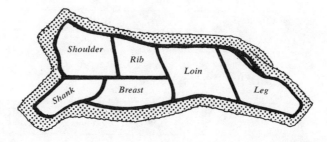

Veal Veal should be roasted until well done or faintly pink, about 25 to 35 minutes per pound, depending on size of roast. It has little fat and should be kept moist and juicy with butter or bacon fat. Veal should be basted frequently with drippings or additional fat.

Veal should never be seared, it should be cooked, uncovered in a 300° to 325° F. oven.

Veal can be roasted, braised, or pan-fried. It is suitable for stewing or cooking in liquid. It is not suitable for broiling except very tender young chops. The best veal comes from animals 4 to 14 weeks old weighing 40 to 100 pounds.

Timetable for Roasting Veal

Market Cut	Approximate Weight in Pounds	Oven Temperature ° F.	Meat Thermometer Temperature	Approximate Total Cooking Time in Hours	Approximate Cooking Time Minutes per Pound
Leg roast, half	3	300-325	170-175	2	40
Leg roast, whole	6-8	300-325	170-175	3¼	25-35
Loin roast	4-6	300-325	170-175	2¾	30-35
Breast, stuffed	3-4	300	170-175	1¾	30
Kidney roast	4-5	300-325	170-175	2-3	35-40
Rib roast	3-5	300-325	170-175	2½	35-40
Rolled shoulder	4-6	300-325	170-175	3½	40-45
Rump	4-5	300-325	170-175	2¾-3	40

Timetable for Braising Veal

Market Cut	Approximate Weight in Pounds	Approximate Thickness in Inches	Approximate Total Cooking Time in Hours
Stuffed breast	3-4		1½-2½
Rolled breast	2-3		1½-2½
Rolled roasts	4-6		3½-4
Standing rump	7-9		3½-4½
Center leg	5-8		2½-3
Shoulder roast	8-10		3½-4
Chops		½-¾	45-60 minutes

Market Cut	Approximate Weight in Pounds	Approximate Thickness in Inches	Approximate Total Cooking Time in Hours
Shoulder chops		½ - ¾	45-60 minutes
Steaks		1-1¼	45-60 minutes
Cutlet		½ - ¾	45-60 minutes
Veal Birds		½	45-60 minutes
Stewing veal (Shank)		1-1½	1-2
Calves liver		½ - ¾	15-20 minutes

Crown Roast

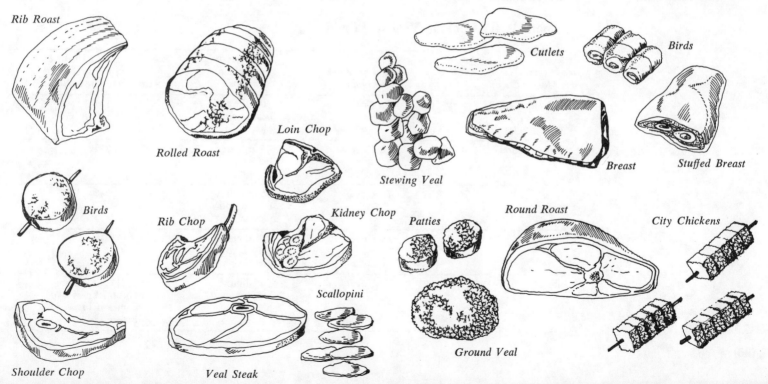

Rib Roast

Rolled Roast

Loin Chop

Cutlets

Birds

Stewing Veal

Breast

Stuffed Breast

Birds

Rib Chop

Kidney Chop

Patties

Round Roast

City Chickens

Scallopini

Ground Veal

Shoulder Chop

Veal Steak

Timetable for Pan Frying

Market Cut	Approximate Weight	Approximate Thickness in Inches	Approximate Total Cooking Time in Minutes
Chops	2½ ounces	½-¾	15-20
Cutlet	1 pound	½-¾	15-20
Scallops		¼	6-12
Calves' liver		½	8-10

Timetable for Cooking Veal in Liquid

Market Cuts	Amount of Water or Liquid	Additions of Vegetables, Potatoes	Approximate Total Cooking Time in Hours
Veal stew, shank	To Cover	30 minutes before completion	1½-3
Heel of round	To Cover	45 minutes before completion	2½
Neck	To Cover	45 minutes before completion	2½
Fore shank	To Cover	45 minutes before completion	2½
Riblets	To Cover	30 minutes before completion	¾-1¼ depending upon thickness (30 minutes if browned before cooking)

Calf or Veal

Veal Brains   8 ounces, ⅓ pound per serving.

Brains must be soaked well in acidulated water, first cold (the skin should be removed at this point) then warm (to remove all traces of blood). Blanch before using.

Veal Hearts   1 pound, ½ pound per serving.

Before cooking wash well in cold running water, making sure to wash out all blood, and remove all fat, veins and arteries.

Veal Kidneys   5–12 ounces, 1 kidney per serving.

Kidneys must be soaked well in cold water, the membrane clipped off, and balanced before cooking.

Veal Liver   2 to 3 pounds, ⅓ pound per serving.

Cut out any tubes and remove any membranes. Liver can be broiled, very quickly (about 1–1½ minutes per side for a ⅓-inch slice).

Sweet Breads (veal)   1 pair serves 2 persons.

Sweetbreads must be soaked in frequently-changed water, blanched, trimmed and refrigerated before cooking.

Roasts and Chops   Cut of veal with bone, ½–1½ pounds per person. Boneless, ¼–⅓ pound per person.

Storing Veal   Do not store veal for more than 2 to 4 days in refrigerator. Rewrap meat loosely in waxed paper or foil and store in coldest part of refrigerator or meat compartment. Loosen wrapper of packaged veal before refrigerating. Veal for freezer should be wrapped tightly in freezer wrapping and kept at 0° F. Do not freeze for more than 6 to 9 months.

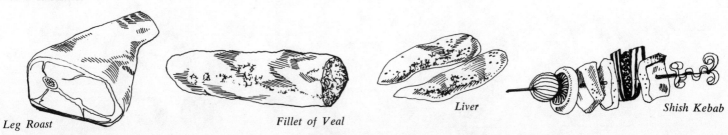

Leg Roast   *Fillet of Veal*   *Liver*   *Shish Kebab*

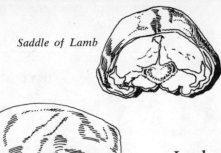
Saddle of Lamb

Leg of Lamb

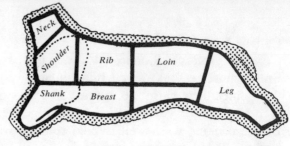

Rack of Lamb

Lamb Lamb is a tender meat and most cuts may be cooked by dry heat. The few less tender cuts should be braised or simmered. Spring lamb is about 12 months old; genuine spring lamb is 5 months old or less. Purchase lamb that is pink-to-reddish with covering of pinkish-white fat.

Lamb Roasts Leg of lamb and lamb shoulder are the best known cuts for roasting. In addition, loin, breast and rib (rack of lamb) are often roasted.

A "Frenched" leg of lamb has had the meat trimmed from the end of the leg bone. An American leg is one in which part of the shank bone has been removed to form a pocket. The shank meat is tucked into the pocket and skewered in place.

Roast lamb with or without removing the "fell" (the thin, paper-like covering). The fell does give the meat a strong taste, which some cooks prefer. Sprinkle roast with salt and pepper. Place, fat side up, on a rack in an open roasting pan. Insert a meat thermometer into the center of the thickest muscle. Roast in a 325° F. oven to an internal temperature of 175° F. for medium-done lamb or to 180° F. for well-done. Do not add water or cover the pan.

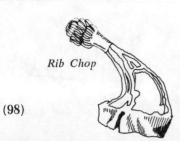
Crown Roast

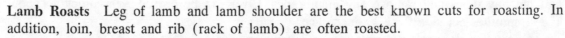

Rib Chop

Loin Chop

Saratoga Chop

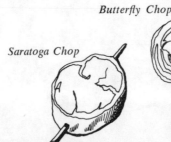
Butterfly Chop

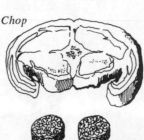
Patties

London or English Chop

(98)

Market Cut	Weight in Pounds	Approximate Roasting Time in Hours	Approximate Roasting Time Minutes per Pound	Internal Meat Thermometer Temperature	Oven Temperature Degrees Fahrenheit
Leg, medium	5-6	2½-3	30-35	175	300-325
Leg, well done	5-6	3¼-3½	35-40	180	325
Leg, medium	6-8	3¼-3½	35	180	300-325
Leg, well done	6-8	3½-4	35-40	180	325
Crown roast	5	3¾	40	175	325
Crown roast, well done	5	4	35-40	180	325
Shoulder, medium	4-6	3	35	180	325
Shoulder, well done	4-6	3¾	35-40	180	325
Shoulder, boned & rolled					
Medium	3	2¼	40	180	325
Well done	4-5	3	40	180	325
Breast, stuffed & rolled	2	2-2¼	35	175	300

Baste lamb only when roasting on a spit or if a flavor or glaze should be added. For rare, or French-roasted lamb, reduce cooking times by 8 to 12 minutes per pound.

Lamb Chops   Lamb chops are cut from the loin, rib, leg and shoulder. (Cuts from the leg often are called leg steaks.)

An English or French chop is cut from the unsplit loin; it is boned and usually wrapped around lamb kidney. A Saratoga chop is a boneless chop from the shoulder.

All lamb chops may be broiled, pan-broiled or pan-fried. Shoulder chops may also be braised.

Broiled Lamb Chops   Place chops on broiler rack so that the top surface of 1-inch chops is approximately 2 inches from source of heat and 2-inch chops about 3 inches from heat. Broil until top side is brown; season with salt and pepper. Turn chops and brown second side; season. Allow 10 to 15 minutes cooking time per side.

Pan-Broiled Lamb Chops Heat a heavy skillet and grease lightly. Place chops in skillet and brown on both sides. Reduce heat and continue cooking until meat is tender, turning occasionally. Pour off fat as it accumulates. Season.

Braised Lamb Chops Brown chops in a little hot fat in a heavy skillet. Season and add a small amount of liquid. Cover and cook over low heat until tender, 30 to 40 minutes.

Timetable for Broiling Lamb

Market Cut	Weight in Ounces	Approximate Total Cooking Time in Minutes	
		Rare	Medium
Shoulder Chops			
1 inch	5-8	10	12
1½ inches	8-10	16	18
2 inches	10-16	20	22
Rib Chops			
1 inch	3-5	10	12
1½ inches	4-7	16	18
2 inches	6-10	20	22
Loin Chops			
1 inch	4-7	10	12
1½ inches	6-10	16	18
2 inches	8-14	20	22
Ground Lamb Patties			
1 x 3 inches	4	16	18

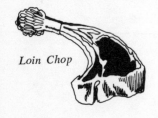

Loin Chop

Rib Chop

Lamb Breast and Riblets Lamb breast may be cooked in one piece or cut into serving-size pieces for cooking. It may be roasted, braised, or stewed in liquid.

Braised Lamb Breast or "Riblets" Cut breast into serving-size pieces or have meat man remove breast bone and cut breast between ribs into "riblets." Brown meat in a little hot fat. Season and add a little liquid, such as barbecue sauce, tomato juice or water. Cover and cook over low heat or in a 325° F. oven until tender, about 1½ hours. Add more liquid as needed during cooking.

Stuffed or rolled breast of lamb may be braised 1½ to 2 hours (see directions above) or it may be roasted (see directions under Lamb Roasts).

Lamb Shanks When buying lamb shanks, plan on 1 shank per serving. The shanks may be braised or simmered in liquid.

To braise shanks, flour, then brown in a little hot fat. Season, add a small amount of liquid and cook, covered, over low heat or in a 325° F. oven until tender, about 2 hours. Add more liquid as needed.

To simmer shanks, cover with hot water. Add desired seasonings. Cover and cook over low heat until tender, 1½ to 2 hours. Vegetables may be cooked with shanks during the last 30 to 45 minutes of cooking.

Ground Lamb Lamb neck, shoulder, flank, breast or shank may be ground for use in loaves, patties or in "mock chicken legs." Patties may be broiled, pan-fried, or braised. "Mock chicken legs" may be braised or pan-fried. Loaves should be baked.

Lamb Stew Lamb stew meat is from the shoulder, neck, shank, or breast. Have meat cut in 1- to 2-inch cubes.

Roll lamb stew meat in flour and brown on all sides in a little hot fat. Season with salt, pepper and desired herbs; add water to nearly cover. Cook, covered, over low heat until meat is almost tender, about 1½ hours. Add vegetables, such as halved onions and potatoes, small carrots or carrot chunks and sliced celery. Sprinkle with salt. Continue cooking until vegetables are tender. Thicken mixture, if necessary, with a flour and water paste. (If desired, omit potatoes and pour stew into a casserole; top with seasoned mashed potatoes and brown in a hot oven.)

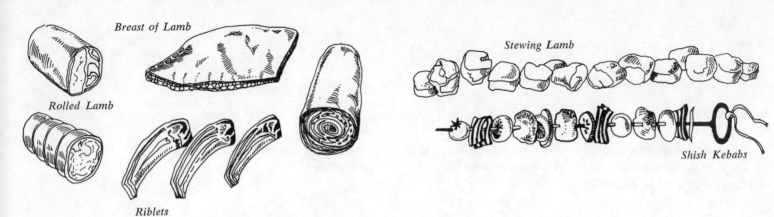

Breast of Lamb

Rolled Lamb

Riblets

Stewing Lamb

Shish Kebabs

Timetable for Braising Lamb

Market Cut	Average Weight or Thickness	Approximate Total Cooking Time in Hours
Breast, stuffed	2-3 pounds	1½-2
Breast, rolled	1½-2 pounds	1½-2
Neck slices	¾ inch	1
Chops	1 inch	1¼
Shanks	¾ to 1 pound each	1-1½
Shoulder chops	¾-1 inch	45-60 minutes

Storage   Loosen wrappers on market-packed meat and store in refrigerator, or wrap meat lightly in paper or foil and store in refrigerator.

Meat Cuts	Refrigerator 38° F.-40° F. in Days	Recommended Maximum Storage Time in Freezer at 0° F. or lower in Months
Lamb roasts	2-4	6-9
Ground lamb	1-2	3-4
Lamb stew		3-4

Pork Columbus is said to have brought 8 pigs to the New World on his second voyage, Cortez brought a drove and DeSoto brought 13 hogs. Pork has been a staple in the American diet ever since. The Eastern Indians learned to roast it and when the covered wagons went West they carried their hogs. Young hogs are usually called *pigs* until they weigh about 120 pounds. A young female which has not produced a litter of pigs is a *gilt*. A mature female is a *sow*. A fully developed male is a *boar,* and a castrated hog is a *stag.*

Fresh Pork Fresh pork should always be cooked until well done. Slow cooking is recommended. Pork can be roasted, braised, fried and cooked in water.

How to Roast Fresh Pork Place the pork fat side up, in a shallow, open pan, on a rack to keep the meat out of the drippings. Insert a roast meat thermometer into the center of the meat, making sure the point does not rest on fat or bone.

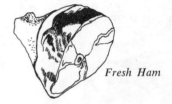

Fresh Ham

A meat thermometer is the most accurate measure of doneness, because it indicates the internal temperature of the meat. Season the meat with salt and pepper, either before or after roasting. The meat needs no flouring, no cover, no water and no basting during cooking. Roast pork at a constant low temperature of 325° F. until the internal temperature shown on the meat thermometer is 185° F. (Fresh pork roasts are excellent for rotisserie cooking. About ⅓ less time is required to bring internal temperature to 185° F. than is required for roasting.)

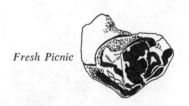

Fresh Picnic

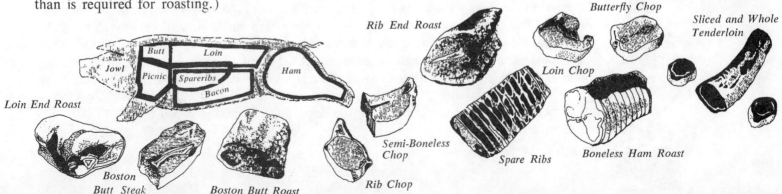

Loin End Roast

Boston Butt Steak

Boston Butt Roast

Rib Chop

Semi-Boneless Chop

Rib End Roast

Spare Ribs

Loin Chop

Butterfly Chop

Boneless Ham Roast

Sliced and Whole Tenderloin

Smoked Ham Slice

Smoked Ham Portion

Smoked Ham Butt Portion

Sliced Bacon

Smoked Picnic

Slab Bacon

Timetable for Roasting Fresh Pork at 325° F.

Market Cut	Weight in Pounds	Approximate Roasting Time in Hours	Internal Temperature in Degrees Fahrenheit	Approximate Roasting Time in Minutes per Pound
Loin roast	8	4½	185	35-40
	10	5½	185	35-40
	14	6½	185	35-40
Loin center	3-5	2¾-3¼	185	45-50
Loin, half loin	4-6	3-3½	185	45-50
Loin end	3-4	2¾-3	185	45-50
Leg, fresh ham, whole	10-14	4-7	185	25-30
Butt or shank portions	4-6	3-3½	185	35-40
Shoulder, butt portion, bone in	4-6	3¾-4¼	185	45-50
Shoulder, butt portion, boneless	4-6	3-4¾	185	45-50
Spareribs	1½-3	1-1½		
Shoulder, picnic, bone in	4-6	3-4¾	185	45-50
Whole tenderloin	1½-2	1	185	60-65 minutes total cooking time

How to Braise Fresh Pork   Brown meat in a few tablespoons of hot fat, or roll meat in flour and then brown in hot fat. Add seasonings and a small amount of water (¼ to ½ cup usually); cover the pan tightly and simmer over *low* heat or bake in a 325° F. oven until meat is tender. Add small amounts of liquid during cooking if necessary. Cooking times vary with the size and thickness of the meat. Pork chops, ¾-inch thick, require from 25 to 30 minutes cooking time, while spareribs need about 1 to 1½ hours. Pour 1 or 2 cups of barbecue sauce over the spareribs at the beginning of cooking if you like.

How to Cook Fresh Pork in Water   Cover meat with hot water, add seasonings, cover pan tightly and cook over *low* heat until the meat is tender. To assure a tender product, do not boil. Cooking times vary with the size and thickness of the meats.

How to Cook Pork Sausage   Cut patties ½ inch thick from pork sausage meat package and shape *gently*. Excessive handling is not recommended for ground meat. Brown lightly in a heavy skillet. Reduce heat and cook *slowly* until well browned on both sides, about 15 minutes.

How to Cook Pork Sausage Links   Place pork sausage links in a cold skillet with 2 tablespoons of water. Cover pan and cook over low heat for 5 minutes. Remove cover and drain off water. Continue cooking links over *low* heat until well browned and thoroughly cooked, turning frequently. Do not puncture skins before or during cooking.

How to Cook Cured, Smoked Ham   There are only two kinds of cured, smoked ham sold in most retail stores today, cook-before-eating and fully cooked. Cook-before-eating hams require additional cooking. Fully cooked hams can be served cold without further cooking, or if you prefer, they may be reheated.

To bake a ham, place the meat, fat side up, on a rack in a shallow roasting pan. Do not add water or cover and do not baste. Insert a meat thermometer into the thickest part of the meat and bake in a 325° F. oven.

Cook-Before-Eating Hams   Should be baked to an internal temperature of 160° F. according to the cooking time indicated below. Center slices can be cooked by oven-baking, broiling, pan-broiling or frying.

Fully Cooked Hams (which include all canned hams)   May be reheated to an internal temperature of 125° F. to 130° F. according to the cooking time indicated below. Center slices can be browned lightly on each side to heat through.

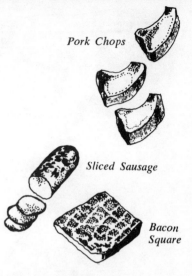

Pork Chops

Sliced Sausage

Bacon Square

Smoked Pork Hocks

Smoked Pork Loin Roast

Sausage

Smoked Boneless Butt

(105)

Smoked Ham

Canned Ham

Smoked Shankless, Skinless Ham

Smoked Boneless Ham

Market Cut	Weight in Pounds	Approximate Roasting Time in Hours 325° F.	Internal Temperature in Degrees Fahrenheit	Approximate Roasting Time in Minutes per Pound
Cook-before-eating hams, bone in	6-8 pound section	3¼	160	24-27
	10-12	3½-4	160	20-25
	12-15	4-4½	160	16-21
	18-22	5-6	160	15-18
Cook-before-eating picnic shoulders bone in	4-6	2½-3	170	25-37
	8-10	4-4½	170	25-32
Cook-before-eating boneless shoulder butt	2-3	2-3	170	50-75
Fully cooked ham, bone in	6-8 pound section	2¼	130	20-22
	10-12	2½-3	130	13-17
	15-18	3½-4	130	12-15
Fully cooked picnic shoulder bone-in	3-5	1½-2	130	21-35
	7-9	2½-3	130	18-23
Canned ham	6	2¼	130	20
	8-13	2-3¼	130	15-20

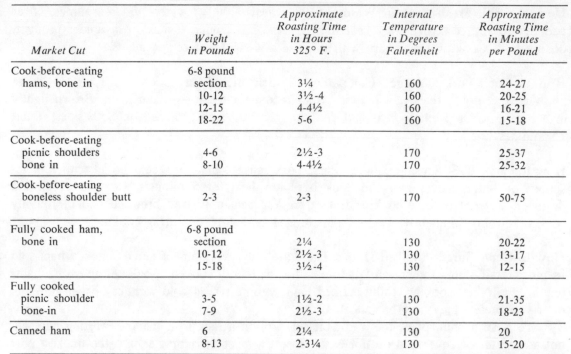

Smoked Semi-Boneless Ham

Canned Picnic

Luncheon Meats

Sliced Ham

Sliced Sausage

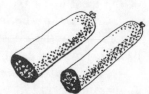

Liver Sausage

Salt Pork

Roasting	Broiling Pan Broiling Frying	Braising	Cooking in Water
Bone-in loin roast	Ham slices	Chops	Spareribs
Boned loin roast	Bacon	Shoulder steaks	Hocks
Fresh ham	Canadian-style bacon	Diced pork meat	Pigs' feet
Smoked ham	Sausage	Tenderloin patties	Boneless smoked butt
Fresh picnics	Salt pork	Whole tenderloin	Ham shank
Smoked picnics	Chops	Spareribs	
Pork shoulder butts	Shoulder steaks		
(Boston butts)	Tenderloin patties		
Whole tenderloin			
Spareribs			
Canadian-style bacon			

Smoked Boneless Ham Roll

How to Cook Smoked Ham Slices   Ham slices may be baked, broiled or pan-broiled. Bake a 2-inch thick fully cooked ham slice on a rack in an open pan in a slow oven (325° F.), 40 minutes. A cook-before-eating ham slice requires 60 minutes. The slice may be studded with whole cloves and topped with a fruit sauce or glaze before baking, if desired.

   Broiled Ham Slice   Slash the fat edges in several places to prevent curling. Broil 3 inches from source of heat. A 1-inch thick slice of fully cooked ham requires 5 minutes per side. Allow 10 minutes per side for cook-before-eating ham slice. Thinner ham slices should be pan-broiled.

Lard

Bacon

   Thin-sliced bacon   Usually packaged in 8-ounce, 12-ounce and 1-pound packages; up to 35 slices per pound.

Larding Pork

Regular-sliced bacon   Usually packaged in ½-, 1-pound and 2-pound packages; averaging approximately 22 slices per pound.

Thick-sliced bacon   Packaged both stacked and shingled in 1-, 1½- and 2-pound packages; up to 18 slices per pound.

Ends and pieces   Available in 1-pound packages and boxes, 3-pound cartons, and 4- and 5-pound boxes.

Slab bacon   Sold by the piece for home or market slicing.

Pre-cooked bacon   Available in cans that require no refrigeration; 18 to 20 slices equivalent to 1 pound of uncooked bacon. Requires heating for only 3 to 5 minutes.

Bacon crumbles or bits   Completely cooked and crumbled, ready to add to casseroles, sandwiches or any dish improved by bacon flavor.

Canadian bacon   Usually packaged in 4-ounce and 8-ounce packages.

How to Cook Bacon

To Pan-Fry   Place bacon in skillet and cook over *low* heat. Separate slices as they begin to cook so that each piece is flat in the pan. Turn slices often. Never let the fat smoke or the bacon will have a burned flavor. When browned evenly, drain on absorbent paper.

To Bake   Arrange bacon slices on rack in shallow pan. Bake at 400° F. for 10 to 15 minutes. This is a good way to cook a quantity of bacon, for the bacon requires less watching and needs no turning at all.

To Broil   Place bacon slices on rack 3 to 3½ inches below heat source. Broil 2 to 3 minutes to a side, turning once. Broiled bacon is well worth the watching this method requires.

How to Store Pork   Cured and smoked pork and fresh pork sausage deteriorate rapidly in flavor when frozen. It is recommended that some of these products should not be frozen and that others be stored in freezer for only limited periods. (see Freezing Section, p. 000) Perishable canned hams—3 pounds and over—should not be frozen; they should be stored at refrigerator temperatures 30 to 40° F. in the unopened can until used.

Market Cuts	Refrigerator 38° to 40° F.	Freezer at 0° F. or lower
Fresh pork	2-4 days	6-12 months
Ground pork	1-2 days	1-3 months
Sausage, fresh pork	1 week	2 months
Sausage, smoked	3-7 days	
Frankfurters	4-5 days	
Bacon	5-7 days	
Whole smoked ham	1 week	60 days
Smoked ham slices	3-4 days	

Kinds of Sausages

Alessandri   Italian-type salami of American origin (see salami, Italian).

Alpino   Italian-type salami of American origin (see salami, Italian).

Arles   Salami of French origin; similar to Italian salami.

Berliner-style Sausage   Cured, coarsely ground pork and some mildly cured, finely chopped beef; no seasoning; smoked and cooked; casings about 3 inches in diameter.

Bologna   Next to frankfurters most popular sausage; cured beef and pork finely ground with seasonings similar to franks; smoked, cooked and ready to serve; ring bologna packed in 1½-inch ring-shape casings; long bologna packed in casings of 2½–5 inch diameter, 18–20 inches in length.

Bologna, Ham Style   Contains large cubes of lean pork; smoked, cooked and ready to serve.

Blood Sausage   Diced, cooked fat pork, finely ground cooked meat and gelatine-producing materials mixed with beef blood and spices; 4-inch casings.

Blutwurst   (See blood sausage)

Bockwurst   Generally contains larger percentage of veal than pork, milk, chives, eggs, and chopped parsley; seasoned similar to franks; links approximate size of small franks; although "scalded" or parboiled, should be cooked thoroughly before serving.

Bologna

Bratwurst   German for pork sausage. Pork or a pork-and-veal mixture, seasoned with sage and lemon juice; packed in casings about 1⅜ inches in diameter, 4-inch links; must be "scalded" or parboiled before eating.

Braunschweiger   Liver sausage which has been smoked.

Cappicola   Dry sausage of Italian origin. Boneless pork shoulder butt seasoned with ground redhot or sweet peppers, salt and sugar; mildly cured; air dried.

Cervelat   General classification for mildly seasoned dry sausage. Ready to eat as purchased but can also be cooked.

Chorizos   Spanish-type dry pork sausage. Meat coarsely cut; highly spiced and hot to palate; size similar to large frankfurters.

Country-style Sausage, Smoked   Similar to smoked country-style pork sausage except that beef is also included.

Farmer Cervelat   Equal parts of pork and beef chopped coarsely; cured, dried; casings about 1½ inches in diameter; delicately seasoned, without garlic.

Frankfurters   The most popular sausage product; usually about 60 per cent beef and 40 per cent pork but can be made of all beef; cured, spiced, encased and linked, smoked and cooked. The terms "frankfurter," "weiners" "hot dogs" and Vienna-style frankfurters are often used interchangeably. Frankfurters are the largest style, about 1-inch diameter and 4-inches long. Weiners were originally braided into groups of links while Vienna-style frankfurters are twisted into a chain of links, about ¾-inch diameter and 4 to 5½-inches long. Frankfurters should be cooked (never boil but simmer in hot water) even if they are to be eaten cold.

Frizzes   Cured lean pork, chopped coarsely and a small quantity of cured lean beef; highly seasoned; dried.

Genoa Salami   (see salami, Italian)

Goettinger Cervelat   High quality dry hard sausage; delightfully spiced.

Goteborg Cervelat   Dry sausage; coarsely chopped, somewhat salty and heavily smoked; of Swedish origin.

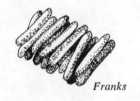

Franks

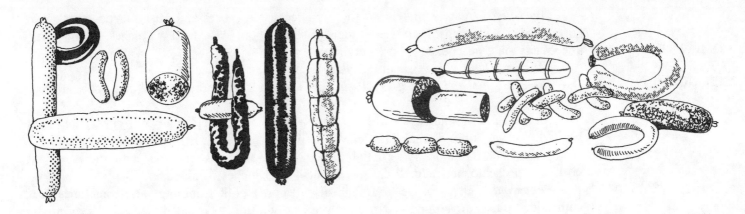

Gothaer Dry sausage; made only of very lean pork, finely chopped and cured.

Head Cheese Hog head meat; cured; casings about 4-inch diameter.

Holsteiner Cervelat Similar to farmer cervelat except packed in ring-shaped casing.

Kielbasa (see Polish sausage)

Knackwurst Similar to frankfurters but contains garlic; encased in wide beef rounds; 3- to 4-inch long links.

Knoblauch Garlic frankfurters. (see knackwurst)

Land Jaeger Cervelat Dry sausage of Swiss origin; filled into casing size of large frank, pressed flat and smoked.

Liver Sausage Finely ground, selected pork and livers; seasoned with onions and spices; cooked.

Luncheon Specialty Fairly large pieces of cured pork pressed together with small quantity of beef; tastily seasoned and ready to serve.

Lyons Sausage Dry sausage of French origin. Made exclusively of pork—4 parts finely chopped lean and 1 or 2 parts of small diced fat, with spices and garlic; large casing; cured; air dried.

Mettwurst   Approximately 60 to 70 per cent cured beef and 30 to 40 per cent cured pork; spiced with pepper and coriander; casings about 1½ to 1¾ inches in diameter; uncooked; must be cooked before serving.

Milano Salami   (see salami, Italian)

Minced Luncheon Specialty   Lean beef and pork trimmings; cured and finely ground; ready to serve.

Mortadella   Italian-style sausage composed of very finely chopped, cured pork and beef with added cubes of back fat; delicately spiced; smoked at high temperatures; air-dried.

Mortadella, German-style   High grade, finely-chopped bologna with cubes of fat pork and pistachio nuts added; casings about 4 to 5 inches in diameter.

Pepperoni   Dry sausage of Italian origin; cured pork trimmings and sometimes beef with added cube fat; ground red pepper used in addition to usual dry sausage seasonings; casings about 1⅜ inches in diameter.

Polish Sausage   Coarsely-ground lean pork with added beef; often highly seasoned with garlic; 1½ inches in diameter; links either 4- to 5- or 8- to 10-inches long; requires cooking.

Pork Sausage, Fresh   Made only of selected fresh pork; sold in links, packaged patties, bulk and cocktail size. All fresh pork sausage must be thoroughly cooked.

Pork Sausage, Fresh Country-style   Made only of selected fresh pork; ground more coarsely than other fresh pork sausage and packed in 1⅜-inch diameter casings; generally sold in unlinked casings but also in bulk and 8 to 10 inch links.

Pork Sausage, Smoked Country-style   Similar to fresh pork sausage except that meat is cured mildly and smoked; casings approximately 1⅜-inches in diameter. Must be cooked.

Salami   General classification for highly seasoned dry sausage with a characteristic fermented flavor.

Salami, Cotto   A cooked, mildly-flavored Italian salami. Yildig, an all-beef salami, is similar.

Salami, German   Less highly flavored and more heavily smoked than Italian salami; contains garlic.

Salami, Hungarian More heavily smoked and less highly flavored than Italian salami; contains garlic.

Salami, Italian Genoa, Milano, Sicilian, southern Italian, etc.; principally cured lean pork coarsely chopped and some cured finely chopped lean beef; frequently moistened with red wine or grape juice, flavored with garlic and various spices; stuffed into large casings; air dried.

Sicilian Salami Calabrese and lola are the two types (see salami, Italian).

Souse Similar to head cheese except for sweet-sour flavor added by vinegar pickle.

Summer Sausage Properly refers to all dry sausage; generally refers to mildly seasoned soft cervelat.

Thuringer Cervelat Medium-dry sausage; distinctive tangy flavor; mildly spiced.

Thuringer-style Sausage, Fresh Made principally of ground pork; may also include veal and beef; seasoning similar to pork sausage except no sage; links generally 1⅜-inches in diameter and 6- to 8-inches long.

Salami

Game Venison and hare can be ordered, frozen, from specialty butchers or from mail-order firms which often advertise before the Christmas holidays. Venison or hare purchased in this manner is well hung and ready for preparation as soon as it is thawed.

Fresh game, which cannot be purchased at butcher shops, should be hung before eating. Follow directions for preparing hunted game in a sportsman's cookbook.

Frozen hare is skinned but the inside skin has to be removed with a sharp pointed knife.

Game should be marinated before larding. Follow specific recipes for marinades, or place hare or venison steaks into buttermilk to cover for 24 hours before larding.

Since game has little fat, it should be larded or barded before roasting (see Dictionary of Cooking Methods, p. 25).

The marinated meat, larded or barded and rubbed either with butter or a preparation directed in a recipe, is usually roasted in an open pan. They can also be stewed.

Cooking   Roast a larded rack or saddle of venison in a 400° F. oven, depending on size, about 15 minutes a pound for rare. Baste frequently.

Larded loin of venison should be roasted in a 450° F. oven for about 1¼ to 1¾ hours in all, depending on size. Baste at least 10 times.

Roast a larded haunch of venison in a 450° F. oven for about 20 minutes a pound, basting frequently.

Roast a larded leg of venison in a 375° F. over for 1½ to 2 hours depending on size.

Use tender cuts of venison for stew. Brown the meat, then stew in the marinade until done, about 1 to 1½ hours in all. The meat of very young animals may be done in 45 minutes.

Roast a larded rack of hare in a 350° F. oven for 1¼ to 1½ hours depending on size. Baste frequently.

Roast a hare in a 450° F. oven for 15 minutes, reduce heat to 350° F. and roast until done, about 1½ to 2 hours, depending on size.

Hasenpfeffer is hare browned and baked in a casserole until tender, about 2 hours depending on size; see a recipe.

Stew hare by simmering for approximately 2 hours, then bake at 350° F. for an additional hour.

Jugged hare is hare baked in a 300° F. oven for about 2 hours; follow a recipe.

There are numerous other wild, edible game in the United States. Follow instructions for preparing, and recipes in a sportsman's or game cookbook. One note of caution, always cook bear meat very well because bear meat can be infected with trichina, an infectious parasite.

From fried chicken to holiday goose, we in America, love poultry. Soups, stock, main dishes, salads, practically anything but a dessert can be made utilizing chicken, turkey, duck, etc.

Game birds, farm-raised or wild, have less fat than chicken or turkey and need special attention when cooking.

Buying and Preparing Poultry

Select   Fresh, plump birds with compact bodies, pliable breast bones and broad breasts. Look for a pale skin, free of blemishes and with enough fat under the skin to make the bird juicy. Too much hard yellow fat, however, is undesirable. Each bird purchased should come with its giblets: gizzard, heart, liver and neck. Giblets should be removed from cavity and refrigerated separately.

Selecting the size and weight of poultry for a specific recipe or family need should be governed by three considerations. The number of people to be served, the recipe that is being prepared and the budget. If, for example, a beautiful and time-consuming Chicken Jeanette is planned, it would be folly to waste the time and energy on a fowl. The recipe deserves the tenderest large broilers or small fryers. Fowl is perfect for long-cooking fricassees, and for recipes requiring ground, boiled chicken, as a mousse or soufflé.

The names and weights of the birds usually suggest their uses. A broiler which is of either sex, should be broiled, but it can also be broiled on a rotisserie, simmered in a strong chicken stock or used for recipes where special tenderness and juiciness are called for. The fryer (a young male) is, of course, for frying, but it is the perfect size for casserole dishes and tender chicken salads. If a hungry family wants broiled chicken, they may not be satisfied with broilers and would prefer small fryers instead. Roasting chickens which are males and capons which are altered males, belong in the roasting pan or on the spit of a rotisserie. There are recipes for braised and poached roasting chickens, and boiled roasting chickens for salads, but on the whole roasting or spit roasting suit them best.

Chickens are usually thought of as "she," but the chickens we eat after they are 7 to 12

Rhode Island Reds

Plymouth Rocks

weeks old and weigh 1 to 2½ pounds are always males, or roosters, except when we specifically ask for a pullet, a 4- to 9-month old hen weighing from 2½ to 5½ pounds, or a fowl which is the hen that goes into the stew pot. A cock, or a rooster over one year old, can also go into the stew pot but is rather tough.

There are differences of opinion regarding the sex of poultry in different countries. The French recommend a tender young hen or one of their famous poulardes. The central Europeans consider a young rooster a far greater delicacy than a hen and Americans eat young roosters without being aware of it. The hen, which should be the tenderest, is not nearly as tender as a young rooster and the capon (altered rooster) is plumper and juicier than either of them.

In turkeys the question of tom, hen or baby is more important. Baby turkeys are not as tender in relation to their size as might be expected and a half turkey is often a better and more economical buy than a baby or small hen turkey. The hen has a broader breast and for that reason more breast meat than the tom. A conscientious butcher will advise, but given a hen and a tom of equal size and raised under the same conditions, the tom will always make the better bird.

Preparing   Wipe poultry pieces with a damp cloth. If necessary wash interior of whole birds with cold water and drain well before stuffing or trussing. Remove pin feathers with a knife or tweezers and singe off fine feathers or hair over an open flame or with a piece of burning paper.

Stuffing   If whole bird is to be stuffed, fill it two-thirds full of stuffing or dressing for the stuffing swells as it cooks and secure the opening with skewers or sew closed with kitchen thread. Stuff the neck cavity, pulling the neck skin over the stuffing and under the bird, then truss.

Trussing   Truss the bird by tying the feet together, leaving two long ends of string on either side. Turn the wing tips in, under the back and pull the neck skin down under the bird. Set the bird on its back and draw the two ends of trussing string across the bird, to hold its legs close to its body. Remove trussing strings before serving cooked bird.

Poultry Weights, Servings, Market Forms and Preparation   (Servings are based on dressed weights of bird before cooking.)

Name and Servings	Approximate Age	Dressed Weight in Pounds	Preparation	Market Form
Broiler (½ per person)	7-12 weeks	1-2½	Broiled, fried, breaded and fried, casseroles, Southern fried in batter	Whole and drawn, split, quartered, parts, legs, breasts, fresh and frozen
Fryers (serves 2-4)	14-21 weeks	2-3½	Frying, braising, casseroles, roasting	Split, quartered or disjointed, fresh or frozen
Roasters (1 pound per person)	5-10 months	2½-5	Roasting, braising, stewing, boiling	Whole, disjointed, fresh or frozen, canned
Capons (1 pound per person)	6-12 months	4-8	Roasting	Whole, fresh or frozen
Fowls (1 pound per serving)	8-12 months	2½-5½	Boil, stew, fricassee	Disjointed
Turkey broiler baby (1 pound per serving)	3-6 months	4-5 5-8	Stew, broil, roast	Whole
Turkey Young toms Young hens Mature (1 pound per person)	6-11 months	8-24 8-12 10-18 16-30	Roasted	Whole, breast, half turkey fresh, frozen, canned, turkey roll
Duckling (serves 2)	12 weeks	2½-4	Roast, broil	Whole, fresh, frozen

Leghorns

Golden Bantams

(117)

Name and Servings	Approximate Age	Dressed Weight in Pounds	Preparation	Market Form
Duck (1¼ pounds per person)	1 year	3-6	Roast, spit roast, stew	Whole, fresh, frozen
Goose (1 pound per serving)	9-10 months	4-14	Roast	Whole
Squab (1 serves 1) regular jumbo (1 jumbo serves 1-2)	28 days	8-14 ounces 12 ounces 14-16 ounces	Roast	Whole
Rock Cornish game hens (1 serves 1-2)	6-8 weeks	1-2	Roast, braise, casserole	Whole, fresh, frozen
Guinea hens baby (1 serves 1) mature (1 serves 2)	8-10 weeks 16-18 weeks	14-16 ounces 2	Roast, braise, casserole	Whole
Pheasant* baby (1 serves 1) broiler (1 serves 2) mature cock (1 serves 4) mature hen (1 serves 3-4)	8-10 weeks 10 weeks 20-22 weeks 20-22 weeks	1-1¼ 1½ 3-3½ 1¾-2	Roast, braise	Whole, brace
Partridge chukar (1 serves 1)	18 weeks	1	Roast, braise, casserole	Whole, brace

Partridge or Grouse

Name and Servings	Approximate Age	Dressed Weight in Pounds	Preparation	Market Form
Wild duck				
mallard	6	2	Roast, broil, braise	Whole (serve
(1 serves 2)	months			breast only)
canvasback	6	2-2½		
(1 serves 2)	months			
teal	6	1½-2		
(1 serves 1)	months			
Wild turkey				
(1 pound serves			Roast, smoke	Whole
1 person)				
mature hen	6	6		
mature gobbler	months	12		
Quail	12-14	4-5 ounces	Roast, braise,	Whole, sold
(1-2 per serving)	weeks	(4 dressed weigh approximately 1 pound 2 ounces)	sauté, broil	in braces

*(If game-farm raised, do not hang any of the following birds. If wild, hang undrawn, in a cool dry place for 1 to 7 days. Do not hang quail.)

Roasting Chart for Poultry

Name	Weight in Pounds	Approximate Total Roasting Time in Hours at 325° F.
Chicken		
broilers	1½-2	1-1½
fryers	2-2½	1½-2
roasters	2½-4½	2-3½
capons	4-8	3-5

Name	Weight in Pounds	Approximate Total Roasting Time in Hours at 325° F.
Duck	3-5	2½-3
Goose	8-12	3-3½
Turkey		
whole fryers	4-6	1-1½
baby turkeys	6-8	3½-4½
young hens	8-10	4-4½
young hens	10-12	4½-5
young toms	12-14	5-5¼
young toms	14-16	5¼-5¾
mature hens	16-18	5¾-6¼
mature toms	18-20	6¼-7½
mature toms	20-24	7½-9
mature toms	24 and over	9 or more
turkey quarters	3½-5	3-3¼
turkey breasts	5-8	3¼-4
turkey halves	6-12	3¾-5
Squab	8-14 ounces	¾-1

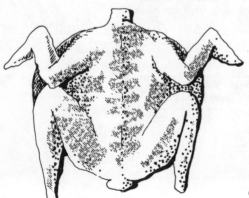

Split Chicken

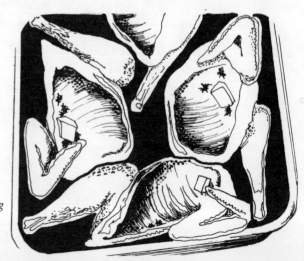

Chicken Prepared for Split Broiling

Deep Fat Frying Poultry Deep fat fry poultry parts at 350° F. Poultry pieces should be dipped in batter or beaten egg and seasoned bread crumbs before being fried in deep fat. Drain on paper kitchen towels before serving.

Roasting Poultry Do not stuff birds until just before roasting. Prepare stuffing or dressing in advance and refrigerate until preparing bird or birds for oven.

Preheat oven to 325° F.; increase heat according to recipe used. Roast duck and goose recipes often call for an increase of oven heat to 425 to 450° F. for last 20 to 30 minutes of roasting time to make the skin, which is fat, crisper and browner.

Most poultry is roasted in an open pan; fat and large birds should be placed on a rack to prevent them from roasting in the pan drippings and prevent skin from sticking to pan. Rack-roasted birds should be turned. Birds may also be roasted on a bed of vegetables to prevent sticking, but vegetables are apt to burn. Recipes sometimes require that the breast of a bird be covered with larding pork, as with game birds, to keep them from drying out, or covered with buttered paper or cheesecloth to keep the breast from getting too brown while a large bird roasts. To roast poultry or game birds wrapped in foil, bring to room temperature before wrapping. Roast at 25° F. higher temperature and open foil during last third of cooking time to allow bird to brown. Baste frequently after foil is opened.

Broiling Poultry Place split broilers, skin side down, on an oiled or foil-covered broiler rack and put a butter pat in each breast cavity. Add any other ingredients or brush bird with any substance that recipe calls for. Place rack in broiler at a level that will put top surface of bird 5 to 7 inches from broiling heat. Broil for approximately 10 to 12 minutes, turn with tongs, brush with butter and broil 10 to 12 minutes more. Turn and brush once more and broil until both sides are golden, about 30 to 50 minutes in all, depending on size of bird.

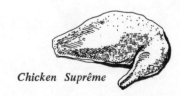

Chicken Suprême

Rotisserie Chart—Poultry Roasting on an Electric Spit or Roto-Broiler

Market Form	Weight in Pounds	Oven Temperature in Degrees Fahrenheit	Approximate Time in Hours
Broiler Unstuffed	2½-3	450	1-1¼
Chicken Unstuffed	3-4	450	1¼
	4-5	450	1½
Chicken Stuffed	3-4	450	1¼-1½
	4-5	450	1½-1¾
Rock Cornish Game Hen	1-1⅛	450	1
Turkey Unstuffed	6-8	450	2¼-2¾
Stuffed	6-8	450	2¼-3
Duckling Unstuffed	4-4½	450	1-1¼
Duck Unstuffed	5-6	450	1¾
Stuffed	5-6	450	1¾-2

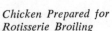

Chicken Prepared for Rotisserie Broiling

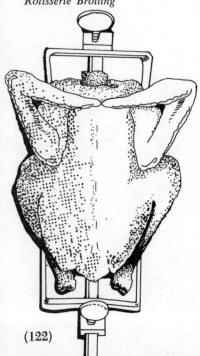

Rules to Observe in Spit-Roasting Poultry

1. Defrost completely and dry well before roasting on spit or roto-broiling.
2. After spit or roto-roasting is completed, let poultry stand from 5 to 10 minutes, depending on size, before carving.
3. Spit or roto-roasting is generally about ¼ to ⅓ faster than oven roasting.
4. When using a sauce in spit or roto-roasting, baste frequently during last 30 minutes of cooking time, unless recipe specifies more frequent basting.

5. Truss securely, as loosened trussing strings can release a wing or leg and interfere with the spit.

Test for Doneness   Leg joints should be flexible. Insert a fork carefully into the fattest part of inside of drumstick; the juices which flow out should be colorless. If they are pink or deep pink, the bird is not done. A meat thermometer is not accurate for poultry.

Roasting Game Birds   Fresh or frozen game birds, whether they are game-farm raised or wild, should be larded or barded before roasting as they have very little natural fat. (see Larding and Barding p. 25)

Roast prepared birds in an open pan, basting frequently.

Young pheasant should be roasted in a 350° F. oven for 45 to 60 minutes. Allow 60 to 75 minutes for a mature pheasant. Baste every 10 minutes while roasting.

Roast quail in a 450° F. oven for 20 minutes, basting almost constantly.

Roast partridge in a 400° F. oven for 20 minutes, increase heat to 450° F. and roast about 10 minutes longer.

Note   Wild game birds differ from game-farm raised birds and cannot be roasted according to specified times. Tests for doneness remain the same and apply to game birds as well as poultry.

Storage of Poultry   Fresh poultry—store in the coldest part of the refrigerator and use within 2 days. Always remove chicken from market wrapping then remove giblets from the cavity of the bird, and rewrap bird loosely before refrigerating—poultry benefits from air circulation in the refrigerator. Giblets should be washed and refrigerated separately or cooked in salted water to cover, until tender. Retain giblets and their broth for gravy.

Leftover Poultry   Cover with foil or plastic wrap, if necessary wrap in several packages, in small quantities. Poultry is perishable and flavor deteriorates rapidly. It may be stored in ice-cube freezer but is best when used or frozen in deep freeze as soon as possible.

If cooked chicken is to be refrigerated, for a period before it is reheated and served, as a casserole or stew, it should be stored in small quantities in separate containers. A large container or casserole of fully-cooked chicken can sour in the time it takes the casserole to be chilled thoroughly.

Frozen Poultry   Wrap tightly in freezer paper, being careful to protect paper from tearing over projecting pieces, as wing tips, legs or cut sections. If a split bird is to be wrapped for freezing, a layer of paper should be placed between the two halves. Pieces may be frozen separately; giblets should always be wrapped separately and then frozen separately or with the bird to which they belong.

It is best to thaw poultry before cooking, except for stews or fricassee. Place frozen bird in refrigerator in original freezer wrapper and allow 2 hours per pound to defrost. Allow 1 hour per pound at room temperature. Slow defrosting is preferable to any other method. A large turkey can require as many as three days in refrigerator to defrost. Never stuff a bird before freezing. (see Freezing Chart p. 273)

Carving Ham, Leg of Lamb, Pork or Venison   There are two school regarding the carving of ham and leg of lamb or pork. One school believes that the meat should be cut down to the bone against the grain, the other believes that meat should be cut with the grain in parallel slices until the bone is reached. Racks for either method can be purchased at the better kitchen-equipment shops. A European ham machine holds the ham or leg of fresh pork firmly level while the carver draws the knife blade towards himself. Proscuitto and Westphalian hams are to be seen in this type of machine at delicatessen shops.

In Scandinavia, where fresh pork roasts are a national dish, and each guest is supposed to be served with a slice of pork with its edge of crisp browned skin, the meat is carved to the bone. The proper way of doing it is so difficult that butchers are paid to slice and reconstruct it before the final heating.

Meat is supposed to be tenderer when cut against the grain. If the meat is stringy, cross cutting is a help. However, if a joint is carved to the bone, each piece has a little of the rarer meat from the bone, especially in the case of lamb, and those who prefer well-done lamb are not able to have those well-done outside slices.

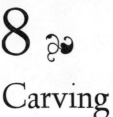

8 ઢ
Carving

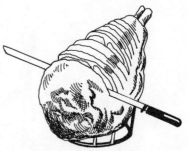

Fresh Leg of Pork or Ham on a Rack

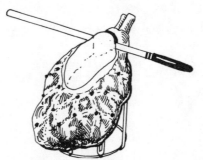

Ham on a Rack Cut with the Grain

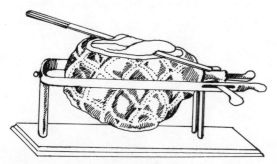

Ham in a German Ham Machine

Racks of lamb, pork, veal or venison are always carved by dividing the chops for each portion and cutting against the grain of the meat. This is also the correct way of carving a crown roast, which is a rack or racks tied in a circle. To fascilitate carving, the butcher cuts the chops at the base, but does not separate them. The carver can cut through the meat with ease after it is roasted.

Saddle of lamb is carved in thin slices with a thin sharp knife cutting parallel to the backbone, or comb. Venison and hare are cut from the ribs in the same way, but the solid piece of meat is then sliced across the grain into small slices.

Ham   Carving ham when not on a rack or in a ham machine:

Place ham, top facing up, on a platter. Hold securely with a two-tined fork and cut a triangular wedge down to the bone just above the shank end. Slice down to the bone on an angle, cutting thin, even slices. In order not to cut the center only—fan out the slicing to take in the two sides. Turn ham and carve in the same way. When ham is half carved turn again and alternate sides until only bone and scraps remain.

Fresh Ham   Place fresh ham on a platter. Cut a wedge from the shank end similar to smoked ham, but slice straight down to the bone instead of slicing on an angle.

Carving a Rack of Lamb

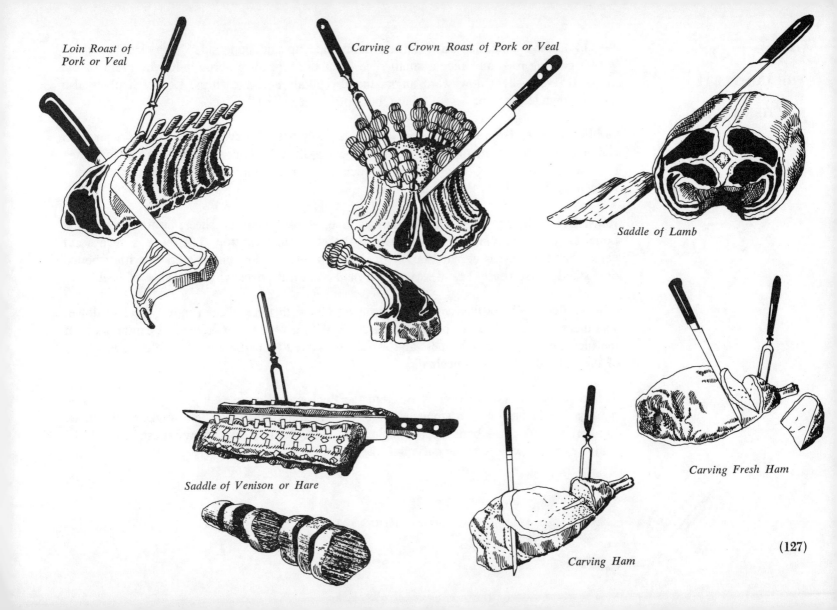

Loin Roast of Pork or Veal

Carving a Crown Roast of Pork or Veal

Saddle of Lamb

Saddle of Venison or Hare

Carving Ham

Carving Fresh Ham

(127)

Leg of Lamb   Place leg on a platter, fleshy side up and bone side down. Hold securely with a carving fork and slice a small slice from the top. Slice across with the grain of the meat at a very slight downward angle, thereby obtaining large slices. Leg of lamb is also carved down to the bone, as fresh ham, but not by the experts.

Saddle of Veal   Hold saddle, meat-side-up, securely with a carving fork. Detach meat from center bone. Start at the top and run knife down against the bone until meat is only attached to bone at the rib end. Cut into slices, as thick as chops running across the grain of the meat. Detach each slice from the rib and serve.

Roast Beef   Slice a rib roast, lying on its face, across into even slices, cutting free of the bone. Or cut a standing rib roast down to the bone from the top. The meat is always cut across but the roast is either "standing" or on its side. Follow either method with a boned or a standing rib roast. Try to serve some of the natural juices with each slice of beef.

Filet of Beef   Slice a filet across the grain into ¾-inch thick slices running straight down. The meat is soft and has to be carved carefully with a very sharp knife. The center slices of the filet are, of course, the finest and should be served first, the carver usually serves some of the natural juices with each slice.

Sirloin Roast   Carve a sirloin roast from the thick end. Remove fat and gristle and loosen the first few inches of meat from the bone. Cut in thin slices, at a slight angle, to the bone. Loosen meat from the bones as the slicing proceeds. Being a large heavy roast, it has to be held very firmly with a strong carving fork.

Leg of Lamb Cut with the Grain

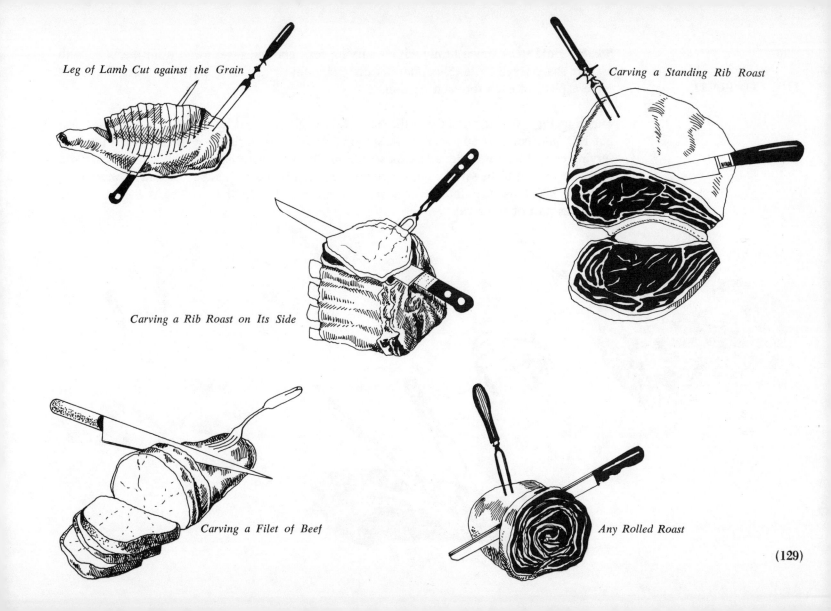

Leg of Lamb Cut against the Grain

Carving a Standing Rib Roast

Carving a Rib Roast on Its Side

Carving a Filet of Beef

Any Rolled Roast

(129)

Steak   Hold steak down firmly with a carving fork and cut meat away from the bone with a short sharp steak knife. Slice the filet or tenderloin or loin into slightly thinner slices and serve a piece of each for each portion.

Suckling Pig   Cut straight down the back, fold back skin and lift away fat if possible, then cut ribs into portions and serve with stuffing. There is so little meat on the ribs that each serving should also include a generous slice of the two miniature hams. The shoulders and neck are the last to be served, but the hams are actually the only large portions of meat on a suckling pig. It is, therefore, always wise to make a stuffing that will be rich and can be served as part of the meal.

Carving a Steak

Carving London Broil

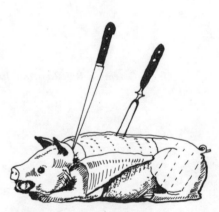

Carving a Stuffed Pig

Carving Chickens and Turkeys Cut legs and wings off first. If the chicken is large enough, separate the second joint and the drumstick. If a large turkey is being carved, meat may be sliced from the second joint and drumstick. The first and second joint of the wing can also be divided. The breast is carved into slices running lengthwise. In small birds the entire breast is lifted off and served as a portion. When the second joint of the wing is left on the breast, it is called a suprême. Small birds are served whole or halved. Broilers are served halved or quartered. All other poultry and game birds are carved in the same way except that in pheasant the host tries to serve only the breast meat and possibly the second joint. Wings and drumsticks are often dry. Duck and goose are carved in the same way, but the wing is not served as it is usually too dry. Half ducklings are served to each guest or, if it is a large duck, breast and leg are considered two servings. On a goose, where the breast is long and wide it is sliced like a turkey, the second joint also makes a serving but drumsticks and wings are usually left for stew with the neck and giblets.

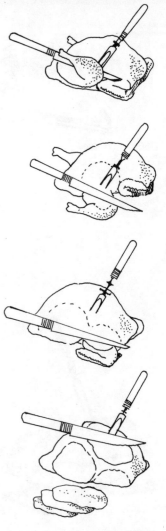

Carving a Chicken

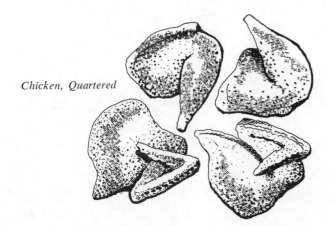

Chicken, Quartered

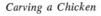

Chicken, Halved

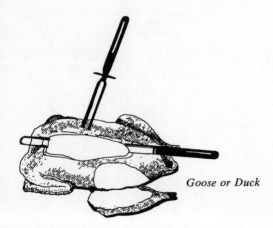

Goose or Duck

Many fresh vegetables are seasonal, and generally prices are lowest and quality highest at the peak of the season. Many vegetables available all year round also have a peak season when the price will drop.

Fresh vegetables are perishable; check the listed information for each vegetable to help avoid those already past their prime.

Do not overcook vegetables—they should retain some crispness.

Vegetables

To Boil Fresh Vegetables   Cook in as little water as needed to prevent scorching. Bring salted water to a boil, add vegetables, return to a boil quickly then reduce heat and cook gently. Root vegetables and lima beans are cooked covered tightly so that the trapped steam will aid the cooking process. Green vegetables are generally cooked uncovered (although there are exceptions, such as asparagus).

Canned Vegetables   Canned vegetables are fully cooked and can be served cold or heated. Here are the most common can sizes and their yields:

Size	Yield in Cups
8-ounce can or jar	1
Picnic can (10½ ounces)	1¼
Vacuum can (12 ounce)	1½ (used largely for corn)
No. 303 can or jar (16–17 ounces)	2
No. 2½ can or jar (1 pound 13 ounces)	3½
No. 10 can (6½–7¼ pounds)	12–13 (restaurant size)

Artichokes

Artichoke   A leaf and bud vegetable. Flower of the thistle plant, native to Africa.

1 whole or 1 half artichoke will serve 1 person.

1–2 Jerusalem artichokes will serve 1 person.

(133)

Jerusalem Artichokes

Artichoke Hearts

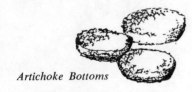

Artichoke Bottoms

Stuffed Artichoke

4–6 artichoke hearts will serve 1 person.

1–2 filled artichoke bottoms will serve 1 person.

Select   Compact, plump globes with large, tightly clinging leaves and good green color. Peak season March to May.

To Prepare for Cooking and Serving   Just before cooking trim stem with a knife, cut off 1 inch of leaves with a kitchen scissors and remove coarse bottom leaves. Boil in acidulated water. The edible part of the globe artichoke is the bottom and that portion of the bottom that clings to the base of the leaves. When served whole, the inner yellow leaves are pulled out while hot and the "hay" or "choke" is scraped out with a silver or stainless steel spoon (other cutlery turns black). This process is simple if the artichoke is sufficiently cooked. Jerusalem artichokes are pared and diced or sliced or left whole.

Test for Doneness   A center leaf pulls out easily and the base is tender when tested with a fork.

Serve   *Hot,* as a separate vegetable course or a vegetable with meat, poultry, fish. *Cold,* as a salad or appetizer.

Happy Marriages   Hot butter sauce, Hollandaise sauce, cold vinaigrette sauce, hard-cooked eggs, garlic, onion, lemon.

Approximate Cooking Times

Marketing Forms	Cooking Forms	Boiling Minutes	Steaming Minutes	Baking Minutes
Fresh	Whole globe	25-45	45	30-60
Jerusalem	Whole,	25-35	30-40	30-60
	sliced,	15-20	20-25	25-35
	diced	12-15	15-20	20-25
Frozen	Hearts	5-8		50

Marketing Forms	Cooking Forms	Boiling Minutes	Steaming Minutes	Baking Minutes
Canned	Deluxe hearts	Heat		10-15
	bottoms	10		10-15
	hearts			8-12 if small
Jarred	Hearts in brine, oil or marinated hearts			

Asparagus   A stalk and shoot vegetable. Cultivated from a wild plant of the fern family. Comes in two varieties, the dark green and the light green or white spears.

1 pound serves 3 persons

Select   Fresh, firm and brittle stalks. Usually sold in bunches of approximately 1 pound, 16 to 20 average stalks. Store in refrigerator in plastic bags and use within 2 days. Peak of season April to May.

To prepare for Cooking and Serving   Cut bunch across and discard woody bases. Trim stalks with sharp knife or peeler. Drain well before serving.

Test for Doneness   Feels just tender when tested with a fork. Never cook until soft.

Serve   Hot, as a separate vegetable course, or as a vegetable with meat, poultry and fish.

Cold, as a salad, appetizer or in salads. Asparagus is also used in soups.

Happy Marriages   Hollandaise sauce, butter sauce, ham, crumbs, eggs, prosciutto, smoked salmon.

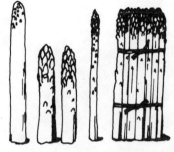

Asparagus

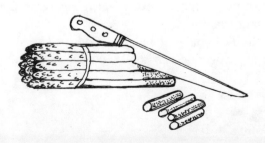

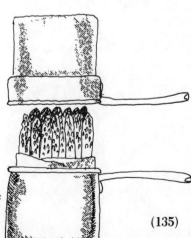

Steaming Asparagus

(135)

Approximate Cooking Times

Marketing Forms	Cooking Forms	Boiling Minutes	Steaming Minutes	Baking Minutes
Fresh	Whole, tips	10-20	12-30	35
Canned	Spears, tips cut spears, green and white	Heat		15
Jarred	Whole, white spears	Heat		15
Frozen	Spears, jumbo, cut pieces	10-12 10-12		55 50

Aubergine, (see Eggplant, p. 150)

Beans Cultivated in the Old World.
    1–1½ pounds green beans, French cut, yield 3–4 cups, will serve 4–5 persons.
    1–1½ pound wax beans, cut, yield 3–4 cups, will serve 4–5 persons.
    1 pound lima beans, in shell, serves 2 persons.
    1 pound lima beans, shelled, yields 2¾ cups, serves 4–5 persons.
    1 pound lima beans, in shell, yields ⅓ pound shelled.
    ⅓ pound lima beans, shelled, yield 1 cup.
    Select   Green, string or wax beans.
Brightly colored beans, green or yellow depending on variety, they should be young and tender, firm and crisp. The beans should snap easily when bent. Avoid discolored, limp, bulging or whitish beans. Store, covered in refrigerator and use as soon as possible.
    Select   Lima beans.
Light green, well-filled, but not bulging, pods. They should be crisp and unblemished or yellowed. Store in refrigerator, in shell, and use in 1 or 2 days.

Soy Beans

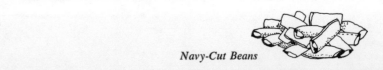

Navy-Cut Beans

To Prepare for Cooking and Serving

Green, string, snap or wax beans Break off both ends and pull off any strings. Cut beans into three thin strips with a bean cutter, French cut into diagonal strips, or straight across with a sharp knife. Cook in cut form, or whole. Drain well before serving.

Lima beans Shell and discard pods. Drain cooked beans well before serving.

Test for Doneness Taste test and drain as soon as beans are tender but not soft. Color should be bright and unfaded.

Serve Hot, as a vegetable with meats, poultry and fish.

Cold, as a salad or appetizer.

Happy Marriages Herbs, butter, toasted almonds, parsley, dressing and hardcooked eggs.

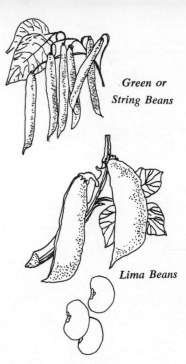

Green or String Beans

Lima Beans

Approximate Cooking Times

Marketing Forms	Cooking Forms	Boiling Minutes	Steaming Minutes	Baking Minutes
Green beans	Fresh, French cut	10-20	20-30	
	cut	15-30	20-30	
Italian green beans	cut	15-30	20-30	
Wax beans	cut	15-30	20-30	
Baby Lima beans	whole	20-30	25-30	
Fordhook Lima beans	whole	20-30	25-35	
Fresh soybeans	whole	20-30	25-35	
Frozen				
Green beans	Navy cut	8-10		20
Green beans	French cut	8-10		20
Lima beans	whole	12-16		35
Fordhook Lima	whole	10-15		45
Baby Lima	whole	12-16		30
Wax beans	cut	8-10		20

Wax Beans

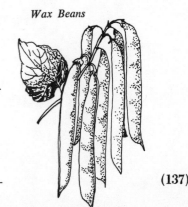

(137)

Beets

Beets   A root vegetable. One of a large variety of roots grown for their sugar or for fodder, the small red sweet beet is used for salads or vegetable dishes. The tops are also edible.

1 bunch, approximately 1½ pounds, will serve 4 persons.

Select   Firm, young beets with good color. Store in refrigerator in vegetable compartment or in a plastic bag and use within 2 weeks. Peak June to October.

To Prepare for Cooking and Serving   Trim beet greens, but leave 2 inches of the tops and the roots on to prevent bleeding and to retain a deep red color. After cooking, slip off skins as soon as beets are cool enough to handle, and cut off stems.

To Test for Doneness   Fork test for tenderness.

Serve   Hot, as a vegetable with meat, poultry, or fish. As a separate vegetable course. *Cold,* as a salad, relish or pickled with meat, poultry or fish. In salads, as an appetizer or relish. Beets are also used in soups.

Happy Marriages   Cloves, sugar, dill, horseradish, orange sauce, vinegar, mustard, sour cream, onions.

Approximate Cooking Times

Marketing Forms	Cooking Forms	Boiling Minutes	Steaming Minutes	Baking Minutes
Fresh	Whole, young	25-35	40-60	30-50
	whole, old	45-90	50-90	40-60
	sliced, diced	15-25	(will lose color)	
Canned	Whole,	Heat		20-30
	whole, small	heat		20-25
	sliced,	4-5		15
	cut	3-4		15
Jarred	Whole, small	Heat		20
	sliced	2-3		15

Belgian Endive (witloof), (see Endive, p. 151)

Boston Marrow, (see Squash, p. 168)

Boletus   An edible mushroom. Any of a large number of mushrooms having pores and not gills on the underside of the cap. The famous French cepe, generally available in this country as a dried mushroom, is a boletus. Many of members of the boletus family are edible and choice, and grow wild in many areas of the country.

Broccoli   A bud and leaf vegetable. Developed in Southern Europe from a cabbage plant similar to cauliflower.

2 pound bunch serves 4 persons.

Select   Fresh, green broccoli with compact buds, dark green, dark sage-green or purplish green. Stalks and stem branches should be tender but firm. Store in a plastic bag in refrigerator and use as soon as possible. Lowest availability June–September.

To Prepare for Cooking and Serving   Trim stems and wilted leaves. Halve thick stems. Drain well before serving. If preferred, stems can be sliced thin and boiled.

Test for Doneness   Sample bud end. Drain as soon as buds are tender and bright green in color.

Serve   Hot, as a vegetable with poultry or fish. As a separate vegetable course. *Cold,* as a salad.

Broccoli is also used for soup and gratineed dishes.

Happy Marriages   Lemon, egg, butter sauce, Hollandaise, almonds, mustard seed, dill, cheese, bread crumbs.

Broccoli

THE COMPLETE

KITCHEN GUIDE

Approximate Cooking Times

Marketing Forms	Cooking Forms	Boiling Minutes	Steaming Minutes	Baking Minutes
Fresh	Whole	10-15	15-20	20-25
	sliced stems	19	22	
Frozen	Spears	8-15		45
	deluxe spears	8-15		45
	chopped	5-10		40

Brussel Sprouts

Brussel Sprouts   A leaf and bud vegetable. A variety of cabbage cultivated for its sprouts. The vegetable originated in China.

Allow 1–1¼ pounds for 4 persons. Sold in 1-pound baskets.

Select   Firm, compact, fresh and bright green sprouts. Store in plastic bag or vegetable compartment in refrigerator no longer than 2 days. Peak season in October and November.

To Prepare for Cooking and Serving   Trim off any poor or yellow leaves. If large, cut in half lengthwise. Drain before serving.

Serve   *Hot,* as a vegetable or parbroiled and baked in casseroles. Brussel Sprouts are also used in soups.

Happy Marriages   Butter and lemon, basil, chestnuts, hardcooked eggs, almonds, dill, thyme, poppyseeds, seedless grapes.

Approximate Cooking Times

Marketing Forms	Cooking Forms	Boiling Minutes	Steaming Minutes	Baking in Casseroles Minutes
Fresh	Whole,	10-20	12-22	40
	halved	8-15	10-18	35
Frozen	Whole,	10-15		45
	deluxe baby	8-12		30

Cabbage   A leaf and bud vegetable. Originated in Asia.

1 pound serves 4 persons.

Select   Solid, hard, heavy, closely-trimmed heads, with stems cut close to head. Early cabbage need not be as solid as late cabbage. Store in a plastic bag in refrigerator, 1 to 2 weeks at most. Available all year.

To Prepare for Cooking and Serving   Trim off wilted leaves, quarter head, remove most of core and wash well. Leave in quarters or shred. Shredded cabbage is used uncooked for cole slaw. Cooked cabbage should be drained well before serving.

Serve   *Hot,* as a vegetable, chopped, stuffed, stuffed leaves, quartered and braised, shredded and boiled, fermented and boiled, sauerkraut.

Cold, shredded and dressed as cole slaw.

Happy Marriages   *Green cabbage:* mustard sauce, apples, caraway seeds, white wine, corned beef, lamb, paprika.

Red Cabbage: red wine, juniper berries, apples, chestnuts, pork, goose and game.

Sauerkraut: smoked pork, bacon, apples, onion, caraway seeds. Cabbage is also used for soups and casseroles.

White Cabbage

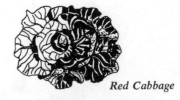

Red Cabbage

Savoy or Curly-Leaved Cabbage

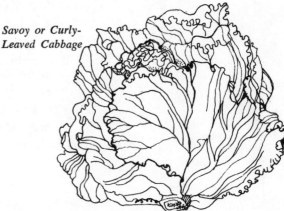

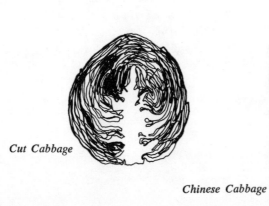

Cut Cabbage

Chinese Cabbage

(141)

Approximate Cooking Times

Marketing Forms	Cooking Forms	Boiling Minutes	Steaming Minutes	Braising Minutes	Baking Minutes
Fresh, green	shredded	4-10	8-12		
green	quartered	10-15	15-20	20-25	25-30
red	shredded	8-12	10-15		
Canned	sauerkraut	30	60	30-40	60-90
Packaged	sauerkraut	20	40	20-30	60-120
Jarred, red	shredded	10	20	15	20

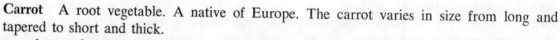

Capsicum   A fruit and pod vegetable. (see Peppers, p. 162)

Carrot   A root vegetable. A native of Europe. The carrot varies in size from long and tapered to short and thick.

1 pound serves 4 persons.

Select   Fresh, smooth, well-shaped and well-colored carrots. Store covered, 1 to 2 weeks, and remove root tips and tops before storing. Available all year.

To Prepare for Cooking and Serving   Wash, scrape or pare. Cut into strips, halves, quarters, slices, cubes, or dice. Drain well before serving.

Test for Doneness   Should be crisp, not soft. Taste.

Serve   Hot, as a vegetable with meat, poultry or fish; or as a soup or soup flavoring. *Cold,* cooked, in salads; or raw in salads or as an appetizer.

Happy Marriages   Sugar and glaze, butter sauce, ginger, dill, peas, mint, parsley. Used in lamb, beef and chicken stews.

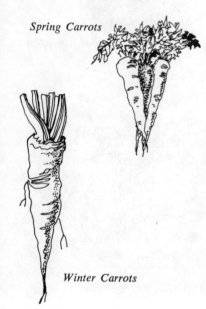

Spring Carrots

Winter Carrots

Marketing Forms	Cooking Forms	Boiling Minutes	Steaming Minutes	Baking Minutes
Fresh	Whole, young	15-20	20-30	35-45
	whole, old	20-30	40-50	60
	young, sliced	10-20	15-25	30-40
	old, sliced	15-25	25-30	40-50
Frozen	Sliced or diced	5-10		35
	whole, small	12-14		45
Canned	Whole, tiny	Heat		25
	sliced	7		20
	diced	7		20
	shredded	5		15
Jarred	Whole tiny	Heat		20
	diced	7		15
	sliced	7		15

Cardoon   A root vegetable. A plant of the thistle family with edible stems and roots. Treat as artichokes. Also called Cardon.

Cauliflower   A leaf and bud vegetable. Originally developed in Asia for its flower and not its leaves. Similar to broccoli but compact and white.

1 head serves 4 persons. 1 large head serves 6 persons.

Select   Clean, white firm and compact heads with fresh, clean and brittle leaves. Store top down and use within 5 days. Peak of season in October.

To Prepare for Cooking and Serving   Trim off leaves, defects and tough stalks. Cauliflower can be cooked whole, or divided into flowerets. Drain well before serving.

Test for Doneness   Done when the stem end yields to the touch of a fork.

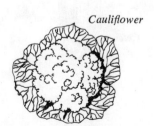

Cauliflower

Serve.   Hot, as a separate vegetable course, as a vegetable with meat, poultry or fish; or in a casserole or soup. Also makes excellent fritters.
Cold, cooked, as a salad, relish or pickle; or raw in salads or as an appetizer.
   Happy Marriages.   Curry sauce, Hollandaise, dill sauce, sour cream, cheese sauce, capers, crumbs, ham, celery seed and mace.

Approximate Cooking Times

Marketing Forms	Cooking Forms	Boiling Minutes	Steaming Minutes	Baking Minutes
Fresh	Whole,	15-20	25-30	30
	flowerets	7-14	10-20	25
Frozen	Flowerets	5-8		45

Celery

Celery, Celery Knob, Celeriac   A stalk and shoot vegetable. European origin. Varieties are Pascal or green celery and also white celery.
   Servings depend on size of bunch. 1 large bunch serves 4 persons.
   Select.   Fresh, crisp, clean bunches, brittle enough to snap easily. Stores well if kept cold and moist. Available all year.
   To Prepare for Cooking and Serving.   Trim off roots and leaves and remove strings with a potato peeler. When celery is to be eaten raw, submerge immediately in cold water and serve on shaved ice. Drain cooked celery well before serving. Parbroil *celery root,* unless very young and tender. Trim off roots and most of skin and boil until tender. Drain well, peel and slice before serving.
   Test for Doneness.   Yields easily to the touch of a fork.
   Serve.   Hot, as a vegetable with meat, poultry and fish; or in soups, casseroles and stews.

Cold, raw, salads, appetizer, snack.

Celery root, *hot,* as a vegetable with meat, poultry, fish.

Celery root, *cold,* cooked, sliced as a salad.

> *Happy Marriages.* Sugar, soy sauce and sesame seeds, olives, radishes, cheese, ham.

Celery Root

Approximate Cooking Times

Marketing Forms	Cooking Forms	Boiling Minutes	Steaming Minutes	Braising Minutes	Baking Minutes
Fresh	Diced, sliced celery root	15-18 30-45	25-30 60	25	30 45
Canned	Whole celery stalks, braised	Heat			45-60
		(see can directions)			

Chard A leaf and bud vegetable. A leaf vegetable of the goosefoot family, known since ancient times in the East. Also called silver beet, kale, Swiss beet or spinach beet.

1 pound serves 2.

Select. Well-colored, firm, crisp-leaved chard. Store in vegetable compartment or plastic bag and use within 2 days.

To Prepare for Cooking. Trim coarse end and root. Parboil, chop and finish cooking in butter.

Test for Doneness. Tenderness of stems, as spinach.

Serve. Hot, as a vegetable with meat, poultry or fish; or as croquettes, fritters and in soufflés.

Happy Marriages. Dry mushrooms, ham and tongue, hardcooked eggs, rosemary, chives, parsley, celery and butter.

Approximate Cooking Times

Marketing Forms	Cooking Forms	Boiling Minutes	Steaming Minutes	Baking Minutes
Fresh	Chopped	4-11	15-25	40
	whole	10-20	45-60	50

Chayotte   A Central American food plant.

Chestnuts, (see Fruits and Nuts, p. 181)   Also rated as a pod vegetable. Slit shell, bake to remove, parboil to remove inner skin, boil or braise and mash.

Chestnuts

Chickpeas   A fruit and pod vegetable.   From Western Asia. Also known as Garbanzos (see Dried Vegetables p. 149). Also comes in canned form and may be added to salads.

Chickory, (see Endive, p. 151)

Chinese Artichoke, (see Stachy, p. 168)

Chinese Cabbage, (see Cabbage, p. 141)

Chives   Similar but smaller than spring onion. The green tops are cut and used in salads, soups, soft cheeses and sauces (see Onions, p. 158).

Collards   Prepare as kale. Frozen collards can be baked in 45 to 60 minutes.

Corn   A fruit and pod vegetable. The tallest grain grass native to America, used for food, animal fodder and decoration. Introduced to Europe soon after the discovery of America.

Meal and flour are made from corn, (see Farinaecous). Corn oil (see **Dairy Products, Fats and Oils**) is also derived from corn. Indian corn and maize are identical.

1–3 small ears serves 1 person. 1 pound cut corn serves 2 persons.

Select   Well-filled ears with plump, milky kernels. Kernels should be firm but not tough. Husks should be fresh and green. Refrigerate and use as soon as possible. Peak of season is July and August.

To Prepare for Cooking   Remove husks and silk, cut off stems and if desired remove tips. Corn can be roasted in the husks, wrapped or unwrapped, buried in hot embers. Kernels can be cut off the ears before cooking. Cut corn should be drained well before serving.

Test for Doneness   Kernels should be tender but not soggy.

Serve   Hot, on the cob, as a vegetable course.

Hot, cut, as a vegetable course or combined for casseroles, fritters, puddings, soufflés, pancakes, soups, chowders, dry, for popping.

Cold, cooked, cut, as a salad, relish or pickle.

Happy Marriages   Butter, lima beans, paprika, green peppers, bacon, tomato sauce.

Approximate Cooking Times

Marketing Forms	Cooking Forms	Boiling Minutes	Steaming Minutes	Baking Minutes	Broiling Minutes
Fresh*	On cob	5-12	10-15	10-12	10
	cut	5-10	10-15	10	
Frozen	Cut, thawed	2		30	
	whole kernel	3-6		45	
	on cob	3-5		45	12
	creamed	12		35	
	deluxe sweet white	2-3		30	

Corn

Marketing Forms	Cooking Forms	Boiling Minutes	Steaming Minutes	Baking Minutes	Broiling Minutes
Canned	Cream	Heat		15	
	whole kernel	7-10	10	15	
	whole white	7-10	10	15	
	on cob	heat	10	20	15

* (Do not add salt to water; corn on the cob can be held in the water it was cooked in for a short while if a pinch of sugar is added to water before it boils. Add 1 tbs. milk to water, optional.)

Courge, (see Squash, p. 168)

Courgette, (see Squash, p. 168)

Cucumber   A fruit and pod vegetable. The fruit of a creeping vine, related to the squash and pumpkin.

1 medium-sized cucumber serves 2.

Select   Firm, well-shaped, bright green cucumbers. Store in vegetable compartment for no more than 5 days. Peak of season in June and July.

To Prepare for Cooking and Serving   Trim, peel and either slice, quarter or halve. Drain well before serving. To prepare for raw cucumber dishes, score skin with a fork or scoring knife and slice evenly, or use a mechanical slicer. For raw salads, salt cucumber slices well, place in colander and weight down to draw off liquid.

Serve   *Hot,* as a vegetable with meat, poultry and fish.
Cold, raw as a salad or salad ingredient; pickled whole cucumbers, as a relish or appetizer. Cucumbers are also used for soups, in mousses and garnishes.

Cucumber

Happy Marriages   Sour cream, chives, fennel, butter, basil, mint, dill, tomatoes and onion, fish, cheese for appetizers.

Approximate Cooking Times

Marketing Forms	Cooking Forms	Boiling Minutes	Braising Minutes	Baking Minutes
Fresh	Whole	15-20	25	20
	sliced	5-10	5	15
Jarred	Relish	Serve as garnish or on relish tray		
	dill			
	sweet			
	gherkins			
	mustard			
	midget gherkins			

Dandelion Greens

Dandelion Greens   A leaf and bud vegetable. Wild growing spring weed, picked before it flowers.

1 pound will serve 4 persons.

Serve   Hot, parboiled and tossed in butter as a vegetable.

Cold, trimmed and wilted for salads.

Happy Marriages   Hardcooked eggs and anchovies.

Dried Vegetables, Beans, Peas and Lentils   Most of the dried vegetables should be soaked before they are boiled. The best rule is to soak overnight in water to cover. Because this is not always convenient, dried vegetables may be boiled for 2 minutes, then soaked for 1 hour before cooking. Lentils and split peas do not have to be soaked but cooking times can be shortened if they are soaked. The following chart gives boiling time and quantities to serve 3 to 4 persons depending on whether vegetable is an accompaniment or a course. Always pick over dried beans carefully to remove stones, straws etc.

Dried Vegetables Cooking Chart

Vegetable	Water in Cups	Additions	Approximate Cooking Time in Hours	Yield in Cups
1¼ cup black beans	3	1¼ teaspoon salt	2	2½
1 cup blackeyed peas, beans or cowpeas	2½	1 teaspoon salt	½	2½
1 cup great Northern beans	2½	1 tablespoon butter 1 teaspoon salt	1¼	2½
1 cup kidney beans	3	1 tablespoon butter 1 teaspoon salt	2	2¾
1 cup lentils	2½	1 teaspoon salt	½	2½
1 cup lima beans, large	2½	1 teaspoon salt	1	2½
1¼ cup lima beans, small	2½	1¼ teaspoon salt	¾	2½
1 cup navy beans	3	1 teaspoon salt	1¾	2½
1 cup pea beans	3	1 tablespoon butter 1 teaspoon salt	1¾	2½
1 cup peas, whole	2½	1 teaspoon salt	1	2½
1 cup pinto beans	3	1 teaspoon salt	2	2½
1 cup split peas	3	1 teaspoon salt	½	2½

Eggplant   A fruit and pod vegetable. Also known as Aubergine. Native of Asia, member of the squash family.

1 average eggplant will serve 3 persons.

Select   Dark, rich purple color, firm, unblemished and smooth. Should feel heavy in

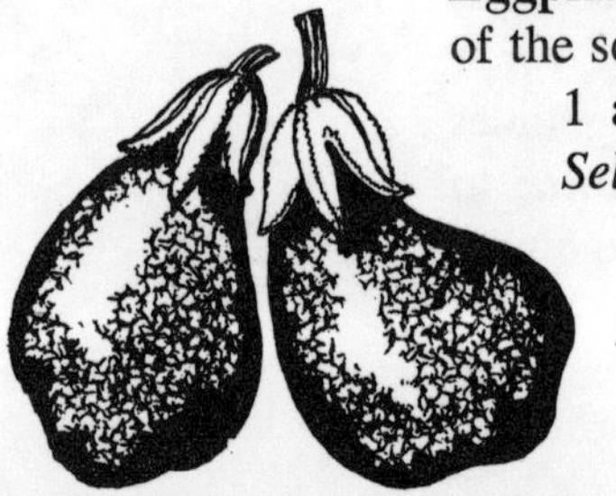

Eggplant

relation to its size. Store in a cool place, but if in a dry room store in plastic bag. Use before eggplant wrinkles. Peak of season is August and September.

To Prepare for Cooking and Serving   Either peel and slice, halve and stuff, peel and chop or cube, unpeeled. Prepare immediately before using as flesh quickly discolors. Boiled eggplant should be well drained before serving. Drain fried eggplant on paper towels before serving.

Serve   Hot, as a vegetable with meat or poultry, or as a separate vegetable course. *Cold,* as an appetizer.

Eggplant is also stuffed and used in casseroles, and is prepared Italian style as a main dish. Makes excellent spaghetti sauce.

Happy Marriages   Oregano, lamb and mutton, mushrooms, tomatoes, zucchini, rice, onions, summer savory, creole sauce, peppers, bread crumbs, mozzarella cheese.

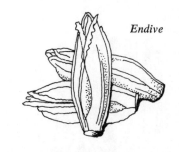
Endive

Approximate Cooking Times

Marketing Forms	Cooking Forms	Boiling Minutes	Steaming Minutes	Broiling Minutes	Frying Minutes	Baking Minutes
Fresh	Sliced	10-20	15-25	6-7	4-5	20-40
	diced	8-15	12-18		4-5	15-35
	halved	20-25	25-35			
	sliced, breaded				6-8	30-45

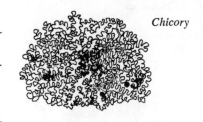
Chicory

Endive, Escarole and Chickory   A leaf and bud vegetable. Chickory and escarole are understood to be in the lettuce family. Belgian endive is sometimes considered an open lettuce head, but is actually a small, cigar-shaped, tightly-leaved lettuce plant. French endive and escarole are salad plants not as frizzled at the edges as the chicory. Chicory can be distinguished by openness of head with bleached center leaves. The straight-leaved type is generally marketed as escarole.

1 pound serves 2 persons.

Escarole

Select   Fresh, clean, crisp and cold greens. Store only briefly in plastic bags in refrigerator. Varying availability.

To Prepare for Cooking and Serving   Trim and parboil for braising and baking. Trim and crisp for salads (serve raw as lettuce).

Serve   *Hot,* as a vegetable with meat, poultry or fish; or as a separate vegetable course. *Cold,* raw, in salads. Cold stuffed Belgian endive is also used as an appetizer.

Happy Marriages   Dressings, ham, hardcooked eggs, soft cheeses, red wine.

Approximate Cooking Times

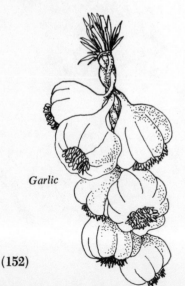

Fennel

Garlic

Marketing Forms	Cooking Forms	Parboil Minutes	Braising Minutes	Baking Minutes
Fresh	Endive, Belgian	6-8	Parboil 5	Parboil 5
	chicory	6-8	before braising	before baking
	escarole	6-8	25-30	30

Fiddlehead Fern   A leaf and bud vegetable. The fern stem has the flavor of asparagus and artichoke. It may be gathered wild or can be found frozen in specialty food stores.

Fennel, Finocchi   A stalk and shoot vegetable. (see Fennel Seed p. 52, and Fennel as a herb, p. 44) Prepare as celery, although it is more pungent in taste. It is used in many Italian recipes. Often eaten raw in antipasto. Most often a flavoring for sauces or liqueurs, the flavor is that of licorice or anise.

Garlic   A bulb and tuber vegetable. A condiment and pungent member of the onion family of Egyptian origin used extensively in Eastern cooking. The whole bulb consists of separate cloves. Remove the membrane of each clove before using whole, crushed or minced. (see Herb chart p. 44) Use in salads, soups and Italian cooking as a flavoring, in sauces, with lamb, tomatoes and snails. The garlic smell can be removed or lessened from the hands by rubbing well with the cut half of a lemon. The smell of garlic can be removed from the breath by chewing on a whole coffee bean.

Greens   Collards, kale, mustard greens, turnip tops, cabbage sprouts, beet tops, dandelion greens, and Swiss chard are cooked in the same manner as Spinach—either chopped, puréed or in some cases raw in salads. Soup greens are not to be confused with greens. Soup greens usually consist of carrots, turnips, onions and celery.

Hearts of Palm   The heart or young terminal bud of a tropical palm tree, usually the cabbage palmetto, available fresh only in Florida. Can be used raw, like cabbage, or cooked, it should be used before it changes color. Available in cans. Suitable for baking in white sauce and gratineeing. Also bound with French dressing or mayonnaise for use as a salad or appetizer. 1 can serves 2.

Hearts of Palm

Herb Bouquet   Also known as Bouquet Garni (see Herbs, p. 42).

Hop Sprouts   A leaf and bud vegetable. Shoots of a climbing plant of the nettle family. Eaten fresh, boiled with melted butter.

Horseradish   A root vegetable. A very strong and pungent vegetable, used for sauces and condiments (see p. 203).

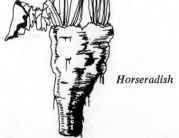

Horseradish

Kale A leaf and bud vegetable. Also known as sea kale or collards. An open cabbage-like plant with green leaves. Use as spinach. Serve with hardcooked eggs or butter sauce. Boil 10 to 25 minutes in salted water and boil chopped frozen kale 8 to 12 minutes. Boil the frozen, chopped collard greens 20 to 25 minutes.

Kohlrabi A root vegetable and a leaf and bud vegetable. Also known as cabbage turnip. It is a hybrid member of the cabbage or brassica family. It is also a cousin of the cauliflower and the broccoli. Although it is a root vegetable the root grows above the ground. The root as well as the stems and leaves are used; it is best when quite young. To prepare, the root is boiled; because it requires a longer boiling time, the leaves are added during the last few minutes of cooking. Boil sliced 20 to 25 minutes, add leaves after 15 minutes. Kohlrabi goes well with butter, cream and garlic.

Leek A stalk and shoot vegetable. A member and the most delicate tasting of the onion family. A cylindrical bulb, the outside and green part of leaves have to be removed and the root trimmed off before cooking. 1 bunch serves 2. (For cooking directions, see Onion, p. 158). Best known for the French leek and potato soup, cold vichyssoise. It combines well with chives, potatoes, ham, butter, cream, mushrooms and hardcooked eggs, and can be used as one would asparagus.

Lentils A fruit and pod vegetable. From Central Asia. (see Dried Vegetables, p. 149)

Kale

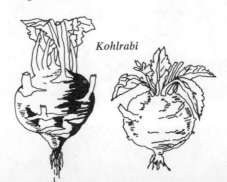

Kohlrabi

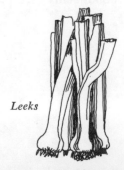

Leeks

Lettuce   A leaf and bud vegetable. There are many different varieties of lettuce. All are related to the cabbage family and are usually considered salad plants. In selecting, always choose good quality, with clean, crisp tender heads, free from rusty appearance. Store in crisper or plastic bags for 1 to 2 days only. Wash salad greens in advance so that they can drain and crisp properly in the refrigerator. Iceberg lettuce should be cored, held under water and drained. The water helps to make the leaves easier to separate. Romaine is torn or laid on its side and cut across with a knife. Bibb is prized for its delicate flavor. Boston is a larger, looser head, and is usually torn to use in tossed salads. Lettuce should be thoroughly dry before being tossed in a salad. Lettuce leaves can be either torn or cut into bite-size pieces. Chicory, escarole and endive are also used for salads (see p. 151).

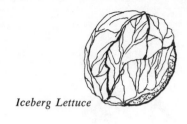

Iceberg Lettuce

1 medium head of lettuce serves 2–3 persons.

Happy Marriages.   All salad dressings, chives, parsley, bleu and roquefort cheese, raw hard-, or soft-boiled eggs, onions, cucumbers, diced green peppers, garlic croutons, crisp bacon, anchovies, leftover vegetables and meats, etc. Lettuce is sometimes stuffed and baked and lettuce leaves are sometimes stuffed, rolled up and baked.

Cos

Marrow, (see Pumpkin, p. 166)

Mushrooms   An edible fungi. The mushrooms available fresh in stores are a cultivated variety of the wild field mushrooms, *Agaricus campestris*. It is not legal to sell wild mushrooms in this country in a market. Canned mushrooms can be used as a substitute for fresh mushrooms, but fresh are preferable. Mushrooms vary a good deal in size, and in stem length.

Boston Lettuce

1 pound of medium mushrooms should serve 4.

Select.   Clean mushrooms with firm flesh. They should be white and the caps should be attached to the stems. If opened, the gills should be pink; brown gills and shriveled caps indicate loss of freshness. Select small mushrooms for buttons, medium mushrooms for

Bibb Lettuce   (155)

Mushrooms

chopping or caps and large mushrooms for broiling or stuffing. Keep refrigerated and use as soon as possible. Do not wash before refrigerating.

To Prepare for Cooking and Serving   Wipe mushrooms clean with a damp cloth or rinse *very* quickly in water; do not soak mushrooms. Peel only if the caps are very discolored. Cut a small slice off the bottom of mushrooms stems and discard the slice. All other mushroom parings can be used in soups if desired. Leave mushrooms whole, or slice with the stems on; remove stems and leave caps whole. Removed stems may be chopped or sliced. Mushrooms may also be chopped, quartered, sliced or minced. They are also fluted to use as a garnish. Dried mushrooms may be kept indefinitely, if tightly covered, To use, simply cover in liquid from ½ to 2 hours, or until soft and pliable. The soaking liquid can be used for added flavor—decrease other liquids accordingly.

Serve   *Hot,* as a vegetable with meat, poultry or fish; as a garnish; stuffed as an appetizer or accompaniment; broiled, as a sauce; baked; as a soup; or in stews, casseroles, etc. *Cold,* raw, as an appetizer or snack; pickled or marinated as an hors d'oeuvre or relish.

Happy Marriages   Butter, bread crumbs, onions and shallots, cream, lemon juice, cheese, tomatoes, veal, chicken, beef, salad dressing, fish.

Approximate Cooking Times

Marketing Forms	Cooking Forms	Sauté Minutes	Bake Minutes	Broil Minutes
Fresh	Whole cap	7-10	15	4-6
	sliced	4-6	10	
	stuffed cap	15-20	20-25	5-8
Canned	Whole	Heat		5
	stems and pieces	3-4		
	sliced	5-7		
	soups	heat		

Marketing Forms	Cooking Forms	Sauté Minutes	Bake Minutes	Broil Minutes
Jarred	Whole	Heat		5
	stems and pieces	3-4		
	sliced	5-7		
	various, in butter	heat		
Frozen	Whole caps	10		35-40
Dried	Sliced, soaked	10-15	15-20	

Okra A fruit and pod vegetable. Hybiscus fruit, also known as gumbo, a member of the mallow family. An edible seed and fruit. Okra is a natural thickening agent, and serves that function in gumbos, soups and creole dishes. There are ridged and smooth varieties. Central American origin.

1 pound serves 4 persons.

Select Medium-sized, tender and fresh pods. Store whole, a maximum of 5 days. Use immediately after cooking to prevent okra's typical "sliminess" from forming. Peak month in July.

To Prepare for Cooking and Serving Trim and cook whole, or trim and slice.

Test for Doneness Cook until tender but not soft.

Serve Hot, as a vegetable with poultry or ham. Okra is used extensively in stews, gumbos and casseroles and all creole cooking.

Cold, cooked, as a salad with French dressing.

Happy Marriages Ham, chicken, tomatoes, filé powder, basil, thyme, almonds, ginger.

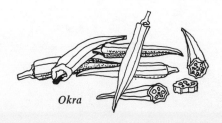

Okra

Approximate Cooking Times

Marketing Forms	Cooking Forms	Boiling Minutes	Steaming Minutes
Fresh	Whole	15-25	
	sliced	10-15	20
Canned	Sliced	Heat	
Frozen	Whole, baby	8-10	
	sliced	10	

Onions A bulb and tuber vegetable. Descending from an Asiatic plant. A vegetable as well as a pungent condiment. There are many varieties of onions.

1 pound serves 3–4 persons.

Select Clean, hard, well-shaped onions with dry skins and without sprouts. Look for green, fresh tops for green onions, spring onions, chives and scallions. Store scallions, green onions in vegetable compartment no more than 1 to 2 days. Store all other onions, except chives, in loosely woven or open-mesh container in a cool place for up to several months. Use before they soften and sprout. Chives are usually obtainable in flower pots and if kept well-watered will grow on a windowsill for weeks. Onions may be chilled before peeling to prevent tears. The peeler may also hold a slice of bread in her mouth.

To Prepare for Cooking and Serving   *Chives:* Cut with kitchen scissors.
Garlic: Divide bulb and peel individual clove; mince, slice or crush. For certain dishes, garlic is crushed with salt.

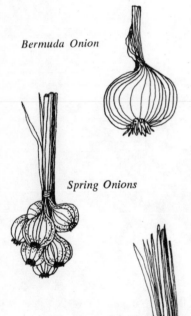

Bermuda Onion

Spring Onions

Spanish Onions

Scallion

Shallots

Green onions, scallions, spring onions and leeks: Trim off root and largest part of green shoot, peel off brown skin, mince or slice for cooking, leave scallions whole for eating raw.
Shallot: Divide clusters, peel and mince. Use as minced onion. The white part of scallions may be substituted in the same proportions.
Small white onions: Trim root end and stem and peel. Small white onions will peel easily if immersed in boiling water for 10 seconds and peeled immediately. Cut a small cross at the root end with sharp knife to keep cooked onions intact.
White, yellow, red, Bermuda and brown onions: Trim, peel, use whole, sliced, chopped, minced, grated or juiced. To juice, press small sections through garlic press or mince until juice is extracted and discard pulp. Used cooked and raw. Bermuda onions are considered sweetest for eating raw on sandwiches and hamburgers.

   Test for Doneness   Test baked onions for tenderness with a fork. Judge fried onions by rich golden color.

   Serve   Chives, garlic, green onions, scallions, spring onions, leeks and shallots are used mainly for seasoning and flavorings in all cooking. Cold, these onions are used in salads and some are used as appetizers and snacks. Small white onions are used primarily for creaming, stews and glazing and some casseroles. All remaining onions are served hot, stuffed and baked, in stews, soups, casseroles; deep fat fried, for smothering, broiled and fried slices, and as a garnish. Cold, raw onion is used in salads, sandwiches, as an addition to meat dishes, and as appetizers. Onions also make excellent soups and sauces, and are always added to the stock pot. They are used widely in poultry stuffing, and pickled onions are used in cocktails and appetizers.

   Happy Marriages   Beef, steaks, liver, mushrooms, crumbs, tomatoes, peas, cheese, walnuts, sage, oregano, butter, cream, potatoes, eggs, all salads and many salad dressings.

Yellow Onion

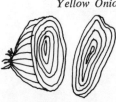

Approximate Cooking Times

Marketing Forms	Cooking Forms	Boiling Minutes	Steaming Minutes	Baking Minutes	Frying Minutes	Broiling Minutes
Fresh	Small white	15-20	25-35	20	15	
Whole	medium yellow	20-30	35-40	40-45		
	brown	30-40	40-45	50-60		
	leek, whole	20-35	25-40			
	yellow, sliced	7	12	20-25	7-10	7-10
	brown, sliced	7	12	25-30	8-12	8-10
	Bermuda, sliced	7	12	30-35	10-15	8-12
	leek, sliced	15	20	20	4-7	
	all diced onions	5			7-10	
Canned		Heat		(see can directions)		
Bottled	Whole, boiled	Heat	15	10-12		
	whole, fancy small cocktail	heat	15	10-12		
Frozen*	chopped	5	7		4-7	
	rings			11 @ 400°	12 @ 360°	2
*(Defrost before using.)						

Oxalis   A bulb and tuber vegetable. Peru, Mexico and Bolivia, a tuber used in the same way as Jerusalem artichoke.

Parsley   (see Herb Chart, p. 46). To store: Wash, discard wilted or yellow stalks, shake off excess water. Place in polyethylene bag, press out air and seal. Store in refrigerator up to 1 week.

Parsley

Parsnip   A root vegetable. Sliced, dipped in batter and fried, or parboiled and baked. If plain boiled, they require a strong sauce. Store at a low temperature.

Patata   (see Sweet Potato p. 163) South American, introduced to Europe before the white potato.

Parsnip

Peas   A root and pod vegetable. Dried peas, originally from China (see Dried Vegetables, p. 149).

½ pound, in pod, serves 1. 1 pound of peas in pod yields 1 cup shelled peas.

Select   Young, tender, sweet peas. Pods should have a fresh appearance and be light green in color. Avoid puffed or swollen pods which may indicate tough peas. Store uncovered in the pod in refrigerator no more than 1 to 2 days. Least available September through December.

To Prepare for Cooking and Serving   Shell peas. It is sometimes possible to obtain such young and tender peas that they are delicious cooked in the pods. Young fresh peas can be eaten raw. Cooked peas should be drained well before serving. It is now possible to buy shelled fresh peas in some markets.

Test for Doneness   Tender but not soft. Taste. For purées and soups, boil until very soft.

Serve   Hot, as a vegetable with meats, poultry or fish; as a separate vegetable course; or in soups and sauces.

Cold, boiled peas for salads.

Happy Marriages   Carrots, onions, mint, lamb, ham, butter sauce, mushrooms.

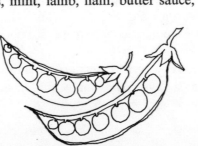

Peas

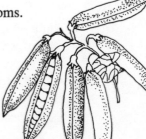

Peppers

Approximate Cooking Times

Marketing Forms	Cooking Forms	Boiling Minutes	Steaming Minutes	Baking Minutes
Fresh	Shelled	8-20	10-20	35-45
Canned	Large	5-6		15-20
	medium, small	4-5		12-15
	very young	3-4		8-10
	mixed sizes	4-5		10-12
Jarred	Small	Heat		8-10
Frozen	Deluxe tiny	2-3		15-20
	regular	5-7		20-25
	purée	6-7		12-15

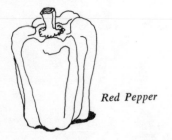

Red Pepper

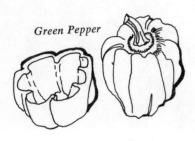

Green Pepper

Peppers   A fruit and pod vegetable. Green and red bell peppers, sweet and hot. Green peppers ripen to red. West Indies and East Indies. Also the capsicum and pimiento. The pepper family is divided into the hot condiment peppers, the sweet bell peppers and the chilis and out of these are derived sweet red paprika, cayenne, allspice and Jamaican peppers.

1 large pepper serves 1–2 persons.

Select   Firm, bright, glossy and deep green peppers; or with more or less red color. Red peppers are mature color form of the green peppers. Store in the vegetable compartment or in plastic bag for no more than 3 to 5 days.

To Prepare for Cooking and Serving   Trim stem, cut in half and remove all seeds and white ribs. If pepper rings are desired, cut into slices before seeding. If the pepper is to be stuffed whole, cut off top and scoop out seeds. Peppers are also chopped or diced for cooking and garnishing.

Test for Doneness   Test for tenderness with a fork or by tasting.

Serve   *Hot,* as a vegetable, usually stuffed or in casseroles.

Cold, raw, in salads or as a garnish.

Happy Marriages Rice, lamb, chopped meat, southern recipes, South American recipes, eastern cooking. Onions, cream cheese, and tomatoes, chili con carne, salads.

Cooking Times Peppers are almost always cooked with other foods, so cooking times vary considerably.

Approximate Cooking Times

Marketing Forms	Cooking Forms	Boiling or Parboiling Minutes	Steaming Minutes	Baking Minutes
Fresh	red green	3-5	10	45-60
Canned Jarred	roasted fried, sweet roasted, sweet picalilli pepper salad	(flavoring, condiment and garnish)		
Pimientos Jarred	whole sliced	To store after opening jar. Retain all liquid in jar, seal tightly, refrigerate and use as soon as possible.		

Pimientos, (see Peppers, above)

Potatoes, White and Sweet A bulb and tuber vegetable. The white potato originated in America, was introduced into France in 1540 and to Great Britain by Sir Walter Raleigh. Among the varieties of sweet potatoes are: Virginian, Algerian, Rose of Malaya and Spanish.

½ pound serves 1 person.

Potatoes

French Fries

Balls

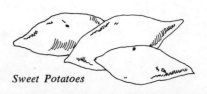
Sweet Potatoes

Chips

Dutchess Potatoes

Mashed

Potatoes Anna

Select   Firm, smooth, unsprouted potatoes with skin intact. Sweet potatoes should be clean, smooth, firm and bright in appearance. Store white potatoes in a cool, dark, well-ventilated place for up to 3 weeks. Use new potatoes immediately. Sweet potatoes can be stored in a cool room for up to several months.

To Prepare for Cooking and Serving   New potatoes need only rinsing before cooking in skins. Start all boiled potatoes in boiling water, dry by cooking a minute after draining; do not cover after draining. Potatoes may also be washed, peeled and cooked whole, sliced, cubed, diced, or cut into balls with a melon baller. Potatoes are often put through a ricer (see p. 18) and served mashed. Sweet potatoes are most often served candied.

Test for Doneness   Squeeze a baked potato to test for softness. Test boiling potatoes with a fork for tenderness, taste a potato ball or cube or dice; judge a fried or French fried potato by rich golden color.

Serve   *Hot,* with meat, fish and poultry, in soups, casseroles and stews, stuffings, and hot potato salads.
Cold, cooked, in salads. Cold sweet potatoes are used pureed as a base for jam.

Happy Marriages   Butter, parsley, onion, herbs, eggs, bacon, cream, chives, cheese, ketchup, mayonnaise, French dressing. Serve Sweet Potatoes with marshmallows, brown sugar, apricots, raisins, brandy, rum, apples, oranges.

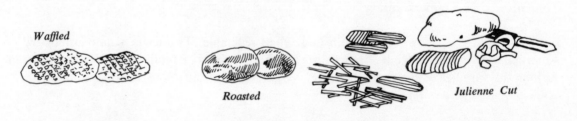

Waffled

Roasted

Julienne Cut

Hash Brown

Home Fries

Baked

Approximate Cooking Times

Marketing Forms	Cooking Forms	Boil or Parboil Minutes	Steam Minutes	Bake Minutes	Fry or Roast Minutes	French Fry 385-395° Minutes
Fresh, white	Whole,	25-45	35-45	45-60	40-60	
	quartered,	20-25	20-30		20-40	5-7
	sliced,	5-7	10-12		10-15	2-3
	diced,	1-2	10-12		7-10	3-5
	cut,	1-2			20	3-7
	balls,	10-15				3-5
	sliced, thin	2-3		20	20	2-3
Fresh, new	whole	20-30		60-75		
Fresh, baking	whole	20-25	35-45	45-60		
Fresh, sweet	whole,	25-35	30-35	30-45		
	sliced,	15-20		20-25		
	quartered	15-25	25-30	20-25		
Canned, white	Sliced,	Heat		20	10	
	whole, small			25	20	
Canned, sweet	whole,	heat		20-25		
	halves	heat		15-20		
Frozen white	Crinklecut,			15-20	5-10	
	thin cut,			12-15		
	potato puff,			10-14		2
	French fries,			15-20	5-10	
	potato patties,					
	shredded potatoes for hash browns,				5-6	
	tiny potato bites,			15		
	cottage fried,			10-15	12	1-2
Frozen sweet	candied			40-45	15	

(165)

Marketing Forms	Cooking Forms	Boil or Parboil Minutes	Steam Minutes	Bake Minutes	Fry or Roast Minutes	French Fry 385-395° Minutes
Jarred white	Whole	Heat		15-25		
Jarred sweet	Whole, sliced	Heat		30		

Radishes

Pumpkin   A fruit and pod vegetable. Originated in China, related to the cucumber, marrow and squash.

Pumpkin is most often eaten in the form of pumpkin pie. Very small pumpkins are sometimes stuffed and baked. Pumpkin also makes a delicious cold soup, and it combines well with allspice, onions and nutmeg. Canned pumpkin is available. (For cooking information see Squash, p. 168.)

Radishes   A root vegetable. Red, white and black. Originated in Asia. It is used as an appetizer, as a garnish (in the form of radish roses) and in salads. It goes well with cold butter and salt. Radishes are rarely cooked.

Rutabaga, (see Turnips, p. 171)

Salsify   A root vegetable. Originated in China. Also known as the oyster plant. Boiled, creamed and gratineed. Good with shallots, chives or parsleys.

Shallots   A bulb and tuber vegetable. The shallot is a compound root bulb, similar to garlic. It lies between the garlic and the onion and originated in Asia. It is used extensively in the

Black Radishes

Salsify

making of sauces, soups, stuffings and veal scallopini, also in meat and poultry dishes. If unavailable, shallots can be ordered by mail (see Onions p. 158).

Spinach   A leaf and bud vegetable. A leafy vegetable native to Asia.

1 pound fresh spinach serves 2 persons.

Select   Clean, fresh, tender leaves of good green color. Wash, drain and remove sand and heavy stems and store in a plastic bag. Use as soon as possible. Available all year.

To Prepare for Cooking and Serving   Remove coarse stems, wash and cook at once without additional liquid, only long enough to wilt and turn bright green. After cooking, either chop or puree or serve in leaf form. Drain well.

Test for Doneness   Taste for tenderness of leaves.

Serve   Hot, as a vegetable with meat, poultry or fish, as a separate vegetable course, spinach puddings, or soufflés.

Cold, raw, as a salad green.

Spinach is also used to make very good soups.

Happy Marriages   Eggs, ham and tongue, bacon drippings, sliced apple, garlic croutons, basil, mushrooms and sherry.

Approximate Cooking Times

Marketing Forms	Cooking Forms	Boiling Minutes	Steaming Minutes	Baking Minutes
Fresh	Whole, chopped or puréed soufflé, pudding	3-10*	5-12	40-60
Canned	Fancy	Heat	(follow can directions)	30
Frozen	whole,	4-6		35
	chopped	4-6		35

(* Boil fresh or washed leaf spinach only in water that clings to leaves after washing. Rewash washed spinach.)

Spinach

Pattypan

Banana Squash

Crookneck

Stachy   A tuber vegetable. Of Far Eastern origin. Parboiling is essential.

Squash and Pumpkins   A fruit and pod vegetable. Among the few cultivated food plants native to America. There are many varieties of squash.

1 medium-sized squash serves 2.

1 medium-sized squash yields 1–1½ cups.

Select   Squash of good color, unblemished and clean, heavy for its size. Keep small tender summer squash covered in the refrigerator for no more than 4 days. Winter squash can be stored at room temperature for 3 to 5 days but if stored in a cool, dry, dark place with good air circulation they will keep several months. Larger or more hard-skinned summer squash will also keep this way.

To Prepare for Cooking and Serving   *Summer squash:* generally sliced, need not be peeled if tender. *Winter Squash:* Halved and seeds removed, cut in serving pieces, diced, sliced.

Serve   Halved, in pieces or mashed as a vegetable with meat, poultry and fish. Squash is also good stuffed, candied, creamed, scalloped and some make excellent puddings and pies.

Happy Marriages   Cheese, tomatoes, pork, sugar, butter, dill, sour cream, onion, almonds.

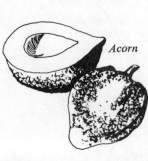

Acorn

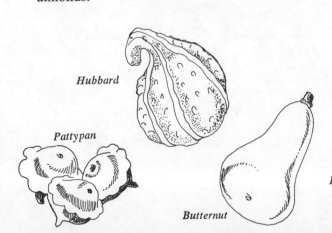

Hubbard

Pattypan

Turban

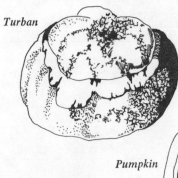

Butternut

Delicious

Pumpkin

Approximate Cooking Times

Marketing Forms	Cooking Forms	Boiling Minutes	Steaming Minutes	400° F. Baking Minutes
Fresh				
summer	Sliced	8-20	15-20	30-60
winter	hubbard, 2-inch pieces	15-20	25-40	40-60
	acorn			30
Frozen	Mashed			
	sliced		(see package directions)	
Canned			(see package directions)	

Swede (*Rutabaga*)

Swede A root vegetable. (Also called Rutabaga, see Turnips, p. 171.) It is boiled or mashed and creamed, parboiled and used in stews, casseroles and for boiled beef.

Tomatoes A fruit and pod vegetable. Red, yellow or green, with many varieties in each color.

1 pound serves 2 persons.

Select Mature, red, ripe, preferably vine-ripened tomatoes. Do not refrigerate tomatoes until they are thoroughly ripe. Let tomatoes ripen at room temperature in a heavy paper bag, away from direct sunlight. After tomatoes are ripe, store in refrigerator and use as soon as possible.

To Prepare for Cooking and Serving To serve raw, remove stem and peel if desired. Serve halved or sliced or quartered. Tomatoes are usually peeled before cooking unless they are stuffed. To peel, immerse in boiling water for 7 to 10 seconds. Draw off skin with a sharp knife.

Serve *Hot,* as a vegetable course, as a vegetable with meat, poultry or fish or eggs. Cooked tomatoes are used in sauces, casseroles, soups, stews, many Italian dishes. They

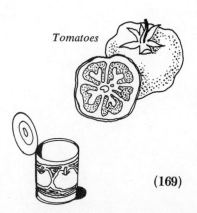

Tomatoes

can be stuffed and baked, sliced and fried, halved and broiled. Sliced and fried green tomatoes are used in condiments.

Cold, raw, as salads, in salads, stuffed, as a garnish, juiced, in aspics and in gazpacho.

Cold, cooked, used in ketchups, chili sauce, relishes, tomato jellies, tomato chutney and in jellied Madrilene.

Happy Marriages Onions, basil, oregano, thyme, bread crumbs, all dressings, mayonnaise, rice, shrimp, garlic, cheese, anchovies, eggs.

Approximate Cooking Times

Marketing Forms	Cooking Forms	Boil Minutes	Steam Minutes	Bake Minutes	Fry Minutes	Broil Minutes
Fresh	Whole, red	7-15	8-16	15-30	6-7	
	sliced, red				6-7	8-10
	sliced, green				6-7	8-10
	halved, red			10-15	8-12	8-12
Canned	Whole peeled, red, sliced baby	Heat	20	35-50		
	Italian peeled with tomato paste puree	15-60 to reduce				
Tomato* paste		Flavoring				
Tomato* sauces	Plain, with cheese	Heat				
Juices*	Cocktail juice	Heat				
Catsup	Plain, hot	Condiment				

*(Store opened tomato paste, sauce and juice in tightly closed jar and bottle in refrigerator.)

Turnips and Rutabagas   Root vegetables of the mustard family.
All carrot preparations are suitable for turnips. Leaves of young turnips can be prepared as spinach or chard. Turnips are particularly well adapted to duck. Boil whole turnips 20 to 30 minutes, and boil sliced 15 to 20 minutes. Steam turnip slices 20 to 25 minutes. Boil frozen pieces 20 to 25 minutes or steam 20 to 25 minutes. 1 pound serves 4 persons. Turnips may also be mashed or stuffed.

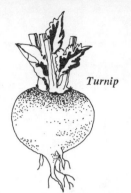

Turnip

Watercress   A leaf and bud salad plant (to store, see Parsley, p. 160). Watercress has a sharp, peppery taste. It is used raw for salads and garnishes, and is cooked for soup. It goes well with apples, cheese, French dressings, cream and bread crumbs.

Yams   A tuber vegetable. Also called a Chinese potato. Originated in the West Indies. It is a large, fleshy tuber, always boiled before it is mashed or baked. It can be used successfully in place of the white potato baked in its shell. Canned halves in syrup are also available.

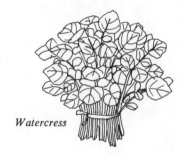

Watercress

Zucchini   A fruit and pod vegetable. A gourd related to the squash and used extensively in Italy.

1 pound serves 2 persons
Select   Firm, dark green, small zucchini; use as soon as possible.
To Prepare for Cooking and Serving   Trim stem ends and slice across or lengthwise. Or use whole, if small and tender. Zucchini can be served raw as an appetizer or cooked in soups, skillet dishes and with meat, poultry and fish.
Test for Doneness   The center of thin slices becomes transparent. As they cook very quickly, watch carefully. Whole zucchini or large slices should be fork tested.
Happy Marriages   Tomatoes, onions, eggplant, lemon, French dressing, butter, oregano, mushrooms.

Yams

Approximate Cooking Times

Marketing Forms	Cooking Form	Boiling Minutes	Baked Minutes
Fresh	Whole	10-15	35-45
	thin sliced	4	15-20
	thick sliced	6-8	20-25
	large stuffed		30-45
Canned	Cut	3-5	(see can directions)
Frozen	Quartered and cut	5-7	15-20

Zucchini

Generally prices are lowest and quality highest when the fruit is at the peak of its season. Fruits are perishable, so buy only what is needed; fruit is not always at eating ripeness in the stores however, so it is often advisable to buy a day or two ahead of time and let the fruit ripen fully at home. Information is given in this chapter on what to look for when buying fruits, and on how to ripen and store.

When buying fruit, make sure you're getting what you want—that is, avoid purchasing "eating" apples if you want to bake them. Ask your grocers advice if unsure. Do not handle fruit excessively and avoid fruit with bruises. If possible, when buying small fruits and berries already packaged in containers, check the lower levels to make sure the fruit is all of desired size and quality.

To keep fruit from discoloring after slicing, peeling, etc., place in lightly acidulated water until needed. Drain and dry well before using.

Fruits and nuts add variety to diet. They are good cooked, as snacks, for desserts, and many other uses. Many fruits are available canned, and many nuts are available in cans, jars and envelopes.

The most common can sizes for fruits are:

Can or Jar Size	Approximate Yield
8 ounce cans and jars	1 cup
Picnic can (10½ ounces)	1¼ cups
No. 300 (14–16 ounces, commonly called the "1 pound" can)	1¾ cups
No. 303 can or jar (16–17 ounces)	2 cups
No. 2 can (1 pound 4 ounces or 1 pint 2 fluid ounces)	2½ cups
No. 2½ can or jar (1 pound 13 ounces)	3½ cups

10 ∂ð

Fruits
and
Nuts

46 ounce can (3 pounds 3 ounces or 1 pint 14 fluid ounces)	5¾ cups
No. 10 can (6½–7¼ pounds)	12–13 cups (restaurant size)

Nuts are generally packed in vacuum cans of 6 to 8 ounces or larger, or envelopes of 1 to 2 ounces or larger. Store nuts in refrigerator to keep them from going rancid after packages are opened. Store envelopes in a canister and do not keep them too long before opening. Store all nuts at temperature just above freezing during summer months.

Almonds   A nut of Near Eastern origin.

Varieties   Sweet, used for cooking and eating. Bitter, used for flavoring. Jordans and Valencias, green almonds.

½ pound in shells will yield approximately ½ cup meat.

½ pound shelled and blanched whole almonds will yield about 1½ cups ground almonds.

1 cup whole shelled almonds weighs about 5½ ounces.

Preparation   To shell: break shell with nutcracker or hammer. Break paper-shells with hands, extract kernel or double kernel, which is the almond meat, and discard the shell. The almond kernel has a tight, brown skin. The almond can be chopped or ground with the brown skin, as used in Linzer tart and spiced cookies, or used whole for parching and certain confections, as praline. For all other purposes the almond kernel is scalded to remove the brown skin. Scalded almonds are also called blanched almonds.

To blanch: pour boiling water over almonds and let stand for 2 minutes. Drain, cover with cold water and squeeze white almond out of the brown skin with the fingers. Blanched almonds are used whole, chopped, shaved, slivered and ground. They can be ground in a regular nut grinder or in an imported Scandinavian or European almond grinder which grinds them as fine as flour. Almond flour is used for finest cookies and small pastries.

Almonds

Market Forms   In shell, loose and packaged; shelled, in cans or envelopes; brown, brown shaved, blanched or slivered in cans or envelopes; dry toasted in jars; flavored almonds and almond confections, such as burnt and Jordan almonds in boxes and jars and occasionally loose; almond paste, loose and in cans; almond extract, bottled; salted and flavored almonds in cans. Can sizes range from 6 to 8 ounces and up; the various almond forms in envelopes are available generally in 1- and 2-ounce sizes.

Serve   Unsalted almonds: to decorate cakes and cookies; roasted and toasted almonds: with vegetables, fish and meat dishes; ground almonds: as a substitute for flour in baking; whole almonds: in fruit cakes, as garnishes and in beverages. Almonds are also eaten as snacks.

Happy Marriages   String beans, trout, veal, chicken, chocolate.

Apples   Fruit mentioned in the Bible. Cultivated in Europe for over 2,000 years. There are thousands of different kinds of apples. Among them are: Baldwin, Jonathan, McIntosh, Northern Spy, Stayman, Winesap (all-purpose apples); Newton Pippin and Golden and Red Delicious (eating apples); Cortlands and Rome Beauties (baking apples). Crab apples (also called lady apples) are descendants of early forms of today's cultivated apples. They are used for decorations and garnishes and are traditionally placed in the suckling pig's mouth before it is served. Crab apples are almost inedible raw, but make excellent preserves, jellies and marmalade. Spiced crab apples are available in jars as a meat accompniment.

3 medium apples weigh approximately 1 pound.

1 pound apples yields about 3 cups peeled and diced apples.

1 pound dried apples yields about 4⅓ cups.

Select   Firm apples of good, glossy color with no bruises or brown spots. Store apples in a cool place until ripe, away from direct sunlight. Apples tend to become mealy if refrigerated before ripe. Least available June through August.

Preparation   Wash before eating raw. Wash and dry and peel, core, slice, quarter or

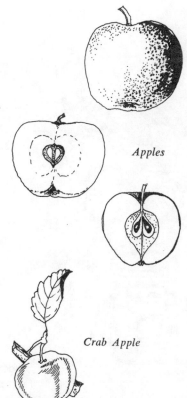

Apples

Crab Apple

cube for cooking. In some cases the peel may be left on. Remove most of the core and peel a strip from the top of the apple for baking. Peeled and sliced apples turn brown upon exposure to air. They should be sprinkled with lemon juice or any citrus fruit juice as soon as they are peeled. The apples which are slow to discolor upon exposure to air are: Red Delicious, Golden Delicious and Cortlands. It is wise to use these varieties for salads, fruit cups and all recipes where the raw, peeled apple is used.

Market Forms   Fresh; sliced in cans, jars and frozen; dried in packages and loose; apple sauce in cans and jars; apple juice in cans and jars; apple cider fresh in bottles and jugs and frozen.

Serve   Cold, cooked as apple sauce or as a relish. Raw, as a fruit, a juice or fermented in ciders. Hot, in slices, cubes, stuffed and baked or whole baked as an accompaniment with beef, poultry or ham or as a dessert. Apples are also used in cakes, as garnishes and, of course, for apple pies and tarts, and apple butter. Dried apples are available loose or in packages. Spiced apples and spiced crab apples are available in jars.

Happy Marriages   Cinnamon, sugar, cream, brown sugar, pork, sauerkraut, caraway seeds, cranberries, cheese and crackers.

Cooking   Bake apples for 40 to 60 minutes at 375–400° F.

Apricots   Originated in China.

8–14 medium apricots weigh 1 pound.

Select   Firm, unwilted apricots of good color, without blemishes. Allow to ripen at room temperature, and do not expose to direct sunlight. After ripening, place in refrigerator and use within 4 days. Peak of season is in June.

Preparation   Cook dried apricots according to package directions. Dried apricots are also pounded into thin sheets and used extensively for confections and baking.

Market Forms   Fresh, by the pound; dried in boxes or bags, usually of 1 pound, candied, canned and in the form of jams and nectars. Both whole and halved apricots are canned in syrup.

Apricots

Serve   As a fresh or stewed fruit; in desserts, as a filling and glaze on meats, baked goods, and as apricot liqueur.

Happy Marriages   With sweet potatoes, pork or ham, cold fruit soups, ice creams and rum babas.

Angelica, (see Herb chart p. 42)

Avocado   Also called Alligator Pear; from California, Florida, Mexico and Central America. Spherical or pear shaped.

1 medium avocado weighs approximately 1 pound.

1 medium avocado will serve 2 when halved, and 4 as a salad.

Select   Green to dark mahogany avocados with no blemishes and just soft to the touch for immediate use. Let hard avocados ripen at room temperature; when ripe refrigerate if not used at once. Available all year.

Avocado

Preparation   Peel and slice or dice. Or leave peel on, halve and remove large pit for scooping out and mashing avocado. Sprinkle cut avocado quickly with lemon juice to keep it from discoloring. Add to cooked and cold dishes just prior to serving. Store cut avocado with pit in, tightly covered in the refrigerator. If avocado is too green when cut, put halves together with seed inside, place in paper bag and leave at room temperature for a day or two to finish ripening. Or dice flesh and marinate for an hour or so in oil and vinegar salad dressing; this softens and ripens the flesh.

Serve   Raw, as an appetizer, in salads, with salad dressings and stuffed as a luncheon dish. There are also avocado soups.

Happy Marriages   Lime and lemon juice, onions, cayenne, chili powder, salad dressings, cold cooked seafoods, chicken, ham.

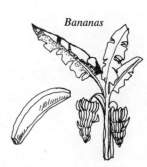

Bananas

Bananas   Of Asiatic origin. Varieties: fig, yellow and red. Plantains (cooking bananas) are larger, coarser and less sweet fruit of the same species as the banana. They are good when

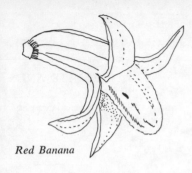

Red Banana

Cranberries

Dewberries

baked, broiled or roasted. Also dried and ground into meal for breads, puddings and as a thickener.

3–5 medium bananas weigh approximately 1 pound.

1 pound bananas will make 2 cups sliced bananas.

1 pound will yield approximately 1¾ cups crushed.

1 pound of dried bananas is approximately 4 cups.

Select   Firm bananas. Bananas are unripe when green, and will ripen successfully at home at room temperature. May be refrigerated for several days once they are ripe. Available all year.

Preparation   Peel and leave whole, halve lengthwise, slice for cooking or mash. Bananas can also be baked in their skins.

Serve   Hot as dessert; broil or fry as an accompaniment with meat dishes and with spicy foods. Cold for cakes, breads, fruit salads, fritters, and chocolate covered and frozen as an ice-cream pop.

Happy Marriages   Butter, brown sugar, pineapple, rum, ice cream, chocolate and fruit sauces.

Cooking Times   Bake at 450° F. for 10 to 12 minutes. Broil at 550° F. for 5 to 6 minutes. Grill, in peels, 18 to 25 minutes.

Berries   Mostly of American and European origin. Usually sold in 1-quart and 1½-quart baskets. Servings vary, but 1 quart usually serves 4.

Select   Large berries of good color, not soft, spotted or mildewed. Keep berries whole and uncovered in the refrigerator and use within 2 days.

Preparation   Wash and remove stems or hull only just before serving. Cranberries cannot be eaten raw and can be stored up to 6 days before cooking.

Market Forms   Fresh, frozen, canned in syrup, in jams, jellies, nectars, toppings, preserves. Melba sauce.

Serve As fresh fruit, as stewed fruits, in desserts, pies, ice creams, sauces, shortcakes, liqueurs, soufflés, puddings, sherberts, in wines, ices and mousses. Cranberries can be cooked in sauces, jellies, stuffings, breads and pies.

Happy Marriages Heavy cream, sour cream, clotted or Devonshire cream, ice cream, sherbert, cold rice, nuts, cinnamon, sugar, brandy and wines.

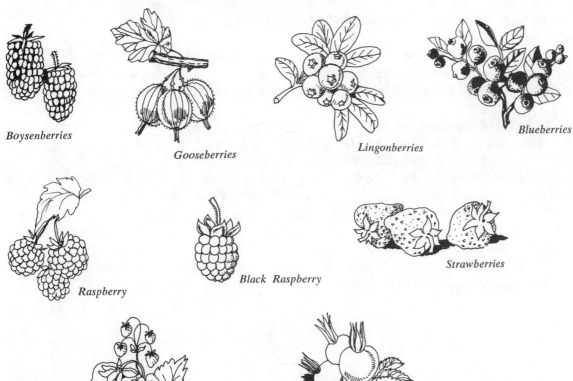

Boysenberries

Gooseberries

Lingonberries

Blueberries

Raspberry

Black Raspberry

Strawberries

Wild Strawberries

Rose Hips

Brazil Nuts

Brazil Nuts   A very hard-shelled nut. Freeze nuts, then break the shell with a nut cracker or hammer. Use the kernel whole or chopped. To slice, bring nuts to boil in water to cover, simmer 5 minutes, drain and slice lengthwise or make curls with a vegetable slicer. Toast slices in a 350° F. oven for about 10 to 12 minutes. Brazil nuts are used as an appetizer, in cakes, fruit cakes, Christmas baking; they may be ground and used in place of flour.

Butternuts   A white walnut (see Walnuts p. 194).

Cashews   A Tropical South American nut; imported from Brazil and India. Used in baking, cooking and for cashew butter. It is served extensively as a snack and is usually available shelled or shelled and salted in envelopes and cans or bottles.

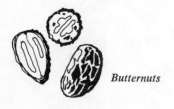

Butternuts

Cherries   Of European origin.
    Varieties   Red, Bing, Oxheart, sour and many others.
    1 pound average cherries, pitted, measure about 2 cups.
    Select   Cherries of good color, glossy and firm, if possible with stems attached. When buying, the larger, darker cherries are usually sweeter. Peak season is June through July.
    Preparation   To pit cherry, use a cherry pitter or cut with a knife and extract pit. Store whole and uncovered in refrigerator and use within 2 days. Wash just before serving or using for cooking.
    Market Forms   Fresh, canned in syrup, preserved, jellies and jams, in ice cream, green and red maraschino cherries, candied.

Cashews

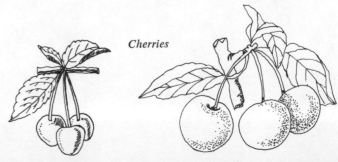

Cherries

Serve   Fresh, as a fruit; stewed, in desserts, .pies, meat and poultry sauces, cakes and tarts, cherry liqueurs, as decorations and garnishes and in cocktails.

Happy Marriages   Ice cream, chocolate, cinnamon, cloves, almonds, fruit cakes, brandy.

Chestnuts   European and Asian origin.

1 pound of chestnuts yield about ⅔ pound shelled chestnuts or 2½ cups.

Select   Large, firm, glossy chestnuts.

Preparation   To shell: cut a cross on flat side of shell with a sharp, pointed knife. Roast in medium oven about 12 minutes or until cut edges turn back and are brittle. Pull off outside shell and as much inner brown skin as possible while nuts are still warm. Boil until inner skins loosen easily. Remove inner skins and drain, or continue to cook until soft and puréed.

Market Forms   Loose by the pound, in boxes, cooked whole in cans, puréed in cans, candied whole in bottles.

Serve   As a stuffing for birds, roasted and peeled as a snack, as an accompaniment with meat and vegetables, puréed, in desserts, riced, candied (Marrons glazes are candied whole boiled chestnuts). There are chestnut cakes and cakes in which chestnuts are substituted for flour.

Happy Marriages   Brussel sprouts, goose and turkey, spinach, butter, brandy, ice cream, sugar.

Chinese Gooseberry   The Carambola of Asiatic origin. Thin, smooth yellow coat, ranges in size from as small as an egg to as large as an orange. Consumed both green and ripe, raw, cooked or in chutneys. Cultivated in Southern California and West Indies.

Citron   A citrus fruit from the Orient. A large fruit with a rough, uneven, thin yellowish-green rind. The edible part of the fruit is small and surrounded with a thick white inner rind. The juice is used in beverages, but citron is best known in its candied or preserve rind form, generally available in jars or packages and used extensively in fruit cakes.

Coconut

Coconut The fruit of a tropical tree. Sizes and weights vary a good deal.

  Select Coconuts heavy for their size. The milk should be heard when the coconut is shaken, or it will be dry. Coconuts are usually marketed without their husks. Should it become necessary to husk one, set the coconut upright, small pointed end down. Using two shovels, back to back, place the tips on the stem and pry husk apart.

  Preparation To open, place in a medium oven briefly to loosen meat from shell. Then break with a hammer or against a pointed, sharp edge or drop from a height onto a hard floor. Pierce two of the soft "eyes" with an ice pick and drain coconut milk into a container with a lid; and refrigerate immediately. Use within 24 hours. Peel the thin brown skin off the white meat with a vegetable parer.

  Market Forms Whole coconuts. Coconut meat is packaged flaked, grated and shredded in cans or packages. It is also available moist and canned. Coconut comes sweetened and unsweetened.

  Serve Raw as an appetizer, topping or garnish. Toasted coconut chips can be used as snacks.

  Happy Marriages Chocolate, chutney, fruits, oranges.

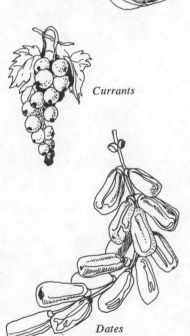
Currants

Dates

Cranberry, (see **Berries**)

Currant, Fresh Small acid berry fruit of bush resembling gooseberry. Sometimes eaten raw, chiefly used for jellies, jams and syrups. Most common are red currants. Green are tart unripened. White and red berries are used for France's famous Bar Le Duc preserve.

Dates Persia, Arabia, Mesopotamia, a Biblical fruit.

  1 pound of dried dates is approximately 60.

Dates are available jarred, spiced and dried. They are eaten as a confection, dried, and are used in baking and in breads. Keep in the refrigerator once package is opened.

Figs   From Asia Minor and Smyrna. Of Biblical times. About 12 figs weigh 1 pound. There are about 42 dried figs to a pound.

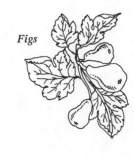

Figs

Figs are amber tinted, greenish-yellow, or black purple, and are ripe when soft to the touch. Stuff fresh figs and serve as a confection, dessert or sweet. They do not need to be peeled. Figs are also available preserved, dried and canned in syrup. They are used as a confection, for desserts, in cakes and cookies and breads.

Filberts   A rich, sweet nut.
1 pound of filberts in shells will yield ½ pound nut meats (see Hazelnuts p. 184).

Grapefruit   Of Chinese origin.
1 medium grapefruit weighs about 1 pound.
Select   Firm fruit, heavy for its size and kept in refrigerator.
Preparation   Cut in half across and loosen individual sections with a sharp knife or grapefruit spoon Or peel carefully and section for fruit salads, removing the white inner peel lining from the fruit sections. Or juice.
Market Forms   Grapefruit comes fresh, white or pink; in cans and jars, in natural liquid, in syrup, sweetened and unsweetened. Fresh grapefruit juice is sometimes available.
Serve   As a fruit, as a juice, in fruit salads, broiled as an entree or dessert.
Happy Marriages   Sugar, mint, honey, maraschino cherries, Cointreau, shrimp, avacado, brown sugar.

Grapefruit

(183)

Grapes

Grapes

Varieties   Among the many varieties are Thompson Seedless, Catawba, Concord, Flame Tokay, Muscadine, white Malagas, Niagras, Delaware, Worden and Barbarossa.

Select   Plump grapes with a bloom; the stems should not be brittle. Ripe grapes are highly perishable and should be refrigerated.

Preparation   Wash before serving; if desired, snip off stems with grapes scissors.

Market Forms   Fresh; in jellies; grape juices in cans and bottles; and fermented as wines and vinegars.

Serve   Cold as a fruit, in salads, as decorations, or frosted; in all "Veronique" dishes. Hot or cooked in stuffings, sauces, with liver and ham, in jellies, juices.

Happy Marriages   Sole, poultry, fruit salads, cantaloupe.

Greengages   A green plum originated in France (see Plums p. 192).

Guavas   A tropical fruit. Guavas vary in color from white to dark red and in size from a small plum to an apple. Guavas are served fresh with other fruits such as bananas and pineapples or alone. They are puréed or peeled and sliced and baked at 350° F. for 30 minutes. Guava is also available as guava jelly and guava paste; both go especially well with cream cheese and crackers.

Hazelnuts   Native to America. Filberts are the European version of our hazelnuts. They are very similar in flavor. Hazelnuts are available shelled in packages and toasted in bottles. The thin brown skin is usually left on but it can be removed in part by parching and then rubbing in a rough towel. They are used in baking, ground in place of flour, used as a decoration or eaten as a snack.

Hazelnuts

Kumquats   Of Oriental origin.

Kumquats are a very small member of the citrus-fruit family, and resemble a small orange. Kumquats are available fresh, preserved and candied. They are served with ham, meat sauces, and whole in Chinese mixed fruits. Kumquats have largish seeds and a very distinctive bittersweet flavor; the entire fruit, rind and pulp, is eaten. Calomondins are a cross between a kumquat and a tangerine.

Lemons   A tropical fruit and member of the citrus family.

1 dozen medium lemons weight about 1 pound.

1 lemon will yield from 3–4 tablespoons juice and about 1 teaspoon grated rind.

Select   Firm lemons of good yellow color and with unblemished skins.

Preparation   Cut lemons in half and squeeze for juice (more juice can be extracted if lemons are rolled against a hard surface to break up the pulp first); slice thin for garnishing; grate the peel with a lemon grater; cut lemon rind with a sharp knife or kitchen scissors. If covered and stored in the refrigerator, lemons will keep for some time.

Market Forms   Fresh; bottled and frozen juice; canned, bottled and cartoned lemonade, fresh and frozen.

Serve   Grated rind, in sauces, marmalade, pies, desserts, drinks, garnishes. Lemon juice is used on fish or scallops, as a vinegar substitute, in sherberts, in cakes.

Happy Marriages   Fish, scallops, butter, veal, poultry, sugar, oil.

Litchi (Lichi or Lee-chee) Nut   Of Chinese origin. Well known here in dried form, a thin brown shell surrounding a shrunken dried fruit surrounding a large seed.

The fresh fruit is imported in canned form. It also makes an excellent preserve.

Limes   A tropical fruit. Select limes of good green color that are heavy for their size. Use as lemons. (The Key or Mexican lime is quite small and yellow when ripe.)

Lemons

Limes

Macademia Nuts Of Hawaiian origin. A gourmet nut. Expensive and usually served as a snack or garnish. Available in bottles and cans.

Mangoes A fruit of a tropical Asiatic tree; grown commercially in Florida, the West Indies, Puerto Rico and Mexico.

There are many varieties of mangoes, the smallest the size of a plum, the largest over 4 pounds. The quality varies greatly. Mango skin is generally orange-yellow. The fruit, itself, is yellow through red and is often black spotted. Mangoes are eaten raw, pickled or in chutneys. To eat, peel and slice neatly or serve as melon, halved with stone removed.

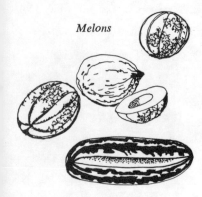

Melons

Melons Of Asian and African origin.

Varieties There are many varieties and strains of melons, among them: cantaloupe (muskmelon), honeydew, Spanish, Casaba (golden and pineapple), watermelon, Cranshaw, Persian, and Christmas.

Select Fragrant melons; watermelons should have a tender skin and sound hollow when thumped. The scar end of a melon should be slightly sunken and well calloused. Melons should be symmetrical. Ripen and store melons at room temperature, and refrigerate before serving.

Preparation Halve small melons and scoop out seeds. Serve halved, in wedges, garnished with lime or lemon, or cut into balls with a melon baller. Slice watermelon, or cut in wedges. Scallop edges of melons, or cut melon baskets for decorations.

Serve By itself, in fruit cocktails, as spiced melons, and melon-rind pickles.

Happy Marriages Fruit salads, smoked ham, salami, crabmeat, shrimp, port wine, cottage cheese, mint, grapes, water ices, chutney.

Nectarines Cultivated in the Western world 2,000 years ago. A cross between a plum and a peach, without the peach fuzz. Freestone and cling types. Use as peaches.

Olives   From Biblical times.

Olives vary greatly in size ranging from 128 to 140 per pound, for small olives to as few as 30 to 32 per pound for super colossal sizes. Olives are available tree ripened, or green, ripe or black, pitted, pitted and stuffed with onions, garlic, capers, etc., or Spanish style, with pimientos.

Olives are used in cooking, in sauces, for garnishes and as snacks. Olive oil is an important oil (see Fats and Oils, p. 247).

The unattractive film that forms in opened bottles of olives is harmless and can be scraped off. Store opened bottles in the refrigerator.

Oranges   From South China. A Citrus fruit.

Varieties   Among the many are: Valencias (juice or sections), Mandarins, Temples (eating), Kings, Navels (eating), Blood, Seville, juice oranges: Hamlins, Parson Brown and Pineapple.

4 medium juice oranges yield about 1 cup juice.

Select   Oranges of good color, unblemished and symmetrical. Store at room temperature. Refrigerate before serving if desired. Keep sectioned oranges and orange juice refrigerated. Available all year.

Preparation   Remove skin by peeling with the hands. Slice in half for juicing, or quarter for eating. Peel and section for fruit salads and remove all the white inner peel from fruit. The peel can be grated; cut the peel for candied orange peel with a sharp knife or kitchen scissors.

Market Forms   Fresh whole or juice; canned and jarred sections; canned and frozen and bottled juices; sections and slices, marmalades, in fruit salads.

Serve   Fresh, as a fruit, as a juice, for beverages, fruit cocktails, salads, sliced as a garnish, especially with ham and duck; fruit soups, icings and cakes, sherbert.

Happy Marriages   Other fruits, ham and duck, vodka, lettuce, Sangria, coconut, French dressing, mint, fruit soups.

Orange

Papaya The fruit of a tropical American tree.

Up to 20 inches in length. Papyas turn from green to soft and yellow when ripe. The flesh is orange. The black seeds can be eaten and are a source of pectin but should be scraped out of melon before serving. The milky papaya juice is very good, and should be chilled before drinking. Eat papya as if it were a melon, garnished with lime or lemon.

Peaches Of Persian or Chinese origin.

Varieties Clingstone (canning); Freestone(canning and eating), white, (eating), Alberta.

4 medium peaches are about 1 pound.

1 pound of dried peaches measure about 3 cups.

Select Firm, well-colored peaches, not green ones. Peaches are ripe when just soft to the touch, and should be refrigerated when ripe. Use as soon as possible. Peak season is July and August.

Preparation Wash before eating. Cut in half and remove pit; peel for cooking or eating if desired. Peel with a knife or vegetable parer or cover with boiling water, boil for 10 seconds and slip peel off. Squeeze half a lemon over sliced peaches if they are not to be eaten at once, to prevent darkening. The pit can be broken with a nut cracker and the bitter peach almond used as a flavorer.

Market Forms Fresh, frozen, canned and jarred. In nectars, preserves, jellies, jams, brandied and in syrup.

Serve Fresh in pies and pastries, jams, filled desserts, fruit salads and cocktails, baked, brandied with meats or as a condiment or dessert, nectars, dried as a confection or for cooking.

Happy Marriages Ham, fruit salads, jams, mayonnaise, crepes, ice cream, grapes, cheese and wines.

Peanuts From South America; also called ground nuts and goobers.

1 pound peanuts in shell will yield two-thirds of a pound shelled.

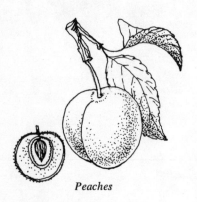

Peaches

1 pound of shelled peanuts measures slightly over 3 cups.

Preparation   Peanut shells break easily with the hands. The inner skin is edible, but is also easily removed if desired. Peanuts are either fresh or roasted if in the shells. Roast peanuts at 300° F. for 30 to 40 minutes in their shells, and 20 to 30 minutes after shelling. Peanuts can be boiled in the shell to prepare them for making peanut paste and similar recipes.

Market Forms   Peanuts are available in the shell or shelled—fresh, roasted or roasted and salted, loose or in packages.

Serve   By themselves for snacks, as peanut oil (see Fats and Oils, p. 247), peanut butter, in cookies, as an icing, in confections and baking.

Happy Marriages   Chocolate, bacon, jellies and jams, marmalade, butter, marshmallows, curries, chicken.

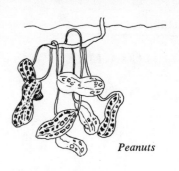

Peanuts

Pears   Of Greek origin.

Varieties   Pears range from the small Seckel pear (cook or pickle), to the large juicy Comice pears (bake or out-of-hand eating). Other varieties include Bartlett (poach or out-of-hand eating), Bosc, Anjous, Nelis.

4 medium pears weigh approximately 1 pound.

Select   Firm pears of good color and shape without bruises. Store pears in the tissue-like papers they come wrapped in, if possible; the papers are generally treated to protect the pears. Ripen at room temperature. Store ripe fruit in the refrigerator and use as soon as possible. Pears held too long at a cool temperature turn brown inside. Peak of season in September and October.

Preparation   Wash pears and serve whole as a snack or with a fruit knife. For cooking use firm pears. Leave whole, core, or peel and slice. Prepare dried pears according to package instructions, or eat as is.

Market Forms   Fresh, sliced and canned or frozen in syrup, as nectar, dried, as whole pears, in syrup or spiced.

Serve   As a fruit, a dessert course, stuffed and baked, with sauces.

Pears

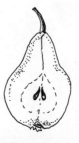

(189)

Happy Marriages   Chocolate sauce, cheese, wine, cream cheese, nuts, pound cake, sherbert.

Pecans   An American Indian nut. Pecans are used as a nut, for snacks, as garnishes in some bakeries, confections and in poultry stuffings and dressings. Pecans make delicious pies. They are available in their shells (they are easy to shell), shelled and halved in envelopes and cans, salted and plain. Pecans also come chopped.

    1 pound of pecans in their shells will yield about ⅓ pound meats. Remove the shells with a nutcracker.

    ½ pound of shelled pecans will measure about 1¾ cups.

Persimmons   The edible fruit of a tree cultivated in southern United States, Japan, China and the Mediterranean region. Persimmons are a small fruit, full of seeds (the oriental Hachiya, often found in the market is almost seedless), and soft and pulpy when ripe. Select ones with unblemished skin and attached stem cap. They are eaten raw as a fruit, in custards, sherberts and other desserts.

Pineapple   A tropical fruit from Central and South America and the Pacific Islands, notably Hawaii.

    Varieties   Cayenne (yellow when ripe), smooth cayenne, Puerto Rico, Red Spanish (pale red when ripe), Sugar Loaf (green when ripe).

    1 medium pineapple weighs about 2 pounds.

    Select   Pineapples are spiny, juicy, sweet fruits and should have a small, compact crown. They should have a good glossy color in the "eye" sections and give off a fragrant odor. The eyes should protrude. Pineapples are ripe when an inner leave can be pulled easily from the crown. The sweeter the smell, the sweeter the fruit. Store at room temperature, away from sunlight, to ripen. Once ripe use within 2 or 3 days.

Pineapple

Preparation   Refrigerate before serving if desired. Cut off top and scoop out fruit.to leave shell intact. Or leave on the top, halve and scoop out or cut into pieces; peel, slice and trim slices and cube if desired. Quarter and cut into slices or pieces. Cook fresh pineapple or canned pineapple before combining with gelatins.

Market Forms   Fresh, whole or halved; canned in slices, cut, crushed, chunks, sweetened or unsweetened; canned juices, candied and candied peel in jars and containers; in marmalades, and frozen juices.

Serve   As a fresh fruit, as a juice, in fruit salads, in cakes and pies, in ice cream, as a topping, as a sauce, garnishing, an appetizer or a dessert.

Happy Marriages   Ham and poultry, in Chinese sweet and sour dishes, other fruits, maraschino cherries, brandy.

Pinenuts   Of Southern European origin. Seed of certain pine trees. Also called Indian nuts, pinons, and pignolia nuts.

Pinenuts have a thin reddish-brown or whitish shell and are quite small, but can be found up to 1½ inches. They are available in shells in envelopes or jarred and are used primarily in cooking, as salted nuts, in confections, in Near Eastern and Mediterranean dishes and as a snack. There are several varieties, and many names. They are also grown in Mexico and the southwestern states.

Pistachio   A nut native to Asia Minor. Pistachio nuts are white, but are most often seen in the red shells, an artificial color. Pistachio nuts are sold loose and packaged in boxes and bags. The nut meat is green; pistachio nuts are also sold shelled in jars and envelopes. They are used primarily as a nut, but are also used in confections and in some cooking. Many famous near eastern rich pastries and cookies contain pistachio nuts.

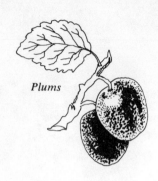

Plums

Plums   Cultivated since prehistoric times.

Varieties   There are over 100 varieties of plums, many of them wild. Among the best are the Damson and the Greengages. Plums vary widely in size. Prunes are dried plums. Beach plums make excellent preserves and jellies

10–15 medium-small plums weight about 1 pound.

Select   Plums of good color, glossy and soft but not mushy. The skins should be taut. A soft tip indicates ripeness. Store in the refrigerator, and use as soon as possible. Peak season in July and August.

Preparation   Wash and dry before eating. Plums may be halved or peeled and the pits removed for salads when slicing.

Market Forms   Fresh, in cans and jars, in jellies. Dried, as prunes (see Prunes, p. 193).

Serve   As a fresh fruit, in fruit salads, as a dessert, in plum puddings, dried as prunes, as jellies and sauces.

Happy Marriages   Cream cheese, whipped cream, cherries, peaches, grapes.

Pomegranates

Pomegranates   Native to semi-tropical Asia. Known in Biblical times.

Pomegranates are about the size of an apple, but with hard, inedible rind that is symmetrical but not round. The fruit consists of many seeds, surrounded by a bright crimson coating that is edible, pulpy and tart. Pomegranates are eaten fresh, and the pulp is made into jellies and grenadine syrup which is used as a flavoring in cocktails, preserves and baking (grenadine is also made from red currants). When eaten raw, discard the seeds eating only the pulp surrounding them. Halve and serve with a spoon. The juice may be frozen into a sherbert; halve and squeeze as for oranges.

Prickly Pear   Large, pear-shaped berry of cactii plants. Also called Indian fig, barbary fig and tuna in cultivated varieties. The fruits are red and yellow. When marketed, the sharp spines have usually been removed. If not, they are easily removed by singeing. Peel prickly pears and eat raw, or boil until tender (see a Mexican cookbook) and use as a vegetable or slice into a salad.

Prunes

Prunes   Dried plums.

1 pound average-sized prunes measures about 2½ cups.

½ pound average-sized prunes, pitted, measures about 1 cup.

Preparation   Cook prunes according to package direction. Prunes may be cooked in fruit juices or wine instead of water. Chop prunes with a sharp knife, or cut with kitchen scissors.

Market Forms   Prunes are generally available whole or pitted in 1- and 2-pound boxes, and pitted in 12-ounce packages. They are also available loose, and as juice.

Serve   Stewed as a breakfast course or a dessert; out of the box if moist as a snack; as prune juice; as a flavoring for yoghurt; in puddings; baking, pies, and infant food.

Happy Marriages   Heavy cream, whipped cream, candied fruit peel, rum and brandy, nut meats.

Quinces

Quince   Of Asian origin and the Mediterranean; known in Biblical times. Quince is used primarily in preserves, jellies and marmalades, but can also be baked plain or stuffed.

Raisins and Currants   Raisins are grapes, of high sugar content, usually dried by the sun. There are several varieties, dark and white. Currants is the name given to small seedless raisins of a particularly firm texture and a sharp flavor, originally grown in Corinth (see Currants, p. 182).

½ pound whole raisins measures about 1⅓ cups.

Preparation   Wash raisins well and remove any stems. Chop if called for; to chop in a blender, freeze raisins, then blend for a second. Soak, drain and dry or dredge before using in cooking if required. Raisins may be plumped in water before adding to recipes.

Market Forms　Raisins are sold in individual-portion boxes; raisins and currants are sold in boxes.

Serve　As a snack or confection, in fruitcakes and coffee cakes, in ice creams, in breads, in cakes and loaf cakes, in sauces, in cold fruit soups, and stuffings.

Happy Marriages　Salted peanuts and almonds, rum and sherry, turkey, ice cream, honey.

Rhubarb　Native to the U.S.

Rhubarb is actually a leaf stalk (the leaf can be mildly poisonous), but is eaten as a fruit product, after cooking. 4 to 8 stalks will weigh about 1 pound. The rhubarb stalks are cut and boiled, and peeled if tough. Serve as a relish or dessert stewed fruit.

Strawberries, (see Berries)

Ugli Fruit

Tangelo　New citrus fruit developed in several forms, usually yellow and the size of an orange. Cross between grapefruit, mandarin, tangerine and satsuma. Good for fruit dishes.

Tangerines　Or Mandarin oranges, North African origin, a member of the Citrus family. Tangerines are available fresh, canned and bottled as sections and mixed with other fruit juices. Use tangerines as oranges. Choose fruit heavy for its size; a "puffy" feel is normal.

Ugli Fruit　Citrus fruit, form of grapefruit. Thick pulpy skin, grotesque exterior, eaten fresh.

Walnuts

Walnuts　One of the most popular and valuable food nuts. There are several varieties. The butternut is a white walnut. The black walnut is also native to North America; the flavor is much more pronounced than that of the English walnut, most often seen in the market.

2 pounds of walnuts in shells will yield about 1 cup meat.

½ pound of walnut meat measures about 2¼ cups and will yield approximately 2¾ cups chopped walnuts.

Preparation   Break walnuts open with a nutcracker. Remove meat from halves. For chopped nuts, use a chopper or put meat through a nut grinder.

Market Forms   Available in shells loose and in bags; halved nut meats are canned and in envelopes; chopped are in cans and envelopes; in syrup as a topping.

Serve   As a nut for snacks or appetizers, in baking, desserts, sauces, stuffings, confections, garnishes, in ice creams and as a topping in syrup, as maple walnuts.

Happy Marriages   Poultry, ice cream, mixed nuts, chocolate, raisins, dates, apples.

Water Chestnuts   Related to the papyrus-giving plant, water chestnuts are actually a tuber. They are available canned and are used extensively in oriental cooking. Once the can is opened, store water chestnuts, covered with water, in the refrigerator.

Watermelon   One of the largest of the melons (see Melons, p. 186).

11 ஃ
Sauces
and
Dressings

The following chart is a guide to the basic ingredients and useages of sauces and dressing, with serving suggestions. All but the condiments can be homemade.

Sauce and Dressing Chart

Name	Main Ingredients	Temperature	Use	Serve With or Over	Market Form
A.1.	See label	Cold	Flavoring, spicings, condiment sauce	Meats	Bottled
Agro Dolce (Italian)	Sugar, raisins, vinegar, wine, shallots, brown stock	Hot	Bitter-sweet flavoring	Italian dishes	Homemade
Aioli (French)	Garlic and oil	Cold	As mayonnaise	Fish	Homemade
Allemandes (French)	Sauce velouté with yolks, cream and butter added	Hot	Binding and masking sauce	A covering and binding sauce for meats, poultry, eggs, vegetables and fish	Homemade
Anchovys	Anchovy paste added to white sauce, mayonnaise or butter	Hot or cold	A sharp sauce for bland dishes	Fish, appetizers, eggs	Tube or jar
Apple sauce	Cooked apples	Cold	A dessert or accompaniment	Pork, duck and goose	Jarred

Name	Main Ingredients	Temperature	Use	Serve With or Over	Market Form
Apricot sauce	Cooked apricots	Hot or cold	A tart sweetening sauce	Desserts, ice creams, puddings	Homemade
Aspic	Gelatin and stock or bouillon	Cold	Masking, garnishing	Cold meats, fish, eggs, molded dishes	Envelopes
Barbecue	Soy sauce, tomato sauce	Hot	Seasoning	Meats, outdoor cooking	Bottled
Bearnaise	Butter, yolks, shallots and herbs	Warm	A favorite herb flavoring sauce	Red meats, fish, eggs	Jarred, envelopes
Bechamel (white sauce)	White sauce made with milk, chicken stock and strained vegetables	Hot	Basic sauce, masking sauce for gratineed dishes, binding sauce for creamed dishes	Vegetables and hot poultry, eggs, veal	Canned, packaged
Berry sauces	Raspberries, strawberries, melba sauce	Cold	Garnisher, sweetener	Desserts	Bottled, homemade, frozen berries, blended
Beurre Manie	Butter and flour	Cold	Thickener of sauces		Homemade
Black butters	Browned butter and vinegar	Hot	A sharp sauce for bland dishes	Eggs, fish	Homemade
Bordelaise	Espagnole or brown sauce, browned vegetables and red wine	Hot	To enhance roast meats	Meats	Homemade
Bourguignonne (French)	Sauce bordelaise highly seasoned and red Burgundy	Hot	A sauce usually part of a large stew	Meat	Homemade
Bread sauce (English)	Milk and fresh bread crumbs	Hot	A mild sauce for well-flamed meats	Game and birds, beef, chicken	Homemade
Brown sauce	Butter, flour, brown stock	Hot	Basic sauce used as gravy or as basis for other sauces	Meats, roasts, potatoes	Packaged
Brown gravy	Pan drippings, flour and liquid	Hot	Enhancing and flavoring	Meats, poultry, stews, and casseroles	Packaged and canned

Name	Main Ingredients	Temperature	Use	Serve With or Over	Market Form
Brown stock	Browned meat and vegetables	Hot	Basis for brown sauces, substitute bouillon or consomme	Broiled beef and vegetables	Cubes, cans
Butters	Butter and flavoring	Hot or cold	Savory flavoring preparations	Meats, fish, snails	Homemade
Butter sauces	Butter	Melted, brown. clarified or black	Delicate form of lubricant sauce	Vegetables or fish	Homemade
Butterscotch	Sugar and butter	Hot	Sweetening	Desserts and ice creams	Bottled or homemade
Caper	White sauce with capers	Hot	A spicing flan for bland meats and fish	Veal, fish, lamb	Homemade
Caramel	Sugar and wine or brandy	Hot	Sweetening	Puddings and ice cream	Bottled
Catsup (ketchup)	Tomatoes	Cold	Condiment sauce	Meats, fish, eggs	Bottled
Chantilly	Whipped cream and sugar	Cold	Garnishing and sweetening	Desserts, fruit	Homemade
Cheese	White sauce and melted cheese	Hot	Flavoring, gratineeing	Italian dishes, vegetables, fish	Canned, homemade, packaged

(199)

Name	Main Ingredients	Temperature	Use	Serve With or Over	Market Form
Cherry, sweet or sour	Brown sauce with sweet or sour cherries	Hot	Enchanced brown sauce	Meats and poultry	Canned cherries
Cherry (sweet)	Black cherries and brandy	Hot	Flavoring	Dessert sauce to enhance ice cream or mousse	Canned cherries
Chili	Tomatoes, peppers see label	Cold	Spicing, savory flavoring	Fish, shell fish, cocktails, appetizers	Bottled
Chocolate	Chocolate, cream, sugar	Hot	Sweetening	Desserts, ice cream	Canned, boxed
Choron	Bearnaise sauce with tomato added	Warm	Flavoring sauce of attractive color	Meats, poultry, eggs	Packaged, bottled
Chutney	Mangoes, oranges, ginger, etc.	Cold	Condiment	Curries and oriental foods	Bottled
Clam sauce	Tomatoes, clams, onions	Hot	Pasta sauce	Italian recipes	Canned
Cocktail	Chili sauce, mayonnaise, condiments and seasonings	Cold	Condiment sauce	Fish and shell fish, appetizers	Bottled
Court bouillon	Fish, vegetables, water	Hot	Basic stock for fish sauces	Fish and shell fish	Homemade
Cranberry	Cranberries, sugar	Cold	Relish sauce	Turkey, poultry	Canned or fresh
Cream	White sauce made with cream or part cream	Hot	As white sauce, binding and masking	Vegetables and fish, poultry, eggs	Canned packaged
Creole	Brown sauce with onions, peppers and mushrooms	Hot	Spicing	Meat	Homemade
Cucumber	Hollandaises and cucumbers	Warm	Flavoring	Chicken, fish	Homemade
Cumberland	Currant jelly, orange, port wine, mustard	Cold	Spicy flavoring	Meats	Homemade and bottled
Currant jelly sauce	Currant jelly and spices	Hot or cold	Sweet-spicy flavoring	Ham and tongue, cold beef	Homemade

Name	Main Ingredients	Temperature	Use	Serve With or Over	Market Form
Curry	Curry powder usually added to white sauce, correctly should be based on coconut milk	Hot for curries, cold for appetizers	Basic flavoring	Curries and eastern dishes, appetizers	Canned or bottled, homemade
Custard	Eggs and milk	Cold	Mild lubricant and flavoring	Dessert	Packaged pudding mixes or homemade
Demi-glace	Reduced meat stock	Hot	Basic sauce	Meats	Jarred
Deviled (diables)	Meat stock, tomatoes and peppers	Hot	A spiced hot sauce	Meats	Homemade
Dill	White sauce or mayonnaise with snipped dill added	Hot or cold	Flavoring	Fish, eggs	Homemade
Drawn butter sauce	Butter, flour, water and lemon juice	Hot	As thin white sauce	Vegetables, fish, potatoes	Homemade
Dressings, French	Oil, vinegar, seasonings	Cold	Seasoning	Green salads, cooked and raw vegetables	Bottled, packaged, homemade
garlic	French dressing with strong garlic flavor	Cold	Seasoning	Green salads, cooked and raw vegetables	Bottled, packaged, homemade
Italian	More highly spiced than French, minced peppers	Cold	Seasoning	Green salads, cooked and raw vegetables	Bottled, packaged, homemade
Roquefort or blue cheese	Crumbled Roquefort or blue added	Cold	Seasoning	Green salads, hot mixed salads	Bottled
Russian	Mayonnaise, pimiento and green pepper	Cold	Seasoning	Green mixed salad	Bottled
Thousand Island	Russian with whipped cream added	Cold	Seasoning	Green mixed salad	Bottled
vinaigrette	Chopped onion, parsley and riced hard-cooked egg added	Cold	Seasoning	Asparagus and cauliflower and artichoke	Homemade

Name	Main Ingredients	Temperature	Use	Serve With or Over	Market Form
Duck sauce	See label	Cold	Condiment	Chinese dishes	Bottled, canned
Egg sauce	White sauce with sliced or chopped hard-cooked eggs	Hot	An enhancing sauce	Fish	Canned white sauce and egg
Egg sauces	(Usually means hollandaise and mayonnaise sauces)				
Escoffier	See label. Add to brown sauces for enrichment	Hot	Condiment sauce	Meats	Bottled
Espagnole (French)	Well-seasoned brown sauce	Hot	Basic sauce for other brown sauces	Meats	Packaged
Fruit sauces	Fruits and raisins in brown sauce or crushed into a sweetened purée	Warm or cold	Flavoring or garnish	Meat and poultry or sweets	Bottled, homemade
Garlic butter sauce	Butter, garlic, salt	Hot	Flavoring	Italian dishes, snails, shell fish, potatoes	Homemade
Giblet gravy	Brown gravy with giblets added	Hot	Meat lubricant	Roast turkey and chicken	Packaged, canned
Gribiche	Hard-cooked egg yolk	Cold	Mayonnaise	Cold beef, fish or shell fish	Homemade
Hard sauces	Butter, sugar and brandy	Cold	Sweetener	Dry puddings and hot desserts	Bottled

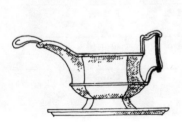

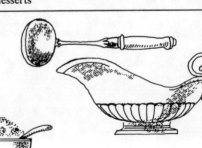

Name	Main Ingredients	Temperature	Use	Serve With or Over	Market Form
Hollandaise	Butter, yolks and lemon	Warm	Popular lubricating and enhancing sauce	Asparagus, artichokes, vegetables	Packaged, jarred, canned
mousseline	Whipped cream added	Warm	Good appearance	Broccolli, eggs, cauliflower	
maltaise	Grated orange rind added	Warm	Flavoring	Asparagus	
chived	Cut chives added	Warm	Flavoring	Chicken	
marguery	Fish stock and oysters added	Warm	Accompaniment	Fish	
cucumber	Chopped cucumber added	Warm	Flavoring	Fish or chicken	
Horseradish I	Grated horseradish in vinegar	Cold	Condiment sauce	Oysters, fish, appetizers	Bottled or fresh grated
II	White sauce and grated horseradish	Hot	Accompaniment	Fish and boiled beef	Bottled or fresh grated
III	Brown sauce and grated horseradish	Hot	Accompaniment	Meat	Fresh grated
Ice-cream sauce	Softened vanilla or coffee ice cream, whipped	Cold	Sweet	Hot puddings, fruit desserts, soufflés	Commercially packed
Italian spaghetti sauces	Tomatoes and meat, mushrooms, or clams	Hot	Flavoring and lubricating sauce	Pastas, rice, meat	Bottled, canned
Lobster	White sauce, lobster, sherry	Hot	Masking	Lobster and bland dishes	Canned
Marinades	Vinegar, wine seasonings	Hot or cold	Tenderizing and flavoring	Meats	Homemade
Maitre d'hôtel butter	Butter, onions, parsley	Cold	Savory flavoring	Meats	Homemade

Name	Main Ingredients	Temperature	Use	Serve With or Over	Market Form
Mayonnaise	Eggs, oil, vinegar	Cold	Dressing and masking or basic egg sauce	Meats, fish, salads	Bottled
caper	Capers added	Cold	Accompanying sauce	Fish	Bottled
tartar	Pickles, onions, capers and chopped herbs added	Cold	Accompanying sauce	Fried shell fish and fish	Bottled
dill	Snipped dill	Cold	Accompanying sauce	Salmon and other fish	Bottled
lemon	Substitute lemon juice for part of vinegar	Cold	Accompanying sauce	Fish and vegetables	Bottled
Mint	Chopped mint, vinegar, sugar	Hot or cold	Flavoring	Lamb	Bottled
Mornay	White sauce or bechamel with cheese	Hot	Masking and binding	Fish, eggs, vegetables	Homemade
Mushroom	Mushrooms	Hot	Flavoring and garnish	Meat, fish, vegetables, soufflés, puddings and pastas	Canned, fresh, packaged
Mustard	Mustard flavored white sauce	Hot	Flavoring	Fish	Jarred
Newburg	Butter, cream, sherry, yolks	Hot	Masking	Lobster	Canned
Normandy	Velouté with fish stock	Hot	Masking and binding	Fish	Homemade
Onion	Onions in white sauce	Hot	Flavoring	Potatoes, fish, meat	Canned, onion soup
Orange	Brown sauce, orange juice, grated rind and orange sections	Hot or cold	Masking, flavoring	Duck	Canned or fresh
	Oranges and sugar syrup		Flavoring	Dessert	
Paprika	Paprika flavored white sauce	Hot	Masking or part of a gulyas dish	Chicken, fish and meat gulyas	Bottled

Name	Main Ingredients	Temperature	Use	Serve With or Over	Market Form
Peach	Stewed peaches	Hot or cold	Flavoring, sweetening, garnishing	Desserts	Jarred
Pepper sauce (Poivre)	Pepper corns	Hot	Spicy hot sauce	Beef	Homemade
Perigueux	Tomatoes, madeira, truffles, meat stock	Hot	Flavoring	Meat, eggs, poultry	Bottled, homemade
Piquante	Butter, onions, peppers, pickles, white wine	Hot	Flavoring	Meat	Homemade
Poulette	White sauce with yolks, cream	Hot	Binding, masking	Chicken, fish	Homemade
Provençale	Tomatoes, mushrooms, bouillon	Hot	Flavoring	Beef and veal	Homemade
Raisin	Brown sauce with raisins	Hot	Flavoring	Tongue, ham	Packaged
Ravigote	Velouté with chives and onions	Hot or cold	Binding, garnish	Fish	Homemade
Rémoulade	Mayonnaise, mustard	Cold	Binding, garnishing	Fish, salads, vegetables	Homemade
Robert	Brown sauce with onions	Hot	Flavoring	Pork, goose	Bottled
Roquefort	French dressing and crumbled Roquefort cheese	Cold	Binding	Salads	Bottled, packaged
Roux	Butter and flour	Warm	Basis for creamed sauces		Homemade
Spaghetti sauces	Tomato sauce with meat, mushrooms or clams	Hot	Flavoring	Pastas	Canned, bottled
Spanish sauces	(see Espagnole)				
Soubise	(see Onion)				
Soy sauce	Soy beans, garlic, seasonings	Cold	Seasoner	Oriental dishes	Bottled

Name	Main Ingredients	Temperature	Use	Serve With or Over	Market Form
Supreme	Velouté with fish, cream added	Hot	Binding as velouté	As velouté with fish	Homemade
Sweet and sour	Vinegar and sugar and brown sauce	Hot	Binder	Chinese dishes	Homemade
Sweet sauces	Sugar, syrup	Cold	Sweeteners	Sundaes	Jarred
Tabasco	Peppers and seasonings	Cold	Condiments, very hot	Meat, fish and soups	Bottled
Tartar	Mayonnaise, herbs, capers, parsley	Cold	Dressing	Fried foods	Jarred
Tomato	Tomatoes	Hot or cold	Binding and flavoring	Italian dishes, casseroles	Bottled, canned
Vanilla	Vanilla, milk, eggs, sugar	Hot	Flavoring and enhancing	Ice creams, pudding	Vanilla pudding or homemade
Velouté	White sauce	Hot	Masking, binding	Vegetables, fish, gratineed dishes	Homemade
Vinaigrette	Oil, vinegar, onions, hard-cooked eggs, parsley	Cold	Dressing	Beet salad, cold aspic, cold artichokes, cold cauliflower	Bottled or homemade
Whipped cream	Heavy cream	Cold	Masking and garnishing	Desserts, fruit	Canned topping, home whipped
White sauce	Butter, flour, milk or liquid	Hot	Masking and binding, basic sauce	Vegetables, fish, poultry, gratineed dishes	Canned, packaged
White stock	Veal or chicken and vegetables	Hot	Basis for many white sauces	Veal, poultry	Chicken consommé or bouillon cube
Worchestershire sauce	See label	Cold	Condiment sauce	Meat, fish, appetizers	Bottled

(207)

Farinaceous foods are simply those which consist of meal or flour. It is hard to imagine a breakfast, lunch or dinner that wouldn't include a farinaceous food. Cereals, pastas, rice, pies and cakes, soufflés, croquettes, breads, etc. are all very much a part of our life.

Wheats That Yield Flour

1. Hard Wheats: hard winter and spring wheats, red or white. Used for bread, all-purpose and bakery flours.
2. Soft Wheats: spring wheat, red or white. Cake, pastry, cracker, bisquit and all-purpose flours.
3. Durum: for making semolina. Semolina is used extensively in making pastas and other Italian dishes.

Flour, Meal and Starch Chart

Name and Marketing Weights	Composition	Substitutions For All-Purpose Flour	Uses
All-purpose flour (2-, 5-, 10- and 25-pound bags)	Hard and soft wheat flours and gluten		Some cakes, breads, pastries, cookies, thickening, dredging
enriched	additional elements		
unenriched	no additions		
instant	free-flowing		thickening only
(13½-ounce container)			
Arrowroot (1-pound boxes)	From the tropical arrow-root plant		Thickening, glazes, puddings, custards
flour			
starch		1 tablespoon=2½ tablespoon all-purpose	
Barley flour (2½ pounds and up)	Hulled barley, processed	1 cup=2 cups all-purpose	Thickener for soups, health soups

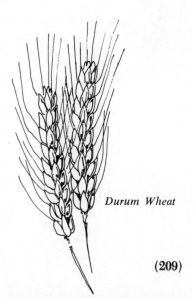

Durum Wheat

12 ♣

Farinaceous Foods

(209)

Rye

Barley

Oats

Name and Marketing Weights	Composition	Substitutions For All-Purpose Flour	Uses
Bran, wheat bran (2 pounds and up)	Outer protective coat of wheat seed		Breads, muffins
Bread flour (usually sold only to bakeries)	Milled hard wheat		Breads, rolls
Buckwheat flour (1 pound and up)	Ground buckwheat seeds and white flour		Pancakes, blini
Cake flour (2-pound boxes)	Milled from highest grade soft wheat	1 cup=⅞ cup all-purpose	Cakes
Corn flour (1-pound boxes)	From corn meal, yellow or white	1 tablespoon=1 tablespoon all-purpose	Baking, Italian recipes, as allergy wheat substitute
Corn meal (1-pound boxes)	Yellow or white corn; plain or enriched		Breads, sticks, crisps, muffins, pancakes
Corn starch (1-pound boxes)	Corn, processed	1½ teaspoons=1 tablespoon all-purpose	Thickener
Cottonseed flour	Cotton seeds		Baking, to increase protein, substitute 2 tablespoons per cup all-purpose flour
Cracked wheat (2 pounds and up)	Cut wheat, not durum; unground		Mix with all-purpose in baking breads
Enriched, (see All-purpose)			
Farina (13½-ounce and 1-pound boxes)	Hard wheat grains		Breakfast cereal, gruels, puddings, gnocchi and Italian foods

Name and Marketing Weights	Composition	Substitutions For All-Purpose Flour	Uses
Graham, (entire wheat, whole wheat) flour (2 pounds and up)	Entire wheat grain, bran and all. Usually hard; not durum wheats	Fine, 1 cup=1 cup all-purpose Coarse, 1 cup=⅞ cup all-purpose	Wheat breads, some pastries, cakes, health foods
Gluten flour (2 pounds and up)	Starch-free wheat, high in protein	13 tablespoons=1 cup all-purpose	Breads (particularly for diabetics)
Hominy 1-pound boxes)	Corn with hull and germ broken		Grits, breads, cereal
Nut meal (usually home ground)	Finely-ground		Flour substitute in some baking, in tortes, cakes and cookies
Oat flour (1-pound boxes)	Ground groats from dehulled oats		Limited
Oat meal (rolled oats) (1-pound containers)	Dehulled oats, groats rolled into flakes		Gruels, cookies
Pastry flour (2-pound boxes)	Soft or winter wheat		Yeast breads, quick breads, pastries
Potato flour and potato starch (14-ounce box)	Dehydrated potatoes	1½ teaspoons=1 tablespoon all-purpose, as a thickener	Soups, muffins, sponge cakes, thickner in pies, and fruit sauces; in European cake recipes
Rice flour (2-pound bags)	Cracked rice grain particles	⅞ cup=1 cup all-purpose	In combination with other flours, eggs and milk
Rye flour (2-pound bags)	Milled rye and gluten	1¼ cups=1 cup all-purpose	With other flours for rye breads

Einkorn

Shot Wheat

Name and Marketing Weights	Composition	Substitutions For All-Purpose Flour	Uses
Rye meal (2-pound bags)	Dark rye flour of whole rye grain		Pumpernickel bread, Boston brown bread
Self-rising flour (2-pound boxes)	Soft wheat flour sifted with salt and baking powder	1 cup=1 cup all-purpose; omit baking powder and salt	Bisquits, cakes, quick breads
Semolina (1-pound boxes and up)	Durum wheat		Pasta, gnocchi, Italian foods
Stone-ground whole wheat, buckwheat (2-pound bags and up)	Ground between stones; unsifted		Superior breads
Soy flour (2-pound bags) full fat low fat	From dehulled soybeans from residue after fat is removed from soybeans	To taste, up to one-fifth flour called for	Alone or combined with wheat flours for baking quick and yeast bread, cakes, pastries
Tapioca flour quick cooking pearl	From the root of the cassava tree	1½ teaspoons=1 tablespoon all-purpose as a thickener	To thicken fruit pies, soups, puddings, sauces, fruit jellies, glazes
Wheat bran, (see Bran)			
Whole wheat, (see Graham flour)			

Bread, Bisquit, Cake and Muffin Mixes There are available packaged mixes for various cakes, yeast and quick breads, coffee cakes, muffins, bisquits, pancakes, waffles, cookies, brownies, popovers and pie crust. Follow package instructions for best results.

Breakfast Cereals Breakfast cereals are made from wheat, rice, farina, oats and other grains. They are served hot, as hot oatmeal, cream of wheat, etc., or cold, as corn flakes,

Corn

puffed rice, etc. They are packaged in 8 ounce to 1 pound and larger boxes, as well as in individual servings. Breakfast cereals are sometimes used in baking, as well as for infant foods, snacks and special diets.

Leaveners These leavening agents produce gases in flour mixtures, causing baked goods to rise.

Name	Composition	Substitutions	Market Forms
Baking Powder			
tartrate	Cream of tartar, tartaric acid	1 teaspoon=¾ teaspoon combination baking powder	6- and 12-ounce cans (1 and 2 cups)
phosphate	Calcium acid phosphate	1 teaspoon=¾ teaspoon combination baking powder	6- and 12-ounce cans (1 and 2 cups)
sulphate-phosphate (double-action or combination)	Sodium aluminum sulfate and calcium acid phosphate	¾ teaspoon=1 teaspoon tartrate or phosphate baking powder	6- and 12-ounce cans (1 and 2 cups)
Baking soda	Sodium bicarbonate	⅓ teaspoon plus ½ teaspoon cream of tartar= 1 teaspoon baking powder	1-pound box (2⅓ cups)
Cream of tartar	Potassium acid tartrate		1¾ ounces (5⅓ tablespoon)
Yeast	Microscopic plant		
compressed cake		1 cake=1 tablespoon jarred or 1 package active dry yeast	1 cake=⅔ ounces 3 cakes=2 ounces
active, dry packaged		1 package=1 cake compressed	1 package=¼ ounce
jarred		1 tablespoon=1 cake compressed; 1 tablespoon=1 package	4-ounce vacuum- packed jar

Household Jellying Agents, Jellies, Jams and Marmalades

Name	Composition	Uses	Market Forms
Gelatin (granulated or in sheet form)	Animal jelly	Aspics and molded dishes, desserts, confections	Boxes of 4, ¼-ounce envelopes 1 envelope=1 table-spoon and will gel 1-pint liquid
Fruit-flavored gelatin	Animal jelly, fruit flavors, sweeteners	Desserts, molded salads	3-ounce packages 3 ounces=7 tablespoons 1 package gels 1 pint liquid
Fruit pectin	Plant tissue obtained from fruits and vegetable	Pectin yields a jelly which is the basis of fruit jellies.	Bottled, 6 fluid ounces
Tapioca quick cooking pearl	Tropical cassava root	Jellying fruit pies, use 1½-3 tablespoon puddings, use 3 tablespoons per quart liquid soups, use 1½ tablespoons per quart liquid use double the amount required of quick cooking tapioca	8-ounce box 8 ounces yields 1½ cups
All fruit jellies, jams, preserves, marmalades, such as apricot jam, currant jelly, orange marmalade and cherry preserves	Natural fruits and fruit juices, pectin, sweeteners, artificial and natural flavorings, preservatives, etc.	Spreads, sauces, desserts, toppings, glazes, confec-tions, baked products, garnishes.	7½, 10 and 12 ounce and 1 pound, 1½ pound and larger jars

Bread

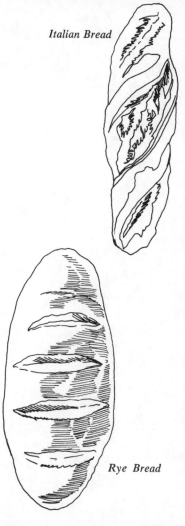

Italian Bread

Name	Market Forms	Weight	Uses
White	Homemade	1-1½ pounds	Accompaniment
white	sliced and unsliced	12-16 slices	with meals,
enriched white	packaged loaves	1 pound	open and closed
sandwich loaves		1 pound	sandwiches,
whole wheat		1 pound	canapés,
cracked wheat		2 pounds sliced	puddings,
rye			sauces,
pumpernickel	packages and loaves		stuffings,
French	loaves		breaded dishes,
Italian	loaves		toppings,
soda	round loaves		substitute for flour in
cheese	loaves	1 pound	baking
raisin	loaves	1 pound	
banana	loaves	1 pound	
cinnamon swirl and many others	loaves	1 pound	
Croutons	Jars	3½ ounce 2 cups	Soups and salads
Fresh bread crumbs	Homemade	1 pound=4 cups	Cooking generally and
Dry bread crumbs	containers	10 ounce	breaded foods, stuffing
Bread stuffings	packages & boxes	1 pound	poultry and meat
Crackers, all varities	Boxed and packaged	2¾, 5½, 7½, 9, 10¼, 10¾, 14 ounces, and 1 pound	Snacks, appetizers, desserts
Cracker crumbs	Boxed	16-18 crackers yield 1⅓	Baking and pie crusts
graham cracker crumbs	homemade	cup=1 pie crust	

Rye Bread

Rice An annual cereal grass grown in low moist land. Cultivated in India 3600 B.C. Has become a staple food in India and all Eastern countries as well as the near East and Mediterranean countries.

Rice

Rice is a starchy grain, sold either coated, uncoated or ground into flour or converted into a breakfast cereal.

1 cup whole grain rice equals a scant ½ pound.

2–2¼ cups equal approximately 1 pound.

1 pound raw rice yields 2 quarts cooked rice or 8 to 12 servings.

Eight servings as a main course, twelve servings as an accompaniment for meat or poultry.

Type of Rice	Market Forms	Weight	Use
Whole grain rice long grain rice yellow rice brown rice precooked rice (minute)	Boxed, bagged and loose	1 pound, 2 pounds 10 ounces, 3 pounds 12 ounces and bag 14 ounces, 1 pound 12 ounces	Accompaniment to fish, meat, poultry, Eastern dishes, Italian and Spanish recipes, breakfast and nursery food, desserts
Flavored rices herbed saffron Italian Spanish and many others	Packages boxed	6 ounce 8-16 ounces	Spanish and Italian saffron rice dishes, curries, risottos and all oriental cookery
Wild rice	Package can	½-1 pound 12 ounces	Serve with game & game birds

Rice flour, (see Flour, Meal and Starch Chart, p. 211)

Macaroni, Pastas   In the United States the term macaroni describes all noodles, spaghetti and pastas which were associated with Italian cookery and have now become an integral part of American cooking.

Macaronis are usually packaged in ½-, 1-, 2- and 3-pound boxes.

Names.

Alphabets
Bows
Broad noodles
Cappelletti
Cavatelli
Elbow macaroni
Fettucini
Fusilli
Green noodles
Lasagna

Macaroni
Macaroni shells
Majalde
Manicotti
Margherite
Noodles
Rigatoni
Spaghetti
Spaghettini
Vermicelli
Zitoni

Alphabet

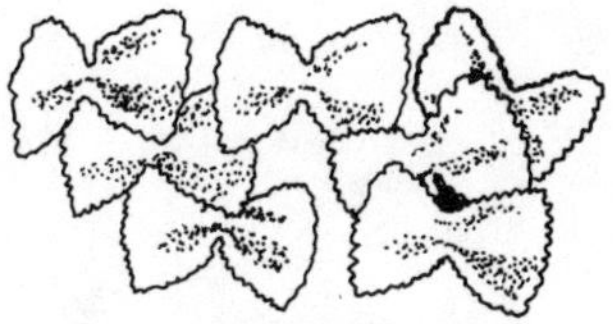

Bow Ties

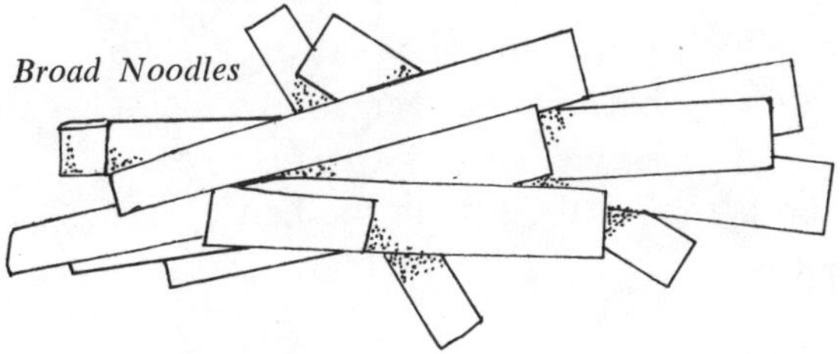

Broad Noodles

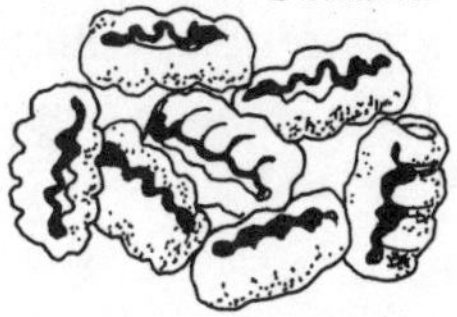

Cavatelli

Cresta Di Gallo

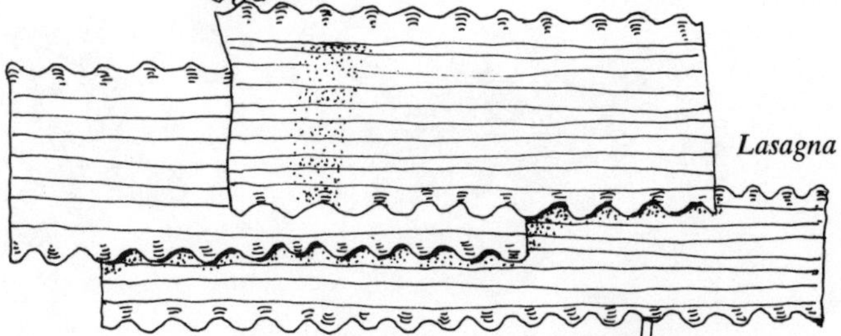

Elbow Macaroni

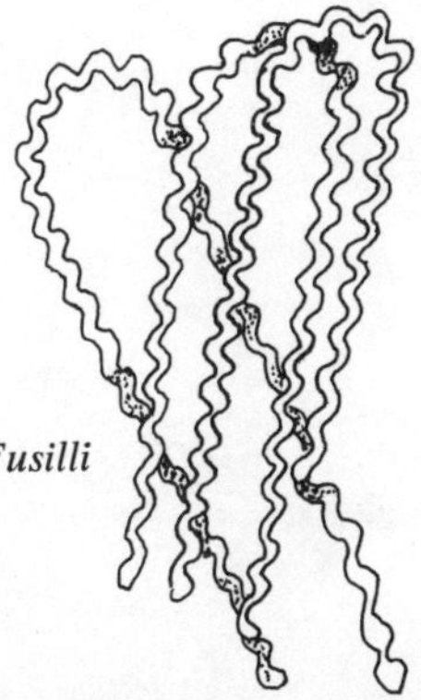

Fusilli

Lasagna

Green Noodles

(217)

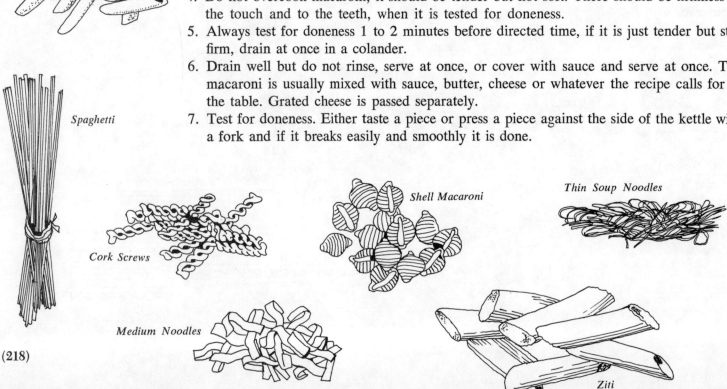

Preparation and Serving   Although most packages and boxes of macaroni carry cooking directions, the following rules should be remembered:

1. Always cook macaroni immediately before it is to be served.
2. Bring salted water to a boil, add macaroni slowly so that boiling is not interrupted. Use about 2 tablespoons salt to 1 gallon water to each pound of macaroni. Add a little oil to water to prevent macaroni from sticking to bottom of kettle.
3. Do not break long spaghetti into pieces, simply lower them slowly into boiling water, then curve them around the kettle as soon as the boiling water softens them.
4. Do not overcook macaroni, it should be tender but not soft. There should be firmness to the touch and to the teeth, when it is tested for doneness.
5. Always test for doneness 1 to 2 minutes before directed time, if it is just tender but still firm, drain at once in a colander.
6. Drain well but do not rinse, serve at once, or cover with sauce and serve at once. The macaroni is usually mixed with sauce, butter, cheese or whatever the recipe calls for at the table. Grated cheese is passed separately.
7. Test for doneness. Either taste a piece or press a piece against the side of the kettle with a fork and if it breaks easily and smoothly it is done.

Mostaccioli

Spaghetti

Cork Screws

Shell Macaroni

Thin Soup Noodles

Medium Noodles

Ziti

(218)

Baking is said to be the most satisfying of the cooking processes. While the process as such includes the cooking of any type of food by dry heat in an enclosed chamber or oven, the word has come to mean all Baked Goods.

Mixes for many of the Baked Goods can now be purchased in package form. Frozen breads, rolls and cookies are available in ready-to-bake as well as heat-and-serve form. Baking adjuncts, garnishes, fillings, frostings, nuts, dried and candied fruits and cake and cracker crumbs are packaged in ready-to-use form.

13 &

Baking

Biscuit

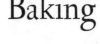
Poppy Seed Roll

Vienna Roll

Baking Adjuncts

Name	Use	Market Forms
Angel flake coconut	Cookies, fillings, toppings	Extra moist, sweetened 3½-ounce can
Biscuit mix	Biscuits, short cakes, crumb cake, muffins, squares	1-2-pound, 8-ounce packages
Bread crumbs	Crusts, cake batters, garnish	10-ounce package
Brownie mix	Brownies, nut squares	9-ounce-1-pound 2-ounce packages
Cake mixes	White cake, yellow cake, chocolate cake marble, loaf, nut and coffee cake, etc.	14½-ounce-1-pound 2½-ounce packages
Decorations: cinnamon imperials, colored sugars, non-pareils, chocolate gems, etc.	Decorating, garnishing	1¾- to 4½-ounce bottles
Fruits, candied Crystallized ginger Mixed candied fruits	Ingredient or decoration	4-ounce jars 3- and 4-ounce packages 1-pound container
Hot roll mixes	Rolls, sweet rolls, coffee cakes	13¾-ounce package

Spanish Bread

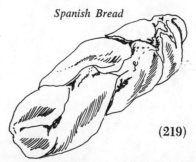

(219)

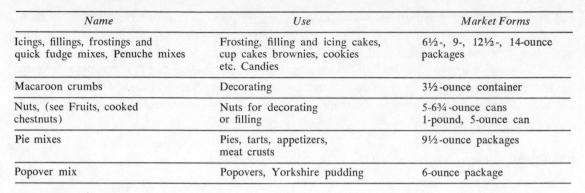

Name	Use	Market Forms
Icings, fillings, frostings and quick fudge mixes, Penuche mixes	Frosting, filling and icing cakes, cup cakes brownies, cookies etc. Candies	6½-, 9-, 12½-, 14-ounce packages
Macaroon crumbs	Decorating	3½-ounce container
Nuts, (see Fruits, cooked chestnuts)	Nuts for decorating or filling	5-6¾-ounce cans 1-pound, 5-ounce can
Pie mixes	Pies, tarts, appetizers, meat crusts	9½-ounce packages
Popover mix	Popovers, Yorkshire pudding	6-ounce package

Baking Timetable

Very slow oven	250° F. to 275° F.
Slow oven	300° F. to 325° F.
Moderate oven	350° F. to 375° F.
Hot oven	400° F. to 450° F.
Very hot oven	475° F. and up

Baked Products	Oven Temperature in °F.	Baking Time in Minutes
Cakes (shortening)		
cupcakes	375*	15 to 25
fruit cakes	250 to 275	2 to 4 hours
layer cakes	350 to 375*	20 to 30
loaf cakes	325 to 350*	45 to 60
oblong cakes	350 to 375*	35 to 50
square cakes	350*	45 to 60

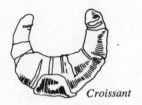

Croissant

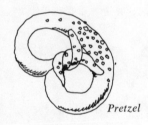

Pretzel

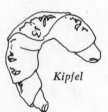

Kipfel

(220)

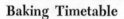

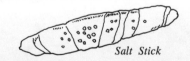

Zopf Braid

Salt Stick

Schnecke

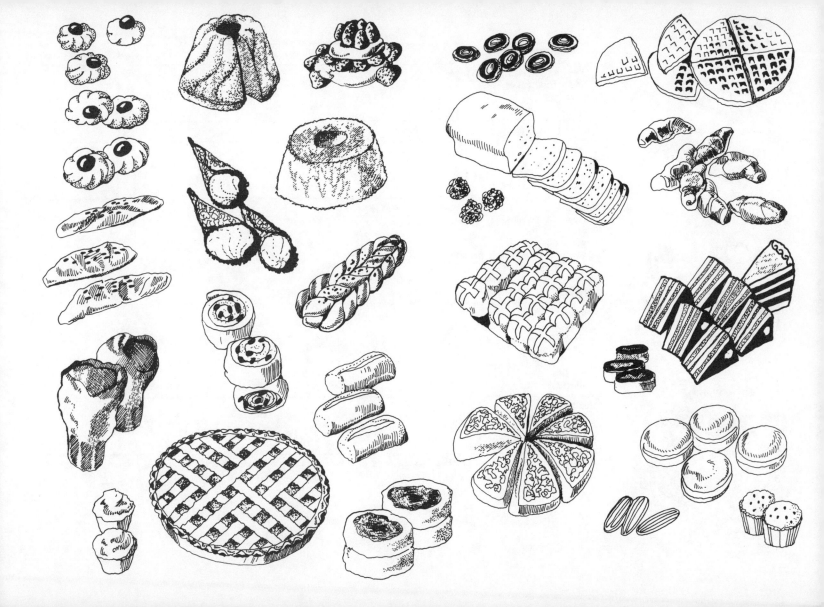

Baked Products	Oven Temperature in °F.	Baking Time in Minutes
Cakes (angel food and sponge)		
angel food cakes	375	30 to 40
jelly rolls	375 to 400	12 to 15
sponge cakes	350 to 375	30 to 40
Cakes (mix) (follow package directions)		
Cookies		
bar cookies	350	25 to 30
drop cookies	350 to 400	7 to 15
refrigerator cookies	350 to 400	7 to 15
Pastries		
custard-type pies	400 to 425	30 to 40
meringue for pies	425	5 to 10
pie shells	450	10 to 12
two-crust pies (with uncooked fruit filling)	425	45 to 60
two-crust pies (with cooked fruit filling)	400 to 425	30 to 45
Quick breads		
biscuits	450	12 to 15
cornbread	400 to 425	25 to 35
gingerbread	350	35 to 50
loaf breads	350	45 to 60
muffins	400 to 425	20 to 25
shortcakes, large	450	15 to 20
Yeast breads		
breads	375 to 400	35 to 50
rolls	375 to 400	15 to 20
sweet rolls	375	20 to 30

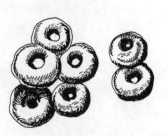

*(When using oven-proof glass baking pans or when baking chocolate cakes, decrease the oven temperature 25° F.)

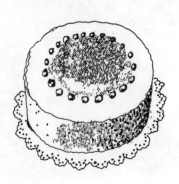

Chocolate is made from the seeds of the cacao tree, and the flavor of chocolate differs according to the quality of the raw chocolate as well as flavorings and complex manufacturing processes.

Avoid chocolate either loose or packaged that looks as if it had melted. The grayish color that occasionally developes on chocolate does not impair the flavor or quality of chocolate. Store chocolate below 75° F.

Cooking Chocolates

Name	Market Forms	Measures	Uses
Unsweetened (bitter)	8-ounce box containing 8 one-ounce squares	1 square=1 ounce 1 square yields about 4 tablespoon grated	Cakes, cooking, sauces, soufflés, puddings
No-melt unsweetened, pre-melted	Boxes of 8 one-ounce packets (semi-liquid)	1 packet=1 square unsweetened	
Semi-sweet	Boxes of 8 one-ounce squares Packages of 6, 12 or 18 ounces or chips	1⅓ ounce=1 ounce bitter chocolate plus 4 teaspoons sugar	Confections, baking, sauces, cookies, as a candy, as a topping
German's Sweet	4-ounce bar		Cooking, baking, dipping confections, eating as candy

If chocolate is to be melted, melt over hot water in the top of a double boiler. Chocolate squares can be melted in their individual wrapping papers and the melted chocolate scraped off. Chill chocolate to be grated.

Sugar derived from sugar beets and sugar cane are identical—99.5% pure sucrose and are totally interchangeable. Cane sugar is produced by evaporating the juices of sugar canes and refining out the components that are not sugar. Molasses and rum are two of the many

14 ❧
Chocolate,
Sugars
and
Syrups

by-products of refining sugar from sugar cane. Beet sugar is also obtained by a refining process.

Chemically, sugars are classed as carbohydrates. Other than beet and cane sugar, the following sugar classifications are also called sucrose.

Dextrose: a crystalline sugar
Fructose: a fruit sugar also in honey
Glucose: a fruit sugar, found particularly in grapes (glucose is found normally in the blood, and an excess of glucose is known medically as diabetes).
Lactose: milk sugar
Levulose: a fruit sugar
Maltose: malt sugar

There are also available artificial sweeteners in tablet, powdered, crystal and liquid forms; they are generally recommended for people who must watch their sugar intake.

Measurements, Substitutions, Uses and Market Sizes

Name	Weights and Measures	Substitutions	Uses
Brown sugar (1- and 2-pound boxes) dark, packed	1 cup=6 ounces 1 pound=2¼ cups	1 cup firmly packed light or dark=1 cup white granulated	Flavoring and coloring in baked goods, candies, with ham, sauces, on grapefruit
light, packed	1 pound=2¼ cups		
granulated		Follow label instructions	
Castor sugar		Powdered sugar	Primarily an English form, similar to U.S. powdered sugar. Used for baking and meringues

Name	Weights and Measures	Substitutions	Uses
Confectioner's 10X sugar (corn starch added to prevent lumping) (1- and 2-pound boxes)			Frostings, icings, dusting over fruits, candy, meringues, some baking
sifted	1 pound=3⅔-4¼ cups	1¾ cups packed=1 cup granulated	
packed	1 pound=3½ cups		
Corn syrup (16-ounce bottles) light dark	16 fluid ounce=2 cups		Cooking, baking, caramels, fudge and other candies
Cube, lump and tablet sugars (1-, 1½-, 2-pounds) ½ inch cube		1=½ teaspoon granulated sugar 1x⅝ inch cube=1 teaspoon granulated	Table sugar, flambeéing beverages
Demerara, a yellow or light brown crystal sugar			Primarily English, used in baking
Granulated sugar (1-pound boxes to 100-pound bags)	1 pound=2-2¼ cups 1 cup=16 tablespoon 5 pounds=11¼ cups	See other columns	Baking, sweetener, coffee, table sugar, jellies and jams, preserves, candies
Honey, many varieties, as alfalfa, clover, etc., strained, homogenized; also in combs (1- to 5-pound jars)	1 pound=1⅓ cups	½ cup=¾ cup sugar and ⅛ liquid	Dressings, sauces, baking, cooking, table spread, in beverages
Maple sugar (strong flavor)		1 tablespoon=1 tablespoon sugar	custards Candies, icings,
Maple syrup (tins and bottles of 12 ounces to 1 gallon)	1 gallon weighs about 11 pounds		Table syrup, pancakes, waffles, French toast

(225)

Name	Weights and Measures	Substitutions	Uses

Molasses
  cane
  cooking (black-strap)
  table
(16 fluid ounce bottles)
	16-fluid ounces=2 cups		Baking, table syrup, desserts syrup, puddings, candy

Powdered sugar superfine (1- and 2-pound boxes)	1 pound=2⅓ cups	1 cup=1 cup granulated sugar	Cakes, mixed drinks, icings sifting over fruits
Sorghum	1 pound=1⅓ cups		Cookies, candies, cakes, table
Treacle, (see molasses)			English name for molasses

Sugar Boiling   Sugar boiled to the syrup or caramel stages is used for desserts, candies, confections, as a sweetener in beverages and as a coloring agent in cooking.

In boiling sugar, use a copper or enamelware utensil and follow recipe directions for amount of water or other ingredient to add to boiling sugar for specified purposes.

Sugar Boiling Chart

Name of Stage or Test	Candy Thermometer in °F.	Description of Test	Use
Clarified syrup or "Pearl"	220		For crystalizing and beverages
Weak thread	225	Cooled sugar syrup spins a 2-inch thread and breaks when a drop is tested between thumb and forefinger, or dropped from end of a spoon.	Syrup

Name of Stage or Test	Candy Thermometer in °F.	Description of Test	Use
Hard thread	230-234	Thread will spin between fingers, as above, without breaking.	For sweetening liqueurs and beverages
Blow	235	Dip a wire loop into sugar syrup, blow through loop and bubbles will float from loop.	Candies, cake icings
Soft ball	234-240	Pour a few drops sugar syrup into a cup of ice water, take out and form into a soft ball.	Fudge, fondant
Soft feather	240		Candying fruits, fondant, creams
Firm ball	244-248	Test as "soft ball;" ball will be firm but pliable.	Caramels
Hard ball	250-265	Test as "soft ball;" drops will be hard.	Marshmallows
Light crack or "soft" crack	270-290	Test as "soft ball;" drops will separate into slivers.	For taffy, butterscotch
Spun sugar	293-295	Sugar spins at this degree, follow recipe directions for spinning.	Decorations for desserts, and confections
Hard crack	300-310	Test as "soft ball;" drops will separate into hard, brittle slivers.	For taffy, nuts, brittles, and drops
Liquefied sugar	320	Sugar liquefies.	Barley sugar
Caramel	338	The liquid sugar turns brown.	Coloring

Dairy products are very versatile foods indeed. The healthy egg becomes the tender omelet, the puffed soufflé or mayonnaise. Cream makes our lovely desserts. Butter isn't just a spread for bread, it is the base of anything from hard sauce or Hollandaise to our flaky pastries. Cheeses no longer go to make merely a quick lunch, but appear instead in Quiche Lorraine, fondues, and cheese cakes.

15 ᕥ

Dairy Products, Fats and Oils

Eggs

Market Sizes and Minimum Weights:

1 Dozen Peewee (Pullets)	= 15	ounces
Small	= 18	ounces
Medium	= 21	ounces
Large	= 24	ounces
Extra-large	= 27	ounces
Jumbo	= 30	ounces

Shell color does not affect weight, quality or nutritive value of eggs, however a brown egg has a yellower yolk and can make cakes and baked products, stuffed eggs and scrambled eggs look richer.

Do not buy eggs that are cracked or soiled. If necessary, use cracked or soiled eggs, but only thoroughly cooked.

Storing   Do not wash—washing removes a thin protective film. Store in refrigerator, covered, with the large end up to keep the yolk centered. For best flavor and quality, use within a week. Store leftover yolks under cold water, refrigerated in a tightly-covered container. Store leftover whites in a tightly-covered container in refrigerator.

How to Break an Egg   Crack center side of egg with blunt knife or by rapping on a thin edge. Hold egg over bowl. Insert thumbs in crack, pull shell apart and allow egg to fall into bowl.

How to Separate an Egg Follow above direction for cracking or rapping the egg. Then hold egg upright over bowl. Remove top half, allow white to run into bowl and retain yolk in lower half of shell. Pour yolk carefully back and forth between the two half shells until all egg white has drained into bowl. Then place yolk in a second bowl.

Be careful in cracking egg, not to cut so deep that the yolk is broken, as the egg cannot then be separated.

If the yolk breaks and a little runs into the white, remove carefully with a piece of paper kitchen towel.

How to Beat Egg Whites Beat in electric beater, at high speed, with a rotary egg beater or a French whisk. Egg whites will not beat up if they contain any yolk.

Preparation and Uses

Boiled, soft-cooked: boiled or simmered in water to cover.

Boiled, hard-cooked: from 10 to 14 minutes depending upon method.

Coddled: egg steamed in shell.

6-Minute egg, also called egg mollet: boiled, cooled slightly, peeled and used instead of poached eggs.

Poached: egg broken into simmering acidulated water and cooked a few minutes.

Fried: egg broken into butter in a pan and cooked until set.

Scrambled: beaten eggs, cooked and stirred in butter or fat.

Baked: cooked in oven in individual or small ramekins.

Omelet: beaten eggs cooked in a pan without stirring, then folded.

Do not use eggs less than four days old for beating, baking or boiling. Hard-cooked fresh eggs are hard to peel and the yolks may turn greenish; fresh eggs used in cakes may cause a cake to rise poorly.

Wash plates used for eggs under cold water; hot water "cooks" the yolk residues onto the plate. Rinse sterling silver immediately after it has been used with eggs, otherwise the egg will tarnish it.

As a thickening agent (egg yolks only) in soups and sauces. To keep the egg yolks from curdling, reduce the heat under the mixture to be thickened to below boiling, stir small amount of hot mixture into eggs, then stir eggs back into hot mixture. The safest method is to add eggs to mixture in top of double boiler over simmering water.

As a leavening agent in angelfood, sponge and chiffon cakes, meringues, soufflés and omelets. The amount of leavening depends upon the amount of air beaten into and retained by the egg whites.

As a binding agent in dry or crumbly mixtures, e.g., croquettes.

As an emulsifying agent to stabilize an oil with a liquid, e.g., oil and vinegar in mayonnaise.

Measurements and Equivalents

To make one cup, use: 7 small eggs

6 medium eggs

5 large eggs

4 extra-large eggs

To make one cup egg whites or yolks, use:

	Whites	Yolks
Small	10	18
Medium	8	16
Large	7	14
Extra-Large	6	12

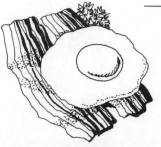

Number of Large Eggs	Equivalents			Approximate Volume
	Extra-Large Eggs	Medium Eggs	Small Eggs	
1	1	1	1	3 tablespoons
2	2	2	3	¼ cup plus 2 tablespoons
3	3	4	4	½ cup plus 2 tablespoons
4	3	5	6	¾ cup plus 1 tablespoon
5	4	6	7	1 cup
6	5	7	8	1 cup plus 3 tablespoons
8	6	10	11	1½ cups plus 2 tablespoons
10	8	12	14	2 cups
12	10	14	17	2¼ cups plus 2 tablespoons

Dried Egg Solids

Equivalents and Reconstitution.

If a recipe calls for Whole Eggs (Large, 24 ounce/dozen)	Use	
	Dried Egg Product, Sifted	Lukewarm Water
1	2½ tablespoons	2½ tablespoons
6	1 cup	1 cup
Egg Yolks		
1	2 tablespoons	2 teaspoons
6	¾ cup	¼ cup
Egg Whites		
1	2 teaspoons	2 tablespoons
6	¼ cup	¾ cup

Equivalents (approximate).

8 ounces dried whole egg solids = 16 large or 18 medium eggs.

8 ounces dried egg yolk solids = 27 egg yolks.

8 ounces dried egg white solids = 50 egg whites.

Store.   In refrigerator, or dry cool place (no more than 50° F.). Good for up to 12 months. Keep opened package refrigerated in a tightly-lidded container.

Check label carefully for specification of rigid bacteriological control.

Reconstituting Dried Egg Solids.   Reconstitute—by blending with water—only the quantity needed. Store opened packages in refrigerator.

Milk

	Milk Fat Content	Marketing Forms	Use
Buttermilk	Soured and treated, skimmed or partially skimmed milk (8.5% milk solids)	Pints, quarts 1 quart=4 cups	Drinking, baking
Condensed	Sweetened whole milk, half water removed, at least 28% milk solids; sugar added	15-ounce cans 1 can=1⅓ cups 1 can=2½ cups milk plus 8 tablespoons sugar	Cooking
Dry, whole milk solids	Whole milk with water removed (at least 26% milk fat)	1-pound boxes (3½ cups) yields 3½-4½ quarts milk ¾-1 cup powder and water yields 1 quart milk	Drinking, cooking
Dry, non-fat milk solids	Fat & water removed from milk (not over 1½% fat by weight)	1-pound boxes (4 cups) 1 pound yields 3½-4½ quarts milk ¾-1 cup and water yields 1 quart milk	Drinking, cooking
Evaporated	Skimmed	6- or 14½-ounce cans (also 128-ounce cans, 15 cups) 14½-ounce can=1⅔ cups 14½-ounce can=3⅓ cups milk	Coffee and miscellaneous uses

	Milk Fat Content	Marketing Forms	Use
Evaporated, whole	Whole milk, 60% water removed, at least 25.9% milk solids	(Same as skimmed)	
Ice milk	Milk solid and fat contents regulated by state laws	1 quart	Substitute for ice cream
Sherbert	Sugar, milk solids, water, etc.; milk solid content 2-5%; milk fat 1-2%	1 quart	Desserts, accompaniment for meats, fruit cocktails, in beverages
Skimmed milk chocolate drink	Whole milk with most fat removed and chocolate added	Quarts 1 quart=4 cups	Drinking, whole milk substitute
Whole milk homogenized chocolate	Cow's milk, sugar and chocolate added	Pints, quarts, gallons, individual containers 1 quart=4 cups 1 quart yields 4, 8-ounce glasses	Drinking, cooking, baking sauces, etc.
Yogurt	Fermented whole milk, fruits or flavors sometimes added	½ pint	Eating, health foods, cooking
Cream			
Light	18-25% milk fat (may be homogenized)	½ pint (1 cup)	Coffee, table, cooking
Light, whipping	30-36% milk fat	½ pint (1 cup)	Whipping
Half & half	10-12% milk fat	1 pint (2 cups)	Coffee
Heavy, whipping	36-40% milk fat	½ pint (1 cup or 8⅓ ounces) 1 cup yields, approximately 2 cups whipped	Garnishing, whipping, desserts, baking, soups, sauces, cream dishes
Ice cream	8-20% (varies according to manufacturers & state laws)	½ pint, pint, quart, gallons, individual portions (1 quart yields 6-8 servings)	Desserts, between meals, beverages, sauces
Sour cream	18-20% milk fat	½ pint, 1 pint	Cooking, eating, sauces, gravies, appetizer dips
Whipped cream topping	(Regulated by State laws)		Garnishing

Natural Cheeses   Natural cheese is made by separating most of the milk solids from the milk by curdling the milk and separating the curd and whey by heating, stirring and pressing.

The distinctive differences between natural cheeses are due to the kind of milk used, the methods of curdling, cutting, cooking and forming the curd, the type of bacteria or molds used in ripening, the amounts and kinds of seasonings added and the conditions of ripening.

Storing   All natural cheeses should be kept refrigerated. Soft, unripened cheeses should be used within a few days. Ripened or cured cheeses can be refrigerated for several weeks if well wrapped.

When possible, leave on the original wrapper or covering; cover cut portions or surfaces of cheese with wax paper, foil or plastic wrap to protect against drying.

Mold which may develop on natural cheeses is not harmful and is easily scraped off cheese surfaces.

Dried cheese may be grated and kept refrigerated in a tightly-covered glass jar.

Store strong-scented cheeses in a tightly covered container.

Wrap cut, ripened or cured cheeses in a soft cloth, wrung out in wine.

Store large uncut cheeses in glass or porcelain containers in a cool dry place, as a cellar. Examine frequently, at least once a week. Wash with salt water and rub surface of cheese with salt water and rub surface of cheese with salt.

Dry cheeses, as cheddar, can be stored in a sort of humidor over wine, vinegar or water, or they can be wrapped as cut cheeses are wrapped in a soft cloth wrung out in wine.

Serve   All natural cheeses—except soft, unripened cheeses such as cottage cheese and cream cheese—should be served at room temperature. This requires from 20 to 60 minutes out of the refrigerator.

Happy Marriages   Cheeses are suitable for any meal of the day, as well as for snacks. Cheese main dishes include fondues, Welsh rarebits, soufflés. Cheese goes well with or in soups, salads and salad dressings, potatoes, rice, pasta and vegetable dishes, fruits, nuts, crackers, hot and cold sandwiches, sauces, gratineed dishes, cheese cookies, cakes, pies and breads.

Ripening Classifications

Soft, unripened (Such as Cream Cheese) Contain relatively high moisture and do not undergo any curing or ripening. They are eaten fresh—soon after manufacture.

Firm, unripened (Such as Mozzarella) Contain very low moisture content, may be used soon after manufacture or may be kept for up to several months.

Soft, ripened (Such as Brie) Curing progresses from the outside, or rind of the cheese, toward the center. Molds and/or bacteria grow on the surface of the cheese and aid in developing the characteristic flavor and body and texture during the curing process. Curing continues as long as the temperature is favorable.

Semisoft, ripened (Such as Bel Paese) These cheeses ripen from the interior as well as from the surface. This ripening process begins soon after the cheese is formed, with the aid of a characteristic bacterial or mold culture or both. Curing continues as long as the temperature is favorable.

Firm ripened (Such as Cheddar) These cheeses ripen throughout the entire cheese with the aid of a bacterial culture. Ripening continues as long as the temperature is favorable. The rate and degree of curing is also closely related to the moisture content; being lower in moisture than the softer varieties, these cheeses usually require a longer curing time.

Very hard, ripened (Such as Parmesan or Romano) These cheeses also are cured with the aid of a bacterial culture and enzymes. The rate of curing is much slower because of the very low moisture and higher salt content.

Blue-vein mold ripened (Such as Roquefort or Bleu) Curing is accomplished by the aid of bacteria and characteristic mold culture that grows throughout the interior of the cheese to produce the familiar and characteristic flavor.

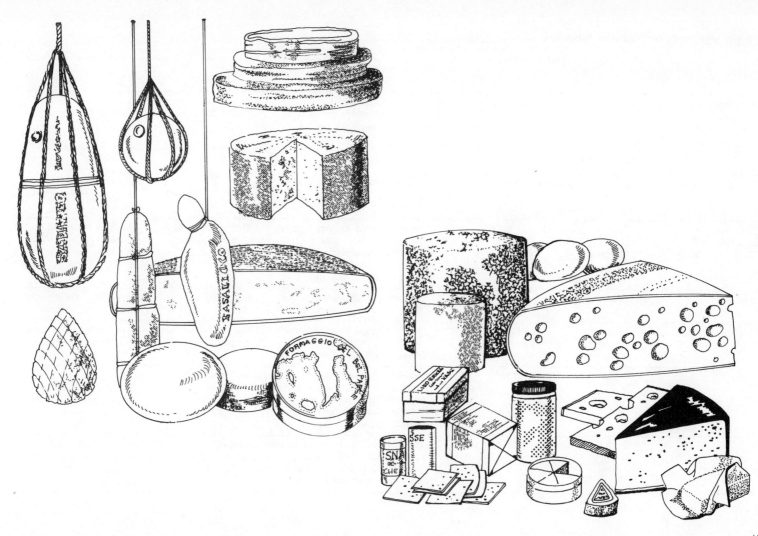

Some Varieties of Natural Cheeses

Cheese	Origin	Milk Used	Variety, Flavor, Body and Color	Packaging	Uses
American	U.S.	Cow's	Firm, ripened; mild to moderately sharp; semisoft to medium firm; light yellow to orange	Slices, wedges, squares, bricks	Snacks, sandwiches, melting & cooking
Bel Paese (Italian trademark)	Italy (licensed for manufacture in U.S. and imported)	Cow's	Semisoft, ripened; mild to moderately robust; soft to medium firm, creamy; creamy yellow interior; slightly gray or brownish surface	Small wheels, wedges, segments	Appetizers, with crackers, snacks, desserts; can be used in place of mozzarella cheese
Blue (bleu on imported)	France, Denmark, Norway, U.S., England	Cow's	Blue-vein mold ripened; tangy, peppery; semisoft, pasty, sometimes crumbly; white interior marbled or streaked with blue veins of mold	Cylindrical, wedges, oblongs, squares, cut portions	Appetizers, salads, salad dressings, with crackers, desserts
Boursault	France	Cow's	Soft, unripened; triple cream cheese, similar to Boursin	Small, round, paper wrapped	Appetizer, cheese tray, with fruits, a spread
Boursin and Herbed Boursin	France	Cow's	Soft, unripened cheese, smooth and creamy white, sometimes flavored with garlic and herbs	Small, round, paper wrapped	Appetizer cheese tray, with fruits, a spread
Brick	U.S.	Cow's	Semisoft, ripened; mild to moderately sharp; semisoft to medium firm; elastic, numerous small mechanical openings, creamy yellow	Loaf, brick, slices, cut portions	Appetizers, sandwiches, snacks, desserts
Brie	France	Cow's	Soft, ripened, mild to pungent; soft, smooth when ripened; creamy yellow interior; edible thin brown and white crust	Circular, pie-shaped wedges	Appetizers, snacks, with crackers & fruit desserts

Cheese	Origin	Milk Used	Variety, Flavor, Body and Color	Packaging	Uses
Caciocavallo	Italy	Cow's milk. In Italy, cow's milk or mixture of sheep's, goat's and cow's milk	Firm, ripened, piquant, similar to provolone but not smoked; firm, lower in milkfat and moisture than Provolone; light or white interior; clay or tan colored surface	Spindle or ten-pin shaped, bound with cord, cut pieces, and braided	Snacks, sandwiches, cooking, dessert; suitable for grating after prolonged curing
Caerphilly	Wales	Cow's	White, granular, and short, semisoft to semifirm	Large, round, 2½-inches thick	Nourishing sandwich cheese, good with freshly-ground pepper, or as a stuffing for celery
Camembert	France	Cow's	Soft, ripened, mild to pungent; soft, smooth; very soft when ripened, creamy yellow interior; edible thin white, or gray-white crust	Small circular cakes and pie-shaped portions	Appetizers, sandwiches, snacks, good with crackers, and fruit such as pears and apples, dessert
Cheddar	England	Cow's	Firm, ripened, mild to very sharp; firm, smooth, some mechanical openings; white to medium-yellow-orange	Circular, cylindrical loaf, pie-shaped wedges, oblongs, slices, cubes, shredded, grated, and spreads	Appetizers, sandwiches, sauces, on vegetables, in hot dishes, toasted sandwiches, grating, cheeseburgers, dessert
Colby	U. S.	Cow's	Mild to mellow, softer and more open than cheddar, white to medium-yellow-orange	Cylindrical, pie-shaped wedges	Sandwiches, snacks, cheeseburgers
Coon	U. S.	Cow's	A fully cured, very sharp cheddar, white with very dark cloth covering	10-ounce stocks wrapped in black film	Use as cheddar
Cottage, plain or creamed. (also called farmer's and pot)	Unknown	Cow's milk skimmed; plain curd or plain curd with cream added.	Soft, unripened, mild, acid; soft, curd particles of varying size; white to creamy white	Cup-shaped containers, tumblers, dishes	Salads, with fruits, vegetables, sandwiches, dips, cheese cake

Cheese	Origin	Milk Used	Variety, Flavor, Body and Color	Packaging	Uses
Cream	U.S.	Cream from cow's milk, and whole milk	Soft, unripened, mild, acid; soft and smooth; white	3- to 8-ounce packages	Salads, dips, sandwiches, snacks, cheese cake, desserts
Crema Danica	Denmark	Cow's	Smooth, white, soft, unripened cheese, very rich	2 foil-wrapped tiles to a box	Essentially a dessert cheese, and may be used as a spread or appetizer with fruit, or as cream cheese
Edam	Netherlands	Cow's milk, partly skimmed	Firm, ripened, mellow nutlike; semisoft to firm, smooth; small irregularly shaped or round holes; lower milkfat than Gouda; creamy yellow or medium yellow-orange interior; surface covered with red wax	Cannon-ball shaped loaf, cut pieces, oblongs	Appetizers, snacks, salads, sandwiches, seafood sauces, dessert
Farmer's cheese	U.S.	Cow's whole or skimmed milk	A white cottage-cheese type of creamy, unripened cheese	Soft roll, usually wrapped in paper or cheese cloth or brick-shaped pieces	Use as cottage cheese
Feta	Greece	Ewe's milk	Flaky, semisoft, white and salty	Thick slices	Nourishing sandwiches and cheese tray; good with Kalamata olives and Greek Retsina wine
Fontina d'aosta	Italy	Cow's and goat's milk	Mild, full milk cheese; yellowish in color; semisoft to hard	Large, round-boxed cheese weighs from 4 to 40 pounds	Table and cooking cheese; topping for polenta and casseroles, or eat with sherry or mixed sweet and dry vermouth

Cheese	Origin	Milk Used	Variety, Flavor, Body and Color	Packaging	Uses
Fromage de chèvre (or chèvre longs)	France	Goat's milk	Chèvre is a name given to all French goat cheese, smooth, strong taste and aroma	Small round cheeses, various wrappings and packaging	Sandwich, spread, cheese tray
Garnished Liptauer	Germany, Hungary, Austria	Sheep's	A crumbly white cheese, usually combined with paprika, capers, onions and other ingredients	Small round, wrapped in paper	Popular spread for black bread and beer
Gervaise	France	Cow's	French equivalent of cream cheese; taste is more pro-ounced	Small tiles or rolls; paper or foil wrapped	As cream cheese, with fruit; a dessert cheese
Gjetost	Norway (imported only)	Whey from goat's milk or a mixture of whey from goat's and cow's milk	Firm, unripened; sweetish, caramel; firm, buttery consistency; golden brown	Cubical and rectangular	Snacks, desserts, served with dark bread, crackers, biscuits or muffins
Gorgonzola	Italy	Cow's milk; in Italy, cow's milk or goat's milk or mixture of these	Blue-vein mold, ripened; tangy, peppery; semisoft, pasty, sometimes crumbly, lower moisture than Blue; creamy white interior, mottled or streaked with blue-green veins of mold; clay colored surface	Cylindrical, wedges, oblongs	Appetizers, snacks, salads, dips, sandwich spread, good with crackers, dessert
Gouda	Netherlands	Cow's milk, whole or partly skimmed	Firm, ripened, mellow, nutlike; semisoft to firm, smooth; small irregularly shaped or round holes; higher milk fat than Edam	Ball-shaped with flatened top and bottom, and loaf shape	Appetizers, snacks, sandwiches, seafood sauces, dessert
Greyerzer	Switzerland	Cow's	Finest of the Swiss cheeses; firm light yellow with holes	40- to 60-pound rounds	Sandwiches, cooking, cheese platter, fondues

Cheese	Origin	Milk Used	Variety, Flavor, Body and Color	Packaging	Uses
Gruyère	Switzerland	Cow's milk, whole or partly skimmed	Firm, ripened; mildly salty, nutlike; firm smooth with smallish round eyes; light yellow	Circular cake 40 to 100 pounds; 3½- to 5-inches high	Appetizers, desserts, salads, snacks, fondues
Liederkranz	U.S.	Cow's	A mild, soft Limburger-type cheese, made of whole milk	Small bricks separately wrapped and boxed	Serve with black bread or with fruit for dessert, good with grapes
Limburger	Belgium	Cow's	Soft, ripened; highly pungent, very strong; soft, smooth when ripened; usually contains small irregular openings; creamy white interior; reddish-yellow surface	Cubical, rectangular	Appetizers, snacks, good with crackers, rye or other dark breads, desserts and beer
Monterey Jack	U.S.	Cow's milk	Soft and semisoft; hard types used for gratineeing	Packaged as cheddar or store cheese	Soft type for sandwiches; hard type for grating
Mozzarella (also called Scamorza)	Italy	Whole or partly skimmed cow's milk; in Italy, originally made from buffalo's milk	Firm, unripened; delicate, mild; slightly firm, plastic; creamy white	Small round or braided form, shredded, sliced	Snacks, toasted sandwiches, cheeseburgers, cooking, as in meat loaf or lasagne
Muenster	Germany	Cow's	Semisoft, ripened; mild to mellow; semisoft, numerous small mechanical openings; contains more moisture than brick; creamy white interior; yellow tan surface	Circular cake, blocks, wedges, segments, slices	Appetizers, sandwiches, snacks, dessert, and with Mozelle wine
Mysost (also called Primost)	Norway	Whey from cow's milk	Firm, unripened; sweetish, caramel; firm, buttery consistency; light brown	Cubical, cylindrical, pie-shaped wedges	Snacks, desserts, served with dark breads

Cheese	Origin	Milk Used	Variety, Flavor, Body and Color	Packaging	Uses
Neufchâtel	France	Cow's	Soft, unripened; mild, acid; soft, smooth, similar to cream cheese but lower in milkfat; white	4- to 8-ounce packages	Salads, dips, sandwiches, snacks, cheese cake, desserts
Parmesan (also called Reggiano)	Italy	Whole cow's milk	Very hard, ripened; sharp, piquant; very hard, granular, lower moisture and milkfat than Romano; creamy white	Cylindrical, wedges, shredded, grated	Grated for seasoning in soups, or vegetables, spaghetti, ravioli, breads, popcorn, used extensively in Italian cooking
Petit Suisse	France	Cow's milk and cream	The fluffiest and lightest of the cream cheeses	Small rolls; paper wrapped	Whipped with sour cream or honey to serve with berries or as cream cheese
Pont-l'Eveque	France	Cow's	Soft cheese, stronger than Camembert	Square, boxed	Serve with apples and wine
Port-Salut	France	Cow's	Semisoft, ripened; mellow to robust; semisoft, smooth, buttery, small openings; creamy yellow	Wheels, wedges	Appetizers, snacks, served with raw fruit dessert
Provolone (smaller sizes and shapes called Provolette, Provoloncini)	Italy	Cow's	Firm, ripened; mellow to sharp, smoky, salty; firm, smooth; light creamy interior; light brown or golden yellow surface	Pear-shaped, sausage and salami-shaped wedges, slices	Appetizers, sandwiches, snacks, soufflés, macaroni dishes and pizza, suitable for grating when fully cured and dried

Cheese	Origin	Milk Used	Variety, Flavor, Body and Color	Packaging	Uses
Ricotta	Italy	Cow's milk, whole or partly skimmed, or whey from cow's milk with whole or skim milk added; in Italy, whey from sheep's milk	Soft, unripened; sweet, nutlike; soft, moist or dry; white	Pint and quart, paper and plastic containers, 3 pound metal cans	Appetizers, salads, snacks, lasagna, ravioli, noodles and other cooked dishes, grating, desserts
Romano (also called Sardo Romano, Pecorino Romano)	Italy	Cow's milk; in Italy sheep's milk (Italian law)	Very hard, ripened; sharp, piquant; very hard granular; yellowish-white interior, greenish-black surface	Round with flat ends, wedges, shredded, grated	Seasoning in soups, casserole dishes, ravioli, sauces, breads, suitable for grating when cured for about one year
Roquefort	France (imported only)	Sheep's	Blue-vein mold, ripened; sharp slightly peppery; semisoft, pasty, sometimes crumbly; white or creamy white interior, marbled or streaked with blue veins of mold	Cylindrical, wedges	Appetizers, snacks, dips, sandwich spreads, good with crackers, dessert
Sapsago	Switzerland (imported only)	Skimmed cow's milk, slightly soured	Very hard, ripened; sharp, pungent cloverlike; very hard; light green by addition of dried, powdered clover leaves	Conical, shakers	Grated to flavor soups, meats, macaroni, spaghetti, hot vegetables; mixed with butter makes a good spread on crackers or bread
Schmierkäse	Germany	Cow's	Soft, often flavored or spiced with onion	Small wrapped tiles	Spread for canapés, sandwiches

Cheese	Origin	Milk Used	Variety, Flavor, Body and Color	Packaging	Uses
Stilton	England (imported only)	Cow's	Blue-veined mold, ripened; piquant, milder than Gorgonzola or Roquefort; semisoft, flaky; slightly more crumbly than Blue; creamy white interior, marbled or streaked with blue-green veins of mold	Circular, wedges, oblongs	Appetizers, snacks, dessert and mellow port wine
Stracchino	Italy	Cow's	Rich, uncooked soft eating cheese, said to be made of milk from tired cows (after their trip down from summer pasture)	Similar to Gorgonzola	Canapés, cheese tray, sandwiches
Swiss, (also called Emmentaler)	Switzerland	Cow's	Firm, ripened; sweet nutlike; firm, smooth with large round eyes; light yellow	Segments, pieces, slices	Sandwiches, snacks, sauces, fondue, cheeseburgers
Taleggio	Italy	Cow's	Uncooked, pale golden color with reddish crust	Small tile	Sandwiches, snacks, appetizers, with fruit, desserts
Tilsiter	Germany	Cow's	Same type as Port du Salut, soft and punctured with tiny holes, piquant flavored	Brick	Appetizers, snacks, with fruits
Tome Au Raisin (or grape cheese) also called Tomme	France	Skimmed cow's milk	A small cheese, ripened in dried grape skins and pips, left over after the vintage, which lends it a characteristic flavor	Medium rolls	With bread or crackers
Triple Cremé	France	Cow's	Similar to Crema Danica, softer, creamier and richer	Small, high round	Use as dessert, spread, appetizer, with fruit or as Crema Danica

Cheese Measurments

1 pound American cheese = 4 cups grated

1 pound Cheddar cheese = 4 cups grated

4 ounces Cheddar cheese = 1 cup grated, sieved or chopped

1 pound Cottage cheese = 2 cups

½ pound Cottage cheese = 1 cup or 8 ounces

½ pound Cream cheese = 1 cup or 8 ounces

6 ounces Cream cheese = 12 tablespoons or ¾ cup

5 ounces Cheese spread = 8 tablespoons or ½ cup

Fats and Oils   Hydrogenation means that hydrogen is added to liquid oil to produce a "fat" that is solid at room temperature.

Store butter, margarine, lard, suet, poultry fats and drippings in refrigerator.

Name	*Market Forms*	*Origin*	*Weight in Cups*	*Substitutions and Smoking Point*	*Uses*
Butter unsalted salted sweet creamery whipped tub canned	1-pound packages or boxes often divided into 4 quarter-pound bars 8-12 ounce paper container or 2¾-pound bar 1 pound 1 pound	Cream	1 pound=2 cups	Above 365° F 1 cup margarine=1 cup butter	Table-baking, frying
Margarine salted unsalted soft	1-pound packages and quarter-pound bars In half-pound containers	Vegetable or animal fats	1 pound=2 cups		
Lard	1-pound packages	Hog carcasses	1 cup=8 ounces	Above 390° F. ⅞ cup+½ teaspoon salt=1 cup butter	Pastry, cookies, yeast breads, quick bread cakes, deep fat frying

Name	Market Forms	Origin	Weight in Cups	Substitutions and Smoking Point	Uses
Suet	By the pound from butcher	Beef fat	1 pound=3¾ cup chopped medium fine 1 cup chopped=4¼ ounce		Puddings
Hydrogenated vegetable shortening	1- and 2-pound cans	Pure vegetable oils, usually cotton seed oil and soybean oil (sometimes peanut and corn oil)	1 pound=2½ cups	Above 390°F. ⅞-1 cup+½ teaspoon salt=1 cup butter	Frying, deep fat frying, baking, salads
Poultry fat	Available at some stores in 8-ounce and 1-pound jars	From chicken, duck, goose or turkey, usually home rendered	1 pound=2 cups	⅞ cup+½ teaspoon salt=1 cup butter	Cooking (Chicken fat is also used as a table spread)
Drippings	Home produced	Beef, lamb (not good for cooking) crackling, pork			Sauce, gravy, breads, sautéing sauces, seasonings
Oils	Bottles: 1 fluid pint, 1½ fluid pint, 1½ fluid quart and 1-gallon cans	Cottonseed, corn, peanut, soybean, safflower, sesame	1 cup=8 ounces 1 pound=2 cups	Can substitute for butter, in small amounts, for frying	Salad dressings, frying, baking
Olive oil	½ pint, pints, quarts, and gallons	Olives	1 cup=8 ounces	Can substitute for part of butter in frying	Salad dressing, frying

Butter   Butter is made from sweet or sour cream and contains not less than 80% milk fat.

Measurements

1 ounce	= 2 tablespoons
1 bar	= 8 tablespoons
	= ¼ pound
	= 4 ounces
	= ½ cup
	= 2¾ ounces, whipped butter only
¼ pound	= 1 bar
½ pound	= 2 bars
	= 1 cup
1 pound	= 2 cups
	= 4 bars

1 pound yields 48, ⅓-ounce squares or 32, 1-tablespoon pats of butter.

Included here is information about the serving of beverages, glasses and bar equipment, the preparation of coffee and tea, the market forms and yields of non-alcoholic drinks and beverage mixes and detailed information on how, when and with what to serve champagne, wine, distilled spirits, beer and other alcoholic beverages.

16 ℘

Beverages

Coffee

Hot Coffee
1 pound + 2½ gallons water makes approximately 50 servings.
1 pound + 2 gallons water makes approximately 40 servings.
¼ cup instant coffee + 1 quart water makes 6 cups.
1 cup instant coffee + 1 gallon water makes 25 cups.
5¼ cups ground coffee = 1 pound.

Iced Coffee   Make coffee for iced coffee stronger than regular coffee as dissolving ice thins the coffee.
A 2-ounce jar instant coffee and 2½ quarts water makes 15 servings.

Coffee Makers and Their Grinds
Percolator = use percolator grind coffee
Drip Pot = use drip grind coffee
Expresso = use Espresso drip grind coffee.
Vacuum Coffee Maker = use fine or drip grind coffee.
Filter Coffee Makers = use drip grind coffee.
Carafe = use instant coffee.
Automatic Coffee Makers = use ½ and ½ Espresso and percolator grind.
Turkish Coffee Makers = finest grind powdered coffee.
Well Known Types of Coffee   Java, Mocha, Arabian, Turkish, Colombian.

Expresso Maker

Turkish Coffee Maker

Market Forms. *Coffee Beans* Beans can be purchased and freshly ground at market or at home. Beans can be blended according to taste.

Ground Coffees
1-pound can vacuum sealed coffee = 5–5¼ cups
1-pound bottle decaffeinated coffee = 5 cups.
2-ounce bottle instant coffee = 60 cups
2-ounce bottle instant decaffeinated coffee = 60 cups
Percolator grind—all purpose
Drip grind—extra fine
Espresso
Silex

	Cans	Jars
½-pound bags	12 ounce	2 ounce
1-pound bags	1 pound	4 ounce
	2 pound	6 ounce
		10 ounce

Tea

1 pound = 6–8 cups tea leaves which makes 250–300 servings.

Black Teas

English "breakfast"	Java
Ceylon	Sumatra

Green Teas

China green	Gunpowder
Hoochows	Imperial
Country Greens	Japanese

Semi-fermented Teas

Oolongs	Formosa oolongs

Scented

Orange Pekoe	Spiced Teas

Indian Teas

Darjeeling	Terai
Assam	Kangra
Cachar	Nilgiri

(The above is only a partial list of teas.)

To Make and Serve Tea

1. Warm a china tea pot.
2. Pour boiling water over leaves and allow them to steep.
3. Use a tea of good quality.
4. Use freshly boiling water.
5. Separate leaves from brewed tea after it is infused.
6. Do not let tea get cold.
7. Make fresh tea, never reheat.

Tea is packaged in 1- and 2-cup-size tea bags, loose in sealed cans or powdered in bottles or package.

Bags

1¼ ounces = 16 bags
3¾ ounces = 48 bags
   8 ounces = 100 bags
Instant tea, powdered – 90 glasses – 2 ounces.
Instant liquid tea – 16 glasses – 1 pint.

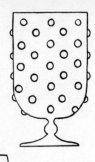

How to Serve Beverages Warm beverages are served in cups or mugs with handles. Tea, coffee, cocoa and hot chocolate are served in cups with handles and saucers. Green tea is served in cups without handles or saucers, black tea is also served out of glasses, placed in handled holders. Iced tea and coffee are served in tall glasses to accommodate the ice.

Milk and milk drinks are served in tall clear glasses, sometime decorated in white or blue.

Fruit ades, juices, summer thirst quenchers should be served in tall clear glasses. Some glasses, as for juleps, are frosted before they are served.

Some brandies are served in large globes, "warmers, snifters or inhalers" which are to be held in both hands to warm the brandy while it is slowly sniffed and sipped.

Beverages are Served From Tea, cocoa, chocolate and coffee pots, urns, samovars. Pitchers, jugs and punch bowls with ladles.

Alcoholic beverages are served out of the original bottle, which can be wrapped in a napkin when it is a cold white wine. Red wine is poured from a bottle held horizontally in a basket to prevent disturbing sediment.

Some fortified wines and whiskeys can be decanted into crystal decanters, but should not be left in a decanter for more than a week.

Milk or Water

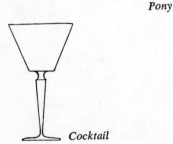

Pony

Cocktail

Cups and Glasses for All Beverages

Cocoa or chocolate cup	5–6 ounces
Black coffee cup or demitasse	2–2½ ounces
Tea cup	6 ounces
Coffee cup	8 ounces
Breakfast coffee cup	8–10 ounces
Breakfast tea cup	8–10 ounces
Milk glass	18–20 ounces
Water glass	16–18 ounces
Lemonade & fruit drink glass	16 ounces

Punch cup	6 ounces
Egg nog cup	6–8 ounces
Tomato juce, fruit & clam juice glass	4 ounces
Wine glass	4 ounces
Sour glass	4 ounces
Collins glass	16 ounces
Whiskey glass	2½ ounces
Old Fashioned	4–8 ounces
Highball glass	14 ounces
Cocktail glass	4–5 ounces
Sherry glass	3 ounces
Champagne glass, hollow-stemmed, saucer or tulip	6 ounces
Liqueur glass	1 ounce
Beer glass, tulip or stein	14 ounces and up

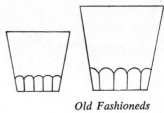

Old Fashioneds

Highball

Bar Equipment

Bar glass with strainer top
Cocktail shaker
Cork screw
Bottle opener
Steel paring knife
Lemon and lime squeezer
Jigger or pony
Ice crusher

Bar spoon with long handle
Muddler
Ice bucket
Ice tongs
Coasters
Trays
Glasses and cups for all beverages

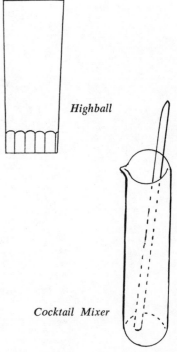

Cocktail Mixer

Bar Measurements

Pony   — 1 ounce
Jigger   — 1½ ounces

Bar Spoon

(253)

Jigger	–	2 ounces
1 Minim	–	1 drop
10 Drops	–	dash
6 Dashes	–	1 teaspoon
60 Drops	–	1 teaspoon
8 teaspoons	–	1 ounce

How to Uncork a Bottle   To open a bottle of wine, draw the cork out of the bottle with a corkscrew. A corkscrew is a tapered metal spiral usually set in a wooden or metal handle. It is about 2½-inches long and should be inserted into the center of the cork. The bottle is then held tightly and the cork is drawn out. Later the cork is removed from the corkscrew and used to recork the bottle if there is wine left over. Champagne is never recorked, and wine should not be stored too long in a recorked bottle.

There are excellent patented corkscrews designed to go straight down the center of the cork. They are equipped with a pair of arms which are lowered and act as levers in drawing the cork out as effortlessly as possible.

It is important to use this type of corkscrew in drawing the cork out of an old bottle of wine which should not be shaken or disturbed, or out of a horizontal bottle of red wine in a wine basket.

Also available on the market is a new type of bottle opener which is equipped with a long needle which is inserted into the cork. The handle is then used to pump a gas into the bottle. The cork is driven up and out. The gas does not effect the taste of the wine in any way and the method is good for many types of corks.

More and more bottles are being sealed with screw-on tops which do not require an opener.

Champagne bottles are opened by breaking the wire sealer and working the cork out very gradually with both thumbs, working all around the bottle and pushing upward from the underside of the cork or plastic stopper. **The cork should come out smoothly and un-**dramatically. It should not be allowed to fly across the room (at any rate, while uncorking, kept the cork away from your face). Properly chilled champagne will not explode out of the bottle.

Champagne Champagne is a white wine which sparkles because it ferments a second time in the bottle.

Champagne

Champagne Classifications

Brut	very dry
Extra Sec	fairly dry
Sec	medium sweet
Demi Sec	fairly sweet
Doux	very sweet

Champagne Bottle Sizes

Split	6½	ounces
Pint	13	ounces
Quart (Regular)	26	ounces
Magnum	52	ounces
Jeroboam	104	ounces
Rehoboam	156	ounces
Methuselah	208	ounces
Salmanazar	312	ounces
Balthazar	416	ounces
Nebuchadnezzar	520	ounces

How, When and With What to Serve Serve chilled. Champagne is a glamorous wine, served at celebrations, weddings and receptions. It can also be served with dessert or throughout a meal. A glass of champagne or a champagne cocktail can be served as an aperitif before a meal.

Well Known Champagnes   The greatest and most expensive champagne is Moët & Chandon's Dom Pérignon which is bottled in a narrow necked bottle with a sealed instead of a wired cork. Other well known imported champagnes are: Perrier-Jouët, Piper-Heidsieck, Veuve Cliquot, Roederer, Mumm and Bollinger. There are excellent American champagnes.

White Wine

White Wines   White wines come from many countries. The most famous imported wines are the French Sauternes of Bordeaux, the Chablis of Burgundy and the German Rhine and Moselle wines. There are Chilean, Italian and South American white wines and many are produced in California and other regions in the United States.

How, When and With What To Serve   Serve chilled. Dry white wines should be served with fish, poultry and white meats (e.g., veal). Sweet white wines should be served with dessert. White wines are combined with champagne, fruit, sparkling water and other ingredients for punches.

Well Known Imported White Wines Are

Bordeaux, Sauternes	Château d'Yquem
	Château La Tour Blanche
	Château Rabaud-Sigalas
	Château Oliver
Burgundy	Chablis
	Pouilly Fuissé
	Meursault
	Montrachet

Rhine Wines (Hock)	Rudesheimer
	Johannisberger
	Hochheimer Hölle
	Rauenthaler Kesselring
Rhine Hesse	Niersteiner
	Liebfrauenstift-Klostergarten
	Oppenheimer Goldberg
Rhine Pfalz	Ruppertsberger
	Deidesheimer
Moselle Wines	Saarburger
	Piesporter
	Erdener Treppchen
	Bernkastler Doktor

Steinweins, Chilean wines, Saar wines and Bochsbeutel are bottled in squat green bottles called Bochsbeutel.

Italian White Wines   Lacrima Christi, sparkling Lacrima Christi, Capri and many other excellent white wines are produced in Italy.

There are many other good white table wines grown in almost all wine-growing countries. The United States produces white wines on the east as well as the west coast.

Red Wines   Red wines come from France, the Mediterranean countries, the United States and all other wine-growing countries. The most famous imported wines are the French Bordeaux and Burgundy wines.

How, When and With What To Serve   Serve at room temperature. Chill Rosé wines or red-wine punches but always uncork a red wine, in the room in which it is going to be served, a few hours before it will be served. (This is called "letting it breathe.")

Red Wine

Well Known Imported Red Wines and Clarets Are

Bordeaux (claret)	Château Margaux
	Château Mouton-Rothchild
	Château Latour
	Pontet-Canet
Burgundy	Chambertin
	Pommard
	Beaujolais
	Clos Vougeot

Rosé Wines   Serve chilled. The Rosé or pink wines are now produced in almost all wine-growing countries, including the United States. The best known are from Tavel, Alsace and Provence.

Fortified Wines   Wines which have been laced with brandy or other spirits. Serve at room temperature.

Port Wine   A sweet dessert wine from Portugal (also made in the United States).
Tawny Port—lighter color.
White Port—made of white grapes.

Sherry   (Jerez or Xeres Wine) A pale gold wine from Spain, served as an aperitif or dessert wine. Serve at room temperature. There are many well-known sherrys as: Amontillado, Manzanilla.

Madeira   A deep golden fortified wine from the Portuguese Island of Madeira. Used as a Marsala. Also used extensively in cooking. Serve at room temperature.

Marsala   An Italian fortified wine from Sicily. Marsala is used as sherry and in cooking. Serve at room temperature.

Sherry

Malaga   A sweet fortified wine from southern Spain. **Serve** at room temperature.

Distilled Beverages   Served as an aperitif, in mixed drinks, as an after-dinner drink. Served chilled, at room temperature or in heated cold weather drinks.

Whiskies
Vodka
Rum
Brandies
Tequilla

Brandy

Compounded Spirits   Served as aperitifs before meals, in mixed drinks and after meals. Served cold, chilled, at room temperature or over crushed ice.

Gins
Bitters
Akvavit
Liqueurs and Cordials

Liqueur

Fermented Beverages Other Than Wines   Served with or after meals, summer thirst quenchers. Always served cold.

Cider
Beer
Ale
Stout
Porter

Sake   Japanese rice wine. Served at room temperature or warmed.

Beer Beer dates back to the Babylonians, 3000 B.C. There are records of the ancient Chinese, the Pharaohs and the Vikings brewing beer or a related beverage.

THE COMPLETE

KITCHEN GUIDE

Beer Tulip

Stein

Serving Beer

1. Almost all beer is served ice cold. A very few people like it over 40°, at room temperature or lightly warmed.
2. Beer cans and bottles should not be shaken before opening and should be opened carefully to avoid foaming.
3. Beer should be poured immediately upon opening.
4. Pour beer slowly down the inside-side of the glass or stein until about ⅔ full, then pour quickly into the center of glass or stein to obtain a "head" or cap of foam.
5. Flat beer is not good, open only as many bottles as will be used immediately.
6. Beer is also used in cooking, as beer soup, Bubble & Squeak, stews and fritter batter.

To Store Bottled or Canned Beer   Beer should be stored in a cool dark cupboard or cellar. Do not chill until it is to be used, then place on bottom shelf of refrigerator. Too long chilling is undesirable, too cold beer will not foam well. Insufficiently chilled beer will foam too much.

Beer Chart

Name	Composition	Use	Market Forms
Beer	A fermented beverage containing grain, malt, hops and yeast	Thirst quench, general beverage	Short and long-necked bottles of 12 fluid ounces, cans of 12 fluid ounces, king size cans of 1 pint, large bottles of 1 quart,
Light beer	More hops	Nourishment and in cookery	
Dark or brown beer	More malt		
Lager			
Ale	English beer, originally brewed without hops	As beer	Bottled as beer
Stout	Heavy malt liquor brewed with some roasted malt	As beer or for health	Bottled as beer or in 8 fluid ounces
Porter	Weak stout	As beer or for health	Bottled as beer

Non-Alcoholic Beverages The following beverages are non-alcoholic thirst quenchers to serve with, after or between meals. They serve also as diluters, nourishers and very mild stimulants. They are rarely used in cooking.

Name	Market Forms	Weight, Measure and Yield	Use

Ades
  fresh fruit
  instant powdered mixes
  frozen
  tablets
	Fresh fruits, juiced
	envelopes & packages
	cans
		3 ounces
		4½ ounces
		
		5 ounces
			Thirst quenchers,
			adjuncts to punches

Beverage drinks
  cola drinks
  ginger ale
  fruit
  root beer
  combinations
	Bottled
	
	canned
		6 bottle pack
		8 bottle pack
		6½ fluid ounces
		7 fluid ounces
		10 fluid ounces
		12 fluid ounces
		12 fluid ounces
			Thirst quenchers,
			for cooking some stews
			and hams

Beverage syrups	Bottled canned jarred	1 pint or 4 quarts 1 pound 1 pound 6 ounces	Concentrates for dilution
Carbonated beverages, sodas and mixes	Bottled canned	8 bottle pack (6½ and 12 ounces) 6 bottle pack (10 and 16 ounces) 7 fluid ounces 12 and 16 fluid ounces 1 pint 12 ounces 12 ounces	Diluters and mixers

Name	Market Forms	Weight, Measure and Yield	Use
Chocolate			Hot and cold beverages, health and nursery drinks, energy drinks, in cold weather
Chocolate drink	Bottled		
Chocolate food beverage			
Cocomalt	can	12 ounces	
Ovaltine	can	6 ounces	
Chocolate malted milk	jar	15 ounces	
Chocolate milk		½ pint, 1 quart	
Chocolate powdered	canned	½ pound, 1 and 2 pounds	
Chocolate syrups	canned	12 ounces, 1 pound	
Clam juice	Bottled	8 fluid ounces	Cocktail or for cooking
Cocoa	Canned	½ and 1 pound	As chocolate
cocoa mix	canned	1 pound	
Cola Drinks, (see Beverage drinks and Carbonated beverages)			
Coolers, fruit flavored	Envelopes non-carbonated beverages	1-3 ounces	Thirst quenchers
Drinks, packaged	Envelopes	3¾-4½ ounces	Thirst quenchers
Egg nog	Bottled	1 quart	Health drinks, punches
Frozen beverages	Cans	9 fluid ounces=6 cups	Thirst quenchers, breakfast drinks
Beverages and reconstituted juices	canned	6 fluid ounces, 24 fluid ounces	
orange		9 fluid ounces, 1½ quarts	
grapefruit		12 fluid ounces, 48 fluid ounces	
lemon		1 pound, 11 ounces,	
lime		6 quarts	
pineapple			breakfast drinks,
pink lemonade			thirst quenchers,
various combinations			punch adjuncts
Grape juice	Bottled	12 ounces and up	Meal or between meal thirst quenchers
	canned	12 ounces	

Name	Market Forms	Weight, Measure and Yield	Use
Juices, fresh fruit			Health drinks,
grapefruit	Fresh fruit	Yields 1 cup juice	thirst quenchers,
lemon		yields 3 tablespoon juice	breakfast drinks,
lime		yields 1½ tablespoon	cooking,
orange		1 orange yields	punch adjuncts,
		6 tablespoon juice	etc.
		4 oranges yields	
		1½ cups juice	
orange	bottled	1 quart	
cranberry	canned	1 pint and 1 quart	
grape	canned	1 pint and 1 quart	
grapefruit	canned	1 pint and 1 quart	
grapefruit & pineapple	canned	1 pint 13 ounces and 1 pint 14 ounces	
lemon	canned	1 pint	
lime	canned	1 pint	
orange	canned	1 pint 13 ounces and 1 quart 14 ounces	
orange & grapefruit	canned	1 pint 13 ounces and 1 quart 14 ounces	
prune	canned	1 pint 13 ounces and 1 quart 14 ounces	
Tomato juice	Bottled	8 ounces, 1 pint 8 ounces, 1 quart	Appetizer breakfast drink, health drink,
	canned	5½ fluid ounces, 1 pint 13 ounces, 1 quart 14 ounces	cooking, soups
Vegetable juice	canned	5½ fluid ounces, 1 pint 13 ounces, 1 quart 14 ounces	
Lemonade, (see fresh and frozen)			
Malted Milk	Jarred	15 ounces	Health drink
Chocolate flavor	jarred	15 ounces	
Vanilla flavor	jarred	15 ounces	

Name	Market Forms	Weight, Measure and Yield	Use

Milk
   buttermilk
   chocolate
   skim
   whole
   malted
	Bottled and in containers	Pints, quarts, and 2-3 quarts (see Dairy Products p. 229)	Thirst quencher, cooking, nursery drink and health drink

Nectars fruit flavors	Canned, bottled	1 quart, 14 fluid ounces	Beverage, cooking
Postum	Jar	4 ounces	As coffee
Sodas, (see Carbonated beverages)			

Tea
   loose
   bags
   powdered
   iced tea mix
	Can
	box
	jar
	bottle and package
		2 ounces, 1-2 pounds
		10-100 bags
		4 ounces
		8-ounce bottle
		3-ounce package
			Hot and cold, health drink

Weights and Measures

Teaspoons
⅛ teaspoon = a few grains
1 teaspoon = 60 drops
1 teaspoon = 5 milliliters
1 teaspoon = ⅓ tablespoon
3 teaspoons = 1 tablespoon

Tablespoons
1 tablespoon = 3 teaspoons
1 tablespoon = ½ fluid ounce
2 tablespoons = 1 fluid ounce
4 tablespoons = ¼ cup
4 tablespoons = 2 ounces
5⅓ tablespoons = ⅓ cup
8 tablespoons = ½ cup
10⅔ tablespoons = ⅔ cup
12 tablespoons = ¾ cup
12 tablespoons = 6 ounces
16 tablespoons = 1 cup
16 tablespoons = 8 fluid ounces

Cups
⅛ cup = 1 ounce
⅛ cup = 2 tablespoons
¼ cup = 2 ounces
¼ cup = 4 tablespoons
⅓ cup = 5⅓ tablespoons

Cups
⅜ cup = 6 tablespoons
½ cup = 4 ounces
½ cup = 8 tablespoons
½ cup = 1 tea cup
½ cup = ¼ American pint
½ cup = 1 gill
⅝ cup = 10 tablespoons
⅔ cup = 10⅔ tablespoons
¾ cup = 6 ounces
¾ cup = 12 tablespoons
1 cup = 8 ounces
1 cup = 16 tablespoons
1 cup = ½ American pint
1 cup = 2 gills
2 cups = 1 pint
2 cups = 1 pound
4 cups = 1 quart
16 cups = 1 gallon

Dry Volume Measure
2 cups = 1 pint
2 pints = 1 quart
4 quarts = 1 gallon
2 gallons = 8 quarts
8 quarts = 1 peck
4 pecks = 1 bushel

17 ❧
Essential Kitchen Information

Liquid Measurements
1 pint or 2 cups liquid measure = 1 pound
2 pints or 1 quart of liquid measure = 2 pounds
1 tablespoon = ½ liquid ounce or 15 grams
1 cup = 16 tablespoons or 8 liquid ounces or 227 grams
2 cups = 1 pint or 16 ounces or 1 liquid pound or 454 grams
4 cups = 2 pints or 1 quart or 32 liquid ounces or 907 grams
1 quart = 64 tablespoons
1 litre = 66⅔ tablespoons

One Cup Ingredient Weight in Ounces

Ingredient	*Approximate Weight in Ounces*
1 cup cake flour	3½
1 cup flour	4¾
1 cup sugar	7
1 cup brown sugar, packed	7
1 cup powdered sugar	2¾
1 cup butter	8
1 cup water	8
1 cup noodles, broken	2⅔
1 cup cottage cheese	8
1 cup ground meat	8
1 cup coffee	3
1 cup corn meal	5
1 cup raisins	5
1 cup almonds, shelled, slivered	5½
1 cup chopped nuts	4¾ to 5½

Ingredient	Approximate Weight in Ounces
1 cup egg whites	8–9
1 cup egg yolks	8⅔
1 cup eggs	10
1 cup dried vegetable	6½ to 7½
1 cup condensed milk	10¾
1 cup honey	12
1 cup macaroni	4
1 cup cracker crumbs	2½
1 cup milk	8⅔
1 cup corn syrup	11½
1 cup ground cheese	4
1 cup rice	7½
1 cup fresh bread crumbs	2
1 cup cocoa	4
1 cup dried fruits	5⅓–7
1 cup melted chocolate	9

Approximate Substitutions

1 teaspoon baking powder – ¼ teaspoon baking soda plus ½ cup buttermilk
— ¼ teaspoon baking soda plus ⅓ cup molasses
— ¼ teaspoon baking soda plus ½ teaspoon cream of tartar

1 cup butter – 1 cup margarine
— 14 tablespoons hydrogenated fat and ½ teaspoon salt
— 14 tablespoons lard and ½ teaspoon salt

1 ounce chocolate – 3 tablespoons cocoa plus 1 teaspoon to 1 tablespoon fat (less for Dutch-type cocoa)

1 cup coffee cream – 3 tablespoons butter and about ¾ cup milk

1 cup heavy cream – ⅓ cup butter and about ¾ cup milk

1 cup all purpose flour – 1 cup plus 2 tablespoons cake flour

1 cup cake flour – ⅞ cup all-purpose flour

1 tablespoon cornstarch – 2 tablespoons flour (as thickener)

1 tablespoon flour – ½ tablespoon cornstarch

1 cup pastry flour – ⅞ cup all-purpose or bread flour

1 tablespoon potato flour – 2 tablespoons flour (as thickener)

1 cup white flour – 1 cup corn meal

⅛ teaspoon garlic powder – 1 small clove

Herbs, ½ to 1½ teaspoon dried – 1 tablespoon fresh

1 cup fresh milk – ½ cup evaporated milk plus ½ cup water

       – ½ cup condensed milk plus ½ cup water (reduce sugar in recipe)

       – 4 teaspoons powdered whole milk plus 1 cup water

       – 4 tablespoons powdered skim milk plus 2 tablespoons butter plus 1 cup water

1 cup yogurt   – 1 cup buttermilk

1 teaspoon sugar – ¼ grain saccharin

       – ⅛ teaspoon non-caloric sweetener

1 cup packed brown sugar – 1 cup granulated

1¾ cups packed confectioners' sugar – 1 cup granulated

1 cup corn syrup – 1 cup sugar plus ¼ cup liquid

1 cup honey – 1 to 1¼ cups sugar plus ¼ cup liquid

Altitude Adjustments

Baking Decrease each teaspoon baking powder or soda by ⅛ to ¼ teaspoon at altitudes from 3000 to 8000 Feet. Decrease sugar by 1 teaspoon to 3 tablespoons per cup at altitudes from 3000 to 8000 feet. Increase liquids from 1 to 4 tablespoons per cup at altitudes from 3000 to 8000 feet.

Boiling   Water boils at 212° F. at sea level. Water boils at approximately 208.4° F. at 2000 feet and at 203° F. at 5000 feet. Water boils at 194° F. at 10,000 feet above sea level.

Above 2500 feet, stews, soup and other liquids require a longer cooking period, as liquids boil at a lower temperature.

Deep-fat Frying   At high altitudes, temperatures for deep-fat frying are lowered by about 8%.

Vegetables   When liquid is used for cooking vegetables, more liquid and a longer time are required. In cooking frozen vegetables, additional cooking time has to be added.

Sugar Syrup   Candy is at the soft ball stage at: 236° F. at sea level,

230° F. at 3,000 ft.

226° F. at 5,000 ft.

222° F. at 7,000 ft.

Deep Fat Frying Temperatures

Food to be Fried	Temperature of Fat Degrees Fahrenheit	Brown a 1-inch Bread Cube Approximate Seconds
Doughnuts	365 3 minutes	50
Fritters oysters, scallops, soft-shell crabs, fish	350-375	60
Potato chips	365 3 minutes	20
Croquettes eggplant, onions, cauliflower	375-385	40
French fried potatoes	385 8 minutes	20

Food to be Fried	Temperature of Fat Degrees Fahrenheit	Brown a 1-inch Bread Cube Approximate Seconds
Croquettes	365 4 minutes	50
Shrimp, raw	365 3-5 minutes	50
Shrimp, breaded	365 4-6 minutes	50
Chicken	365 11-15 minutes	50

Oven Temperatures

Description	Fahrenheit	Temperatures in Degrees Centigrade	Regulo
Plate warming	200		
Cool oven	225-250	107-121	0-½
Very slow	250-275	121-135	½-1
Slow	275-300	135-149	1-2
Slow	300-325	149-163	2
Very moderate	325-350	163-177	3
Moderate	350-375	177-190	4
Moderate	375-400	190-204	5
Moderately hot	400-425	204-218	5-6
Hot	425-450	218-233	6-7
Very hot	450-475	233-246	7-8
Very hot	475-500	246-600	8-9
Extremely hot	500-550	600	9

Fahrenheit to Centigrade Conversion Chart

°F Degree Fahrenheit	°C Degree Centigrade	°F Degree Fahrenheit	°C Degree Centigrade	°F Degree Fahrenheit	°C Degree Centigrade
32	0.0	205	96.1	380	193.3
35	1.6	210	98.8	385	196.1
40	4.4	215	101.6	390	198.8
45	7.2	220	104.4	395	201.6
50	10.0	225	107.2	400	204.4
55	12.7	230	110.0	405	207.2
60	15.5	235	112.7	410	210.0
65	18.3	240	115.5	415	212.7
70	21.1	245	118.3	420	215.5
75	23.8	250	121.1	425	218.3
80	26.6	255	123.8	430	221.1
85	29.4	260	126.6	435	223.8
90	32.2	265	129.4	440	226.6
95	35.0	270	132.2	445	229.4
100	37.7	275	135.0	450	232.2
105	40.5	280	137.7	455	235.0
110	43.3	285	140.5	460	237.7
115	46.1	290	143.3	465	240.5
120	48.8	295	146.1	470	243.3
125	51.6	300	148.8	475	246.1

°F Degree Fahrenheit	°C Degree Centigrade	°F Degree Fahrenheit	°C Degree Centigrade	°F Degree Fahrenheit	°C Degree Centigrade
130	54.4	305	151.6	480	248.8
135	57.2	310	154.4	485	251.6
140	60.0	315	157.2	490	254.4
145	62.7	320	160.0	495	257.2
150	65.5	325	162.7	500	260.0
155	68.3	330	165.5	505	262.7
160	71.1	335	168.3	510	265.5
165	73.8	340	171.1	515	268.3
170	76.6	345	173.8	520	271.1
175	79.4	350	176.6	525	273.8
180	82.2	355	179.4	530	276.6
185	85.0	360	182.2	535	279.4
190	87.7	365	185.0	540	282.2
195	90.5	370	187.7	545	285.0
200	93.3	375	190.5	550	287.7

Freezing   All foods to be frozen should be wrapped securely in freezer paper or any moisture- and vapor-proof wrapping, and placed as soon as possible in a freezer capable of maintaining a temperature of 0° F. or lower. The freezing compartments of most refrigerators are *not* capable of maintaining a temperature of 0° F., and it is not advisable to attempt to freeze foods in a refrigerator freezer for any great length of time (usually no more than a week).

Bacon, fresh pork sausage, frankfurters, some sausages and luncheon meats lose a good deal of flavor if frozen, and freezing these meats is not recommended.

Recommended Maximum *Storage Times at 0° F. or lower*

Smoked hams and bacons	No more than 2 months
Cured and smoked meats	No more than 2 months
Fresh pork and veal	3–4 months
Ground beef	3–4 months
Lamb	6–7 months
Beef	6–8 months
Chicken and turkey	6–12 months
Poultry giblets	4 months
Fish and shellfish	4–6 months
Breads (packaged)	1–2 weeks
Breads, rolls, pies	2–3 months
Cakes (frosted)	6 months
Cookies	9–12 months
Prepared sandwiches	2 weeks

To Thaw and Cook   Thaw frozen foods in the refrigerator   (allow 1 to 2 hours per pound for meats). If a faster thaw is desirable, all frozen foods—except, of course, baked goods and sandwiches, etc.—can be thawed by placing under cold running water for as long as necessary. Thawing at room temperature is not recommended for any frozen foods, because the possibility of spoilage exists.

Thawed foods should be cooked as soon after thawing as possible although some foods can be cooked still frozen, or partially thawed.

Cook frozen meats and shellfish according to usual cooking methods, but allow extra time. There is no hard and fast rule to follow for cooking frozen meats—but the use of a roasting thermometer when cooking frozen roasts is invaluable. Do not, however, attempt to insert the thermometer until the meat is sufficiently thawed in the center to allow the thermometer to be inserted easily. Additional cooking times for roasting will be about one-third to one-half again as long. Steaks require from none to one-third more time.

Refresh frozen breads and pies and other baked goods in the oven at about 325° F.

Frozen fish is also handled the same as fresh fish, but the increase in necessary time is generally less than for meats. However, frozen fish can be thawed quite quickly under cold running water (except for very large pieces of fish) and this is preferable.

Cooking foods frozen does not detract from taste, although it is easier to judge the cooking times for unfrozen foods, which is the big argument in favor of defrosting.

Foods With Low Caloric Content   All vegetables except lima beans, corn and dried vegetables. All fruit except avocados, bananas, persimmons and dried fruits. All lean beef, lamb and veal. All shellfish. All fish except tuna, salmon and fishes packed in oil. All poultry except duck and goose.

Also, eggs, buttermilk, skim milk and skim milk cottage cheese. Bouillon, consommé, broth, clear vegetable and chicken soups. Gelatin.

Foods With High Caloric Content   Pork, smoked pork sausages, breads, candies, ice cream, fountain drinks, peanut butter, sauces and gravies, sugars and syrups, nuts, pies and cakes, milk, cream and butter and alcoholic beverages.

Foods Low in Carbohydrates   Cheese, vegetables, fish, berries, avocados, cantaloupes, shellfish, duck, fats and oils, gelatin, milk, meats, poultry and alcoholic beverages.

Foods High in Carbohydrates   Cakes, pies, apples, bananas, dried fruits, cookies, canned fruits and syrups, bread, breakfast cereals, flours, candies, corn, dates, figs, cranberries, ice cream, scallops, sweet potatoes, tapioca, rice, jams, molasses, pastas.

A.C.	alternating current	imp. gal.	imperial gallon	**ESSENTIAL**
bkt.	basket	in.	inch	
b.p.	boiling point	k.	kilogram	**KITCHEN**
br.	broil; broiler	kg.	kilogram	
bu.	bushel	kilo	kilogram	**INFORMATION**
c.	cup	l.	liter	
° C.	degrees centigrade	lb.	pound	
cal.	calorie	liq.	liquid	
cc.	cubic centimeter	lit.	liter	
cent.	centigrade; centimeter	m.	meter	
cm.	centimeter	mg.	milligram	
D.C.	direct current	min.	minute	
deg.	degree	M.S.G.	monosodium glutamate	
doz.	dozen	pkg.	package	
env.	envelope	pt.	pint	
° F.	degrees Fahrenheit	qt.	quart	
fl. oz.	fluid ounce	reg.	regulo; regular	
ft.	foot; feet	sec.	second	
g.	gram	tbs.	tablespoon	
gal.	gallon	tbsp.	tablespoon	
hhd.	hogshead	tsp.	teaspoon	
hr.	hour			

A

Al Dente — Italian "to the tooth." Used to describe pastas which are cooked until just tender but not soft.

A l'anglaise — French "In the English manner," meaning simply cooked.

Allumettes — French "match sticks," a way of cutting potatoes, puff pastry, etc.

American Plan — Hotel term meaning "meals included."

Antipasto — Italian "before the meal." A plate or selection of first course appetizers.

Aspic — French. A gelatin glaze used over cold meats, fish, eggs, poultry.

Asti Spumante — Italian, white, sparkling wine.

Au Jus — French "with juice." Said of roasts served with their natural juices instead of a sauce or gravy.

B

Baba — French, a savarin-like yeast cake usually saturated with rum while still hot. Also called Baba au Rhum.

Babka — A Polish yeast cake usually baked in a fluted tube form.

Baking Blind — To bake an empty pie shell before filling it. In order to keep the shell from rising, it is usually covered with paper and weighed down with raw rice or washed cherry pits, or it may be pricked heavily with a fork.

Ballotine — French for a boned meat roll. Less rich than a gallantine.

Barbecue — Meat cooked in a pit or over live coals.

Baron — A double cut of meat, consisting of both sirloins joined by the backbone.

Barquette — French "Boat." A boat-shaped pastry tart.

Bavarois — Bavarian cream. A sweet custard cream stiffened with gelatin and served with whipped cream.

Beignets — French light fritters.

Beurre Manie — French butter and flour creamed together, used to thicken sauces.

Glossary

Bisque	French. A purée or thick shellfish soup.
Bisquit Tortoni	Italian. A frozen vanilla mousse flavored with liqueur and sprinkled with macaroon crumbs. Usually served out of paper cases.
Blind	See *Baking Blind*.

C

Cassoulet	French. A famous stew, specialty of Toulouse, contains haricot beans.
Chantilly Cream	French. Whipped cream.
Charlotte	A hot or cold dessert made in a border of biscuit slices or lady fingers.
Chateaubriand	Steak cut from thickest part of beef filet. Usually broiled or grilled.
Chaud-Froid	Poultry or game masked in a cold white aspic or chaud-froid sauce.
Chou Paste	Cream puff dough, used for profileroles, cream puffs, French fritters.
Court Bouillon	A strong bouillon made from fish and vegetables, used as a base for fish sauces.
Crème	French cream, creamed soup or sweet liqueur.
Crepes	French. A thin, small pancake.
Croissant	French crescent-shaped roll of puff paste.
Croutons	Bread cubes, fried or toasted and served in soups, salads or omelettes.
Crown Roast	American roast of lamb or pork. The whole loin is tied into a circle with rib bones projecting and center filled with ground meat, vegetables or mashed potatoes.

D

Daube	French. Braised beef or mutton with red wine.
Demitasse	French-American term for a small cup of after-dinner coffee.
Devonshire Cream	English. Obtained by heating fresh full milk after standing for at least 12 hours in a warm place. The cream is skimmed off and served with fruits and fresh berries.

Duchesse	French. Mashed potatoes, plain or with additions, piped and browned in the oven.
Duxelles	French. Chopped mushrooms and onions cooked in butter.

E

Echalote	French. Shallots.
Eclair	French. Cream puff pastries, long and narrow and filled with vanilla or flavored custard.
Entrecote	French. Sirloin steak.
Entrée	French. Has come to mean main course of a dinner.
Entremets	French. Has come to mean sweet course or dessert.
Estragon	French for tarragon.
European plan	Hotel terms for a la carte service.

F

Fines Herbes	French. Minced parsley, chives, chervil and tarragon. Used in omelettes, salads and sauces.
Flan	French. A pastry or tart shell filled with custard, cream, fruit or cheese.
Filet (or Fillet)	French. A strip of meat. The tenderloin.
Fillet (or Filet)	A boneless strip of fish.
Fondue	French and Swiss. A cheese custard cooked with wine, or meat cooked in oil.
Forcemeat	Finely chopped meat, mixed with herbs and flavorings for stuffings, dumplings and farcés.
Frangipane	Italian. Sweet almond cream used to fill cakes and pastries.

G

Galantine	A boned meat or poultry roll, stuffed and flavored and glazed. Richer than the Ballotine.

Garnishes or Garnitures	Colorful decorations and edible accompaniments of main dishes.
Gateau	French cake, torte.
Gelee	French, jelly.
Genoise	A special sponge dough used for layer cakes and small pastries.
Gespritzter	Austrian or German. White wine and seltzer water. (Fine Gespritzter Champagne and seltzer water)
Glacé	French glaze on ice cream.
Gnocchi	Italian. Semolina or farina dumplings covered with cheese and browned before serving.
Gratin or Gratineé	A layer of grated cheese placed over food and browned in oven or under the broiler just before servings.
Grissini	Italian. Bread sticks.
Guglhupf	German. Plain or yeast cake baked in a fluted tube pan.

H

Hors d'oeuvre	French. "Over the meal." Always in the singular. A small dish or selection of dishes to be served before a meal.
Huitre	French. Oyster.

J

Julienne	French. Finely shredded vegetables.
Jus	French. Meat juice.

K

Kebabs	Oriental origin. Highly spiced meat prepared on skewers.
Kougelhupf	See Guglhupf.
Kuchen	German. Plain cake, coffee cake.

L

Lady Fingers	Double strips of sponge cake, shaped in fingers, used for dessert and charlottes.
Lebkuchen	German. Honey and spice cakes, usually baked at Christmas time.
Legumes	French. Vegetables.

M

Macaron **or Macaroon**	French. Semi-hard biscuit of almond paste, sugar and egg whites.
Macedoine	French. Mixture of hot or cold vegetables or cold fruits.
Madeleine	Parisian small cake baked in an oval shell mold of a special sponge-type dough.
Marmite	French. Cast iron or earthenware soup pot with lid. Usually used to cook Marmite or Pot-au-feu.
Mignonette	French. Means coarsely ground pepper.
Mouli	French device, kitchen utensil for mincing parsley. A food mill.
Mousse	French "froth" or whipped mixture of eggs, cream, gelatin used for molded fish or vegetable dishes or desserts.
Mousseline	French for a whipped or frothy mixture, usually sauces.

N

Noix **or Noisette**	French "Nut." Also means small tender pieces of meat.

O

Omelette	French. Eggs whipped and lightly fried in butter, turned with two folds. Resembles a combination of soft scrambled eggs and pancake. Plain or filled with any of countless fillings.

P

Panettone	Italian. A yeast bread—specialty of Milan.
Pâte	French. Batter or dough for pastry.
Pâté	French. Mixture of sieved liver, herbs, meats, baked in a pastry shell or terrine, served as a first course or savoury.
Petits Fours	French. Very small cakes served at tea or with desserts.
Petits Pois	French. Very small green peas.
Pilaf, Pilau, Pilaw	Plain Turkish rice, or rice cooked with meat, poultry or fish.
Potage	French. Soup.
Puff Pastry	Dough folded over butter puffs and separated into layers or leaves or flakes when baked. Used for French pastries, pastry shells and flakey crusts.

Q

Quiche	French. An open custard tart, specialty of Lorraine.

R

Ragout	French. A navarin or stew of meat in a rich sauce.
Risotto	Italian. Rice fried and cooked with broth and other ingredients. Specialty of Milan.
Roti	French. A roast of meat.
Rotisserie	French. A meat grill or roasting device; a restaurant that grills meat on a rotisserie.
Roux	French. A mixture of butter and flour. Used as a base for thickening sauces and soups.

S

Sauté	French. To cook rapidly and lightly in an open pan or *Sautoir* with a very small amount of fat.
Savarin	French. Yeast cake, baked in a crown or ring mold, similar to the baba.
Savouries	English. Highly seasoned. A piquant. Small dishes served as the last course of a meal or similar to appetizers.
Schnecke	German-snail. A coffee cake or sweet roll dough rolled up, cut into rounds and baked; iced with sugar glaze.
Sourdough	Bread made of a fermented sourdough. Sourdough starter is kept from baking to baking. Some French and Italian breads are made of sourdough.
Speculacius	German flat cookies shaped in wooden molds at Christmas time.
Spumone	Italian. Ice cream.
Stollen	German. A Christmas braid or bread.
Streusel Kuchen	German. Streusel is a combination of flour, sugar, and cinnamon spread over sweet yeast cake before baking.
Suprême	French. Wing and breast of chicken or game bird—a fillet of sole or fish.

T

Tarhonya	Hungarian. A pasta prepared from flour and egg, rubbed through a sieve and dried. Later cooked in soups or as an accompaniment to meat dishes. Also called egg barley.
Terrine	A liver or game pâté baked in a tart.
Tournedos	A steak cut from filet of beef.
Torte	German. Plural: torten. Elaborate layer cakes, highly decorated.
Tortoni	See bisquit tortoni.

Truffle — French. A flavorful black underground tuber grown in France and Italy and used often in foie gras—goose liver—and gourmet recipes.

Z

Zabaione — Italian. Egg yolks beaten with wine and sugar over hot water.

Zwieback — German—"baked twice." A sort of dry toasted semi-sweet bread slice.

Index

THE COMPLETE

KITCHEN GUIDE